I0752598

IMAGES
of America

MIDDLETOWN OHIO

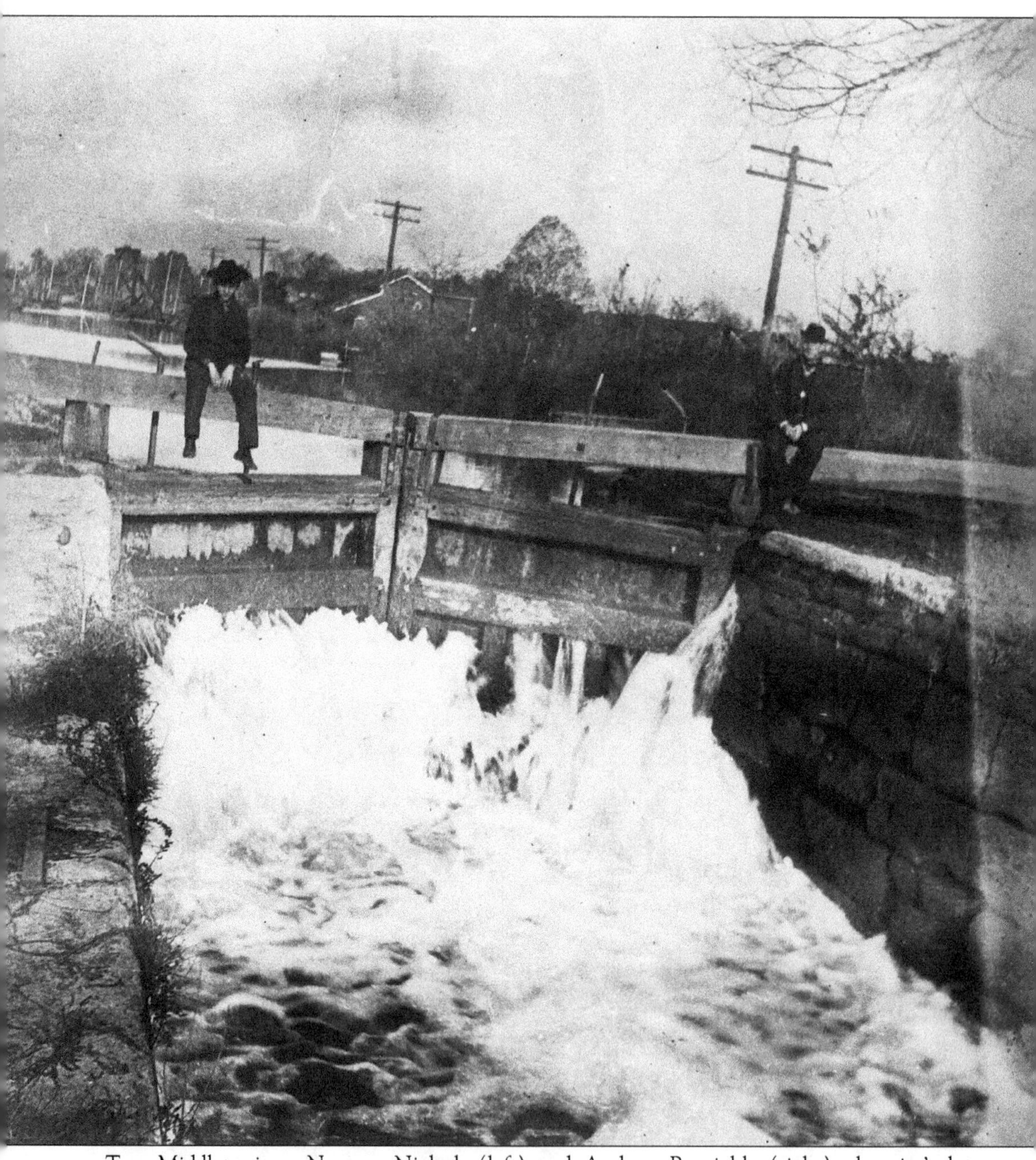

Two Middletonians, Norman Nichols (left) and Andrew Barnickle (right), the city's last locktenders, are shown at the old Doty Lock. It was the third lock completed on the Miami-Erie Canal. The first is still standing at the Excello Locks Park at Dick's Creek. The canal was the main thread in the first two hundred years of the city's history. Groundbreaking for the historic waterway was held July 21, 1825, on Doty's farm where, 104 years later, on November 2, 1929, it would be officially closed, later to be converted into a modern highway (Verity Parkway). State history books have singled Middletown out as the site where the Miami-Erie Canal began.

IMAGES
of America

MIDDLETOWN OHIO

Roger L. Miller and George C. Crout

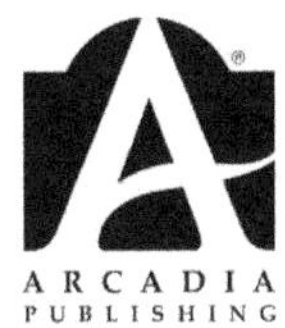

ISBN 978-1-5316-6566-1

Published by Arcadia Publishing
Charleston, South Carolina

Library of Congress Catalog Card Number: 98-86558

For all general information contact Arcadia Publishing at:
Telephone 843-853-2070
Fax 843-853-0044
E-mail sales@arcadiapublishing.com
For customer service and orders:
Toll-Free 1-888-313-2665

Visit us on the Internet at www.arcadiapublishing.com

Contents

ACKNOWLEDGMENTS

A photographic history of a community is not the work of two people, but many, for each photo represents the work of some individual with a camera. Representative photographs were chosen from among thousands viewed in order to best illustrate the highlights of local history in the years leading to the Millennium. The pictures came from many sources, so it would be impossible to give proper credit to all. When possible, the authors have contacted the photographers responsible, or their descendants, for permission to use the photographs. We appreciate their granting the privilege to include them here.

Among the organizations opening their files and granting permission for use of material are: *Middletown Journal*, Middfest International, Middletown Public Library, Middletown Historical Society, Middletown City Schools, Middletown News-Agency, City of Middletown, Armco Steel Corporation, and Aeronca Inc.

Individuals, some now deceased, who through the years have contributed photographs from personal collections to the authors for historical files include: Maynard Alexander, William Alford, Bernard and Gloria Annenberg, Robert Barnett, Elsie Bates, DeWitt Chapple, William Culbertson, Herbert Fall, William Harrison, June Hill, Harold Kramer, Jerry Nardiello, Mrs. Paul Perkins, Laura Riley, Peter Rudokas, Steve Schelb, Ralph Sebald, Everett Sherron, Margaret Ann Stevens, William Thomson, Scott Tobias, Wilfred Vorhis, Robert Wall, Bill Weith, and Earl Whitt. The original photographs or negatives of the pictures in this book will be placed at the local public library in the Crout Collection.

A special note of appreciation is due to Mrs. Roger "Penny" Miller for her help, assistance, and support in preparing the manuscript for publication.

Note: Further information about the pictures in this book or about Middletown history can be found at the local library. Also, local history can be accessed on the internet at http://www.journalink.com or other local internet addresses.

INTRODUCTION

Middletown, Ohio is located between Cincinnati and Dayton, along Interstate 75—the Nation's Main Street. Nestled among rolling hills, it is drained by streams which flow into the Great Miami River. It is likely that the town's name was due to its central location. It began with a simple log cabin in 1791 erected on the river bank, and grew eastward. The river provided an early transportation route to the markets of Cincinnati, the early metropolis of the Midwest. Flatboats gave way to canal boats, with water being drawn from the river to provide its flow. The Miami-Erie Canal began to lose trade when the Cincinnati, Hamilton, and Dayton Railroad was built in 1851, along the river's flood plain. Eventually a network of highways would carry most of the passengers and much of the freight of the area, with Interstate 75 being the main artery.

Censuses record the growth of the town. Beginning with about 50 people clustered around the crossroads, now known as Main and Central and marked by a black granite monument, by 1830 the number rose to 314. The Census of 2000 will show over 50,000 inhabitants. Middletown was populated in pioneer days by emigrants from New Jersey, Virginia, Pennsylvania, Massachusetts, and Kentucky. They cut trees, cleared the land, and a few entrepreneurs such as Stephen Vail and Bamboo Harris built small, water-powered mills along the rivers. These were used to grind grain, saw logs, and process wool. Later came the Irish, who built the canal, and then the hard-working Germans who cultivated farms. As industry developed people from other sections of the country, as well as other nations, came to lend their skills. The first industry was pork packing, followed by papermaking. Tobacco processing would dominate the industrial scene in 1900, to be replaced by the steel industry—the city's major enterprise at the Millennium.

As the city's industrial base grew, so did its political structure. The village became a town in 1833, and then a city in 1886. Its infrastructure kept pace with its growth—schools, utilities, health facilities, and other civic necessities arrived.

While many families came and went, a few remained through the generations. The city's first settler, Daniel Doty, still has descendants here, including the Harrison family in its eighth generation. Descendants of Stephen Vail, who platted the town, have also reached the eighth generation, such as the Greathouse's. Each generation has watched changes take place that transformed a frontier hamlet into a major city. People have always been the city's major resource, and the names of many leaders will show up in the pages of this book. Books have preserved the city's development in words, but this one is the first to record it graphically through a series of photographs. One picture is said to be worth a thousand words. Each picture will be provided with a legend, but your eyes and mind must construct the rest of the story. Now is a good time to pause and look back to reflect on Middletown's progress as it makes brave new plans for the next Millennium.

THE PHOTOGRAPHERS

Old pictures bring to mind the prominent photographers of years past, who did so much to preserve a visual record of the city. The first major, professional photographer to record scenes around the city was William Edward Watson, some of whose work appeared as illustrations in *Middletown in Black and White*, printed in 1906. His camera also recorded the great 1913 flood and thousands of his postcards are still among family souvenirs. He operated a studio on the southwest corner of Central and Curtis Streets. Elmer Sherman, at 404 East Central, advertised "Bring in the Whole Family," and Watson's ad said, "Bring in the Babies." As a family photographer, Watson took thousands of photographs still yellowing in family albums. Another widely published photographer of the area was Thomas Clyde Portsmouth, whose pictures are preserved in old Armco Bulletins and other company publications.

Many local citizens still identify the name of Tobias with photography. Ed Tobias had been a photographer in Kokomo, Indiana. His son, Hayden, decided to locate in Middletown. In April 1926, he arrived here to begin work at Paul Barnaby's Studio at 104 South Main. The next year he purchased the business, which he moved to 30 South Main, next to the U.S. Hotel. His son, Macyln "Mac," began helping his father as a boy of eight, assisting in developing and delivery. Then, after a stint in World War II, Mac joined his father as a partner. Now his son, Scott Tobias, operates the studio, and some of his work is included in this book.

The first photographer on record in the city is J.B. Nunneley, who ran an advertisement in the local newspaper in 1869 noting the location of his "Photographic Gallery" in the Leibee Building at Main and Central.

The first city directory appeared in 1891, and under the photographers heading are listed Lawson and Mathews, George Long, and W. Slater. Some examples of their work are included in this book. By 1914, the directory listed W.E. Watson, Elmer Sherman, and Alexander and Livsey—all with studios along Central, which then went by the name of Third Street. By 1917, amateur photography had become popular, with supplies being sold by Watson, Dysert, Fay's Drug Store, and the Book Shop. Knoll, Bell, and Schiebert also had opened studios around town.

In 1928, Watson was still in business. Tobias had a new studio, and their competitors were Alexander, Nickolis, Dysert, and Parker—the town's first woman photographer. In 1932, Howard Murray, who did both studio and industrial work, moved from Hamilton to locate in Middletown on North Broad. Others on the local scene have imprinted their work with the names of Kramer, Osborne, Easterling, Reeder, Michele, Jordan, Fitzpatrick, Yoder, and Randenheimer. Olan Mills of Springfield has maintained a local studio. Other local photographers work out of their homes, or specialize in portrait work. Journal newspaper photographers through the years have produced some outstanding shots, now a part of this record.

One

Images before Photography

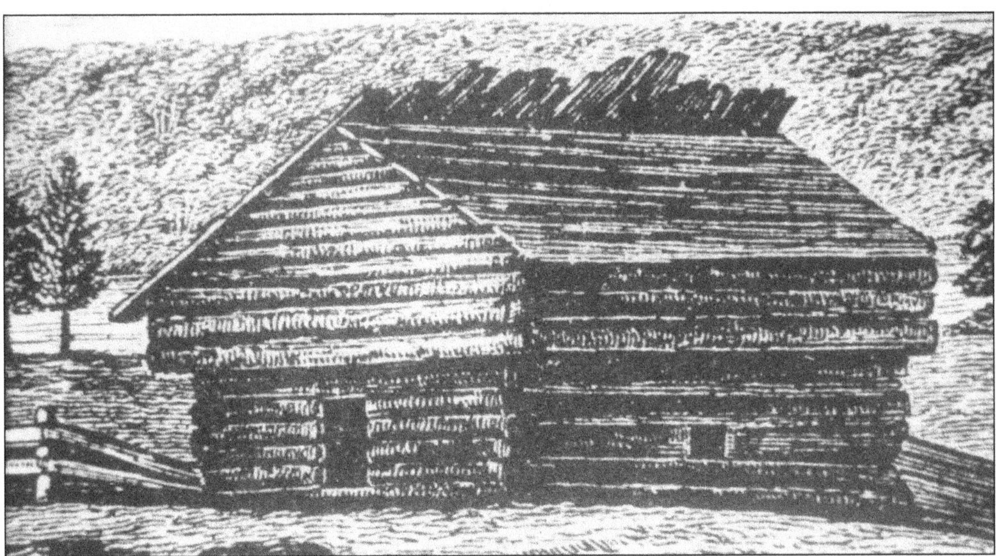

Since Middletown's early years predate the introduction of photography (1839), other graphic arts must provide visual images of that era. Woodcuts, folk art, and charcoal sketches, along with artist's re-creations, are among these techniques. Shown here is a wood engraving made by Henry Howe, pioneer Ohio historian, in 1846. It is of a blockhouse which stood at Columbia, now part of Cincinnati, and was duplicated in some 39 stockades in the western wilderness from Cincinnati to Miamisburg. A blockhouse stood along Dicks Creek at Middletown with a detachment of soldiers from Fort Hamilton, protecting the area from surprise attack by hostile Native American tribes.

The blockhouse was located just south of the present Excello Locks Park, and is now marked with a granite monument. Known as Morrell's Station, it took its name from Dr. Calvin Morrell, who purchased the land in 1791, and it stood until all danger was past in 1805. In late 1791, Daniel Doty erected a log cabin along the banks of the Great Miami River, just above Morrell's Station. From it grew the present city of Middletown. The blockhouse at the station not only provided the Doty family with security, but three of the Doty children were also born there under the professional care of Dr. Morrell. When he closed the station, Dr. Morrell joined the Shaker community, west of Lebanon.

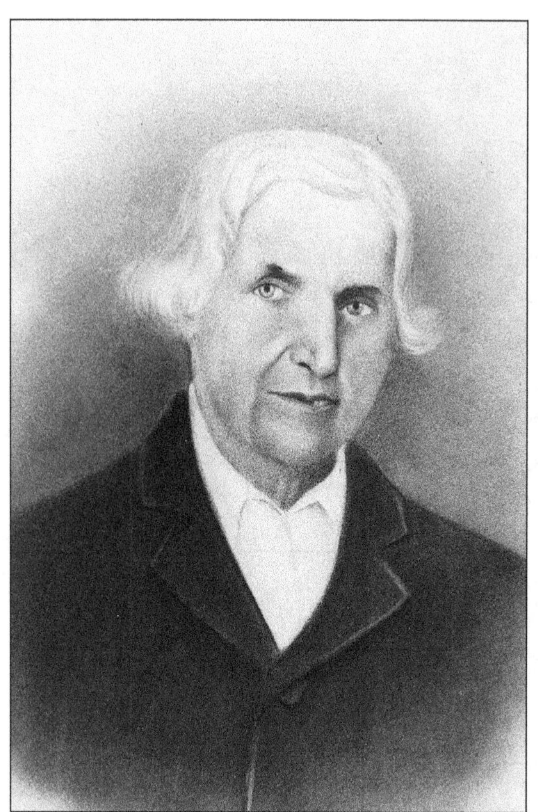

Daniel Doty, who had emigrated from New Jersey to Columbia, followed General Harmar's military trace up the valley. At a site now known as Thorny Acres, he built his first cabin, but the dense forest caused him to seek a better farm site. He then located on the banks of the Great Miami River. His portrait is from a charcoal sketch.

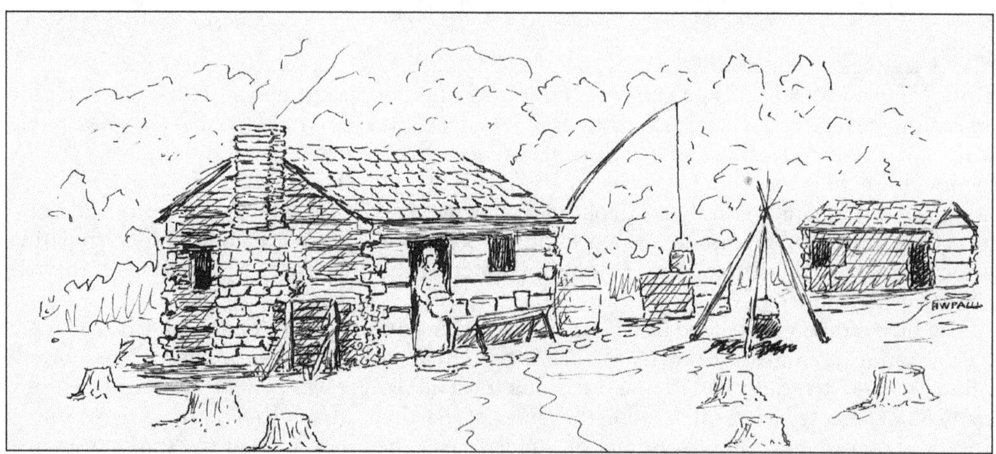

Doty's second cabin stood at the site now marked as 1106 South Main Street. It was typical of those in the new West. In 1815, Doty moved his growing family to a farm to the east and constructed a brick house. The sketch is by local artist Herbert Fall, a Doty descendant.

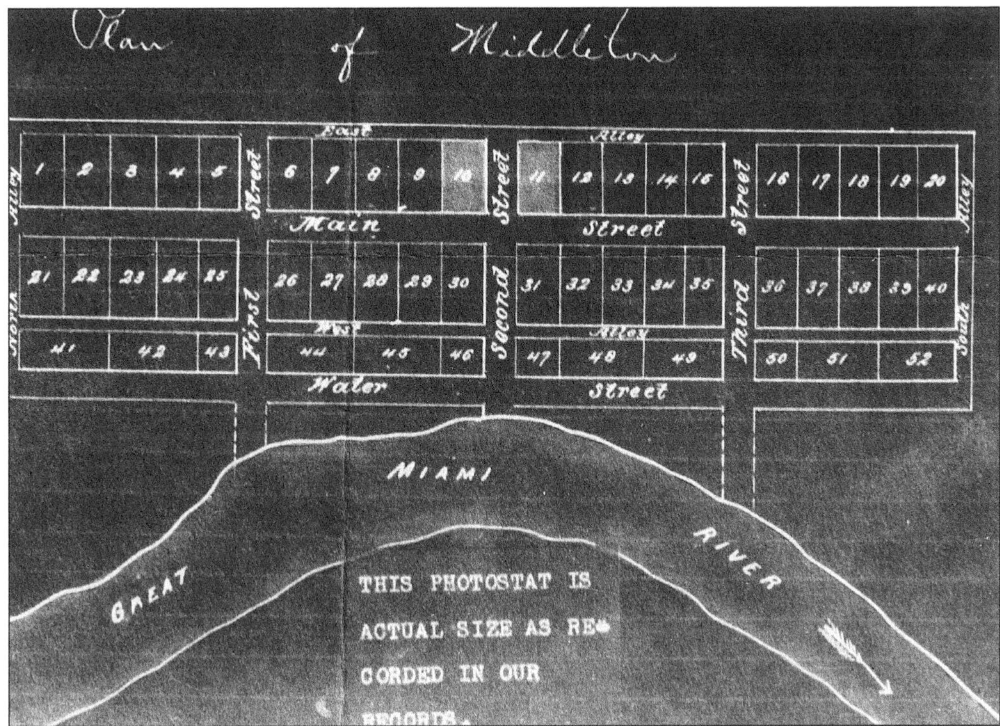

This plat was drawn by Stephen Vail, who took it by horseback to the Hamilton County Courthouse, Cincinnati, where it was recorded on November 1, 1802. Thus, Middletown became a dot on the Ohio map. Vail then built a dam across the Great Miami River, along with a raceway, and built three mills which signified the beginning of industry here.

MIDDLE-TOWN.

THE ſubſcriber has laid off a town on the eaſtern bank of the Great Miami river, about one mile above the big prierie, where lots are now offered for ſale.

The town is beautifully ſituated, on ground high and dry, which has heretofore proved healthy. There is adjoining the town a griſt, ſaw & fulling mill, all going. Water of a good quality may be had by digging from ſixteen to twenty feet. From its central ſituation, and many other advantages which it enjoys, ſanguine expectations are entertained that it will become the ſeat of juſtice of a county as ſoon as a diviſion takes place; and for this it is calculated—ground for a court houſe, jail, grave yard, church, &c. having been laid off in eligible ſituations. The terms of ſale may be known, and a plan of the town ſeen, by applying to the ſubſcriber on the premiſes.

STEPHEN VAIL

November 2, 1802.

This advertisement appeared in the *Western Spy and Hamilton Gazette*, an early Cincinnati newspaper, on November 2, 1802. In it, the people of the Northwest Territory were told of the advantages of settling in Middletown. Vail, a Quaker, arrived here in 1800.

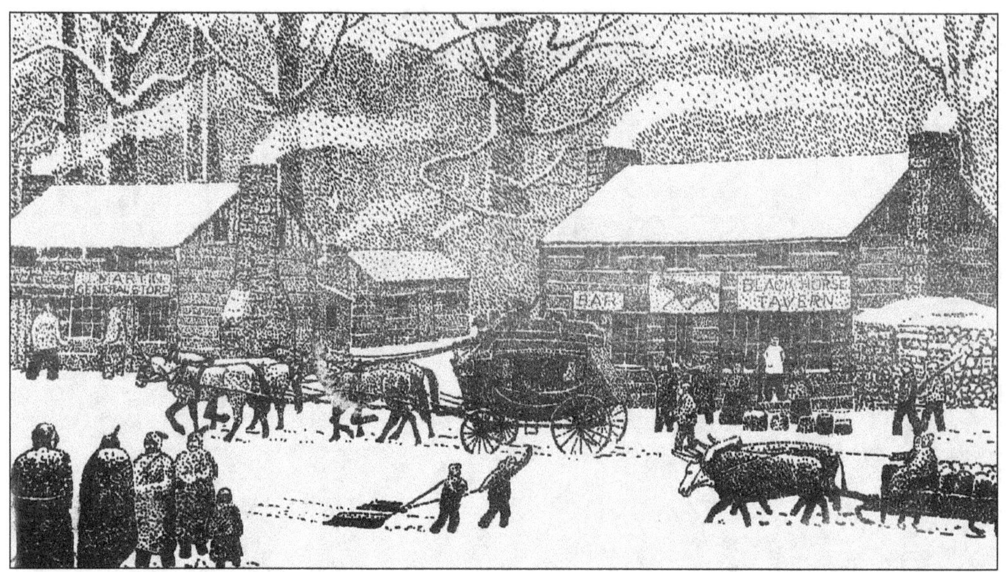

The town grew around the southwest corner of what became Central and Main, where Vail built his cabin. It was at the crossroads of the road from Cincinnati and Hamilton, and the one leading to Lebanon. Artist Fall sketched it as it may have appeared in 1815, when the first stagecoach arrived.

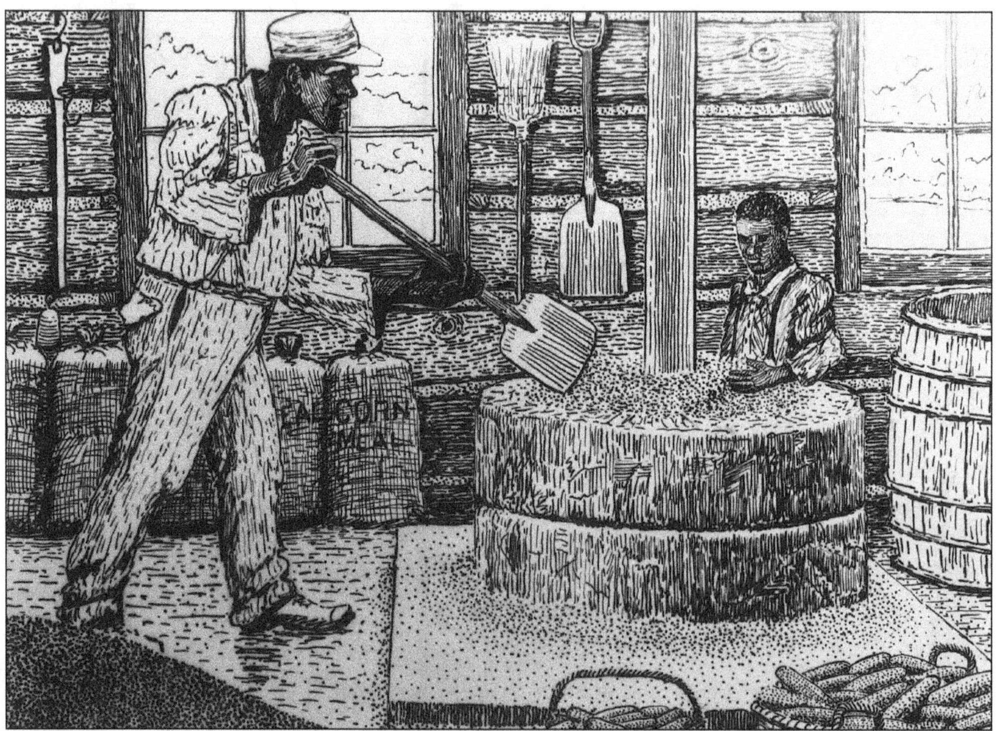

In 1800, settlement also began on the west side of the river, where Bamboo Harris, an African-American engineer, built the first gristmill in the area—the closest at that time being near Cincinnati. It would grind either corn into meal or wheat into flour, depending upon the mill stone used. Fall sketched the mill from descriptions of it given by his grandfather.

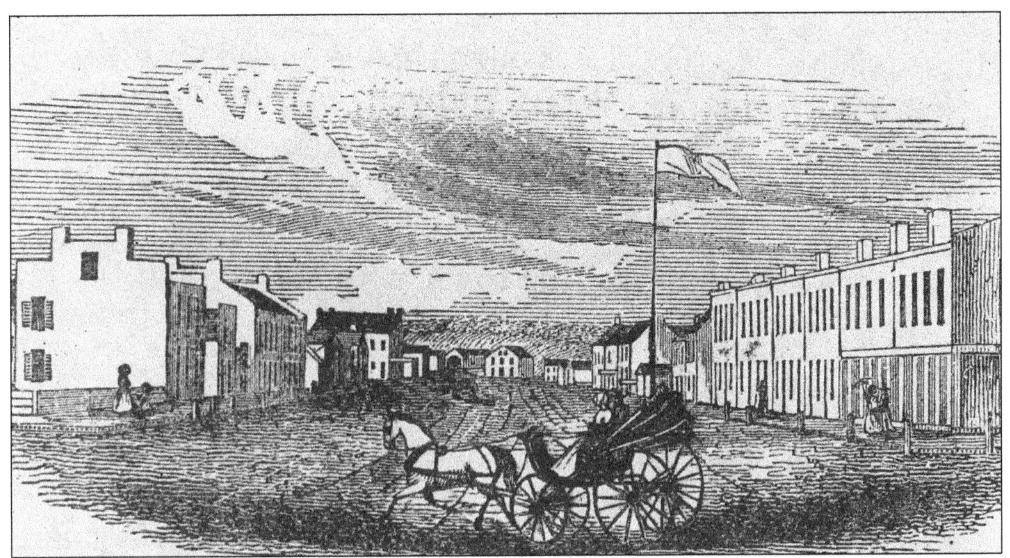

This sketch of the downtown was made by Henry Howe, pioneer Ohio historian, on a visit to the village. It is one of 177 such wood engravings that appeared in his book. The long row building on the right was known as the Leibee block, part of which is still standing. Note the covered bridge, built in 1832, over the Great Miami River, just south of Deardorf's gristmill.

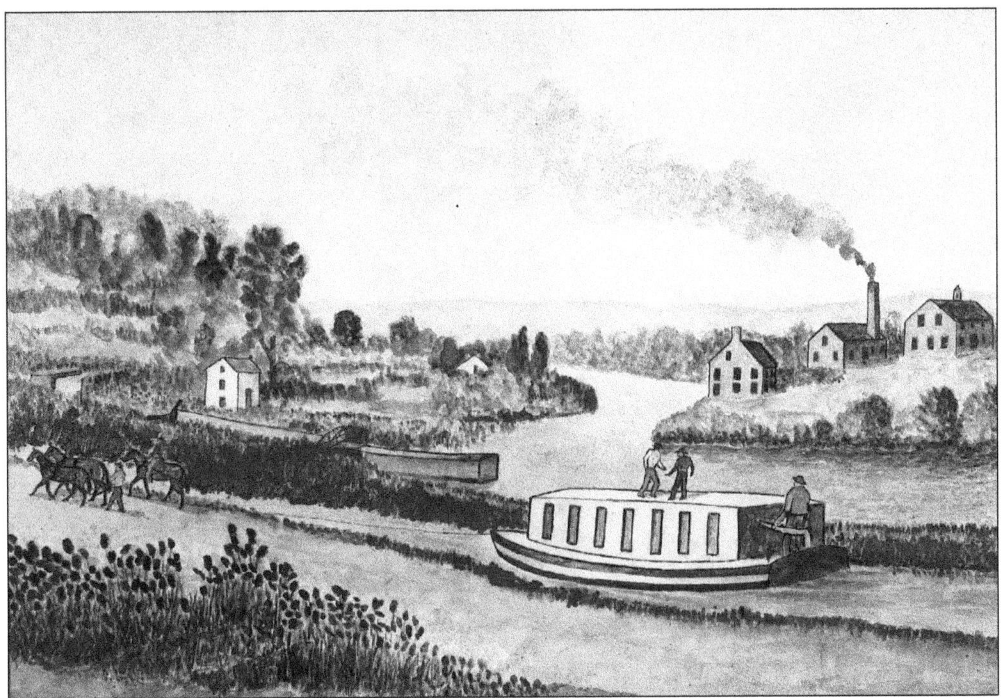

Here is a photograph of a Fall painting based on an engraving found on an old $5 bill that was issued as legal tender by a local bank in 1841. Pictured is the Doty lock area. Fall enlarged the engraving by using a slide for his model, creating a picture that is historically accurate.

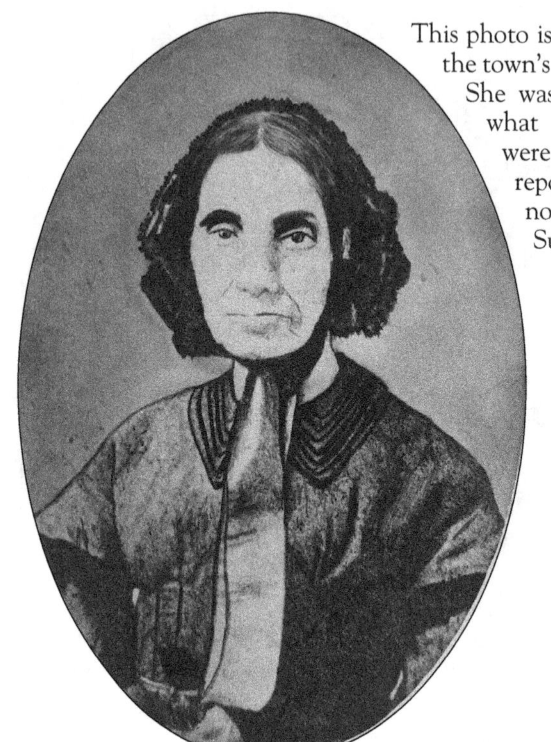

This photo is based on a painted portrait of Jane Potter, the town's first-born. Her birth date was April 2, 1797. She was born in a log cabin near the corner of what is now Main and Ninth. Her parents were Moses and Rhoda Potter. Her mother, reportedly, was the first white woman to live north of Fort Hamilton. Jane married John Sutphin in 1815.

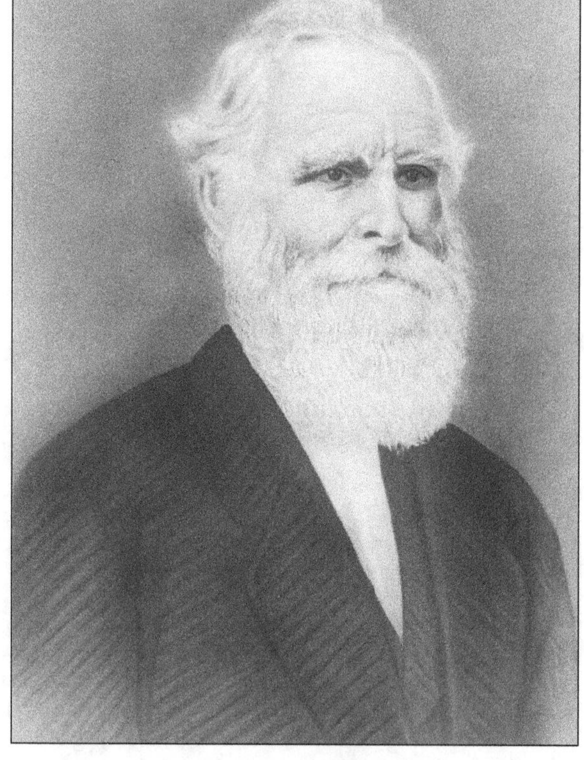

Thomas C. Reed, born October 3, 1797, was the second to be born in Middletown. He was born on a farm on Yankee Road, just north of Dicks Creek. He would help organize the Butler County Fair and become its president. As a young man, he split logs, burned bricks, and built flatboats on which he carried flour to New Orleans from the Dickey Mill at Amanda.

Two

Studio Photographs and Paper Moons

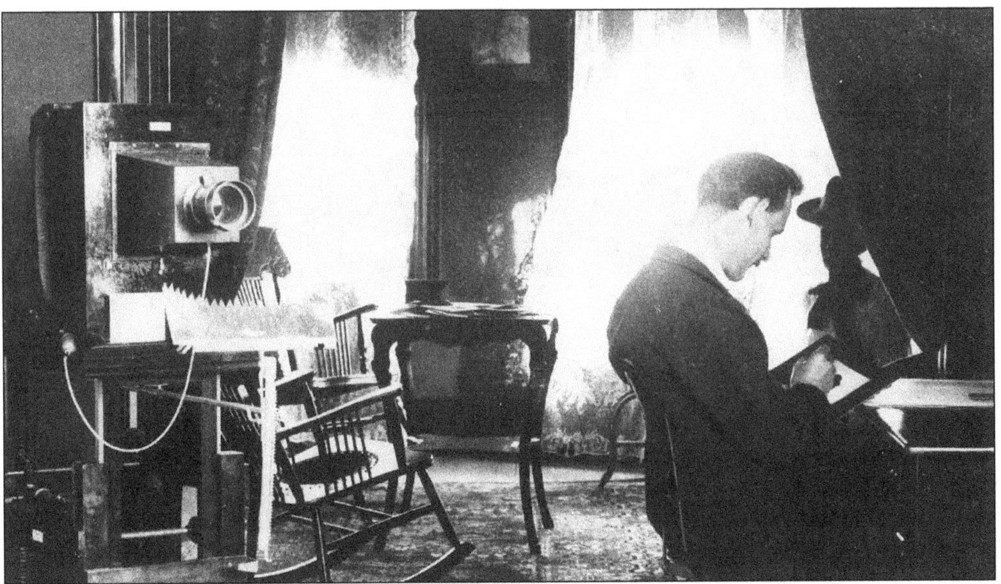

In 1839, Louis Daguerre, after improving upon the experiments in photography by Niepce, who died in 1833, was ready to produce daguerreotypes in a studio for the public. At first, people were skeptical—some warning that the invention was an insult to God, fearing his image might be caught by the camera. But that feeling soon gave way to the desire for a permanent family portrait that might last for generations. Improvements followed, and the tintype became popular. But this involved process kept most of the photography in the studio. To bring in the trade, studio photographers created all kinds of scenery to enhance the background and props such as stationary airplanes and paper moons.

Around 1850, stereoscopy was developed by an Englishman, Sir Charles Wheatstone, and photography went outdoors as, between 1850 and 1920, millions of views were taken and shown in a stereoscope. It was an activity which provided many hours of entertainment in the days before radio and television.

Enter the studio of local photographer Rudolph Schiebert, and look around. From this and other studios here, many pictures have survived and been hidden away as family treasures. In this chapter, such studio work is on display along with a couple of locally produced stereographs.

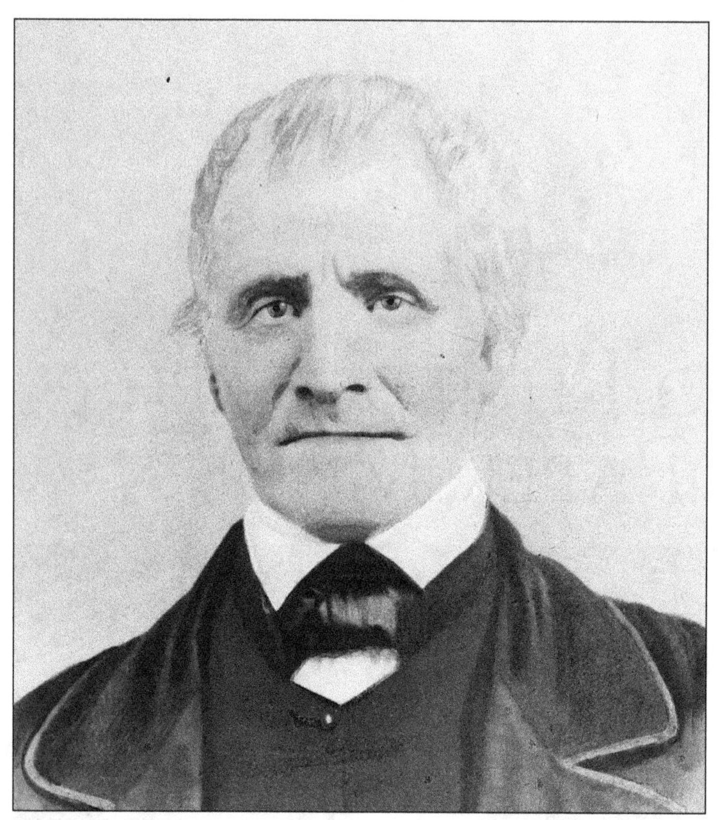

No known picture of Stephen Vail, who platted the town, exists; however, this one of Hugh Vail, one of his three sons, was handed down through the family. Hugh, one of ten children, came here with his father in 1800. He built the large house on the southeast corner of Curtis and First, which has been remodeled as the Knights of Columbus home.

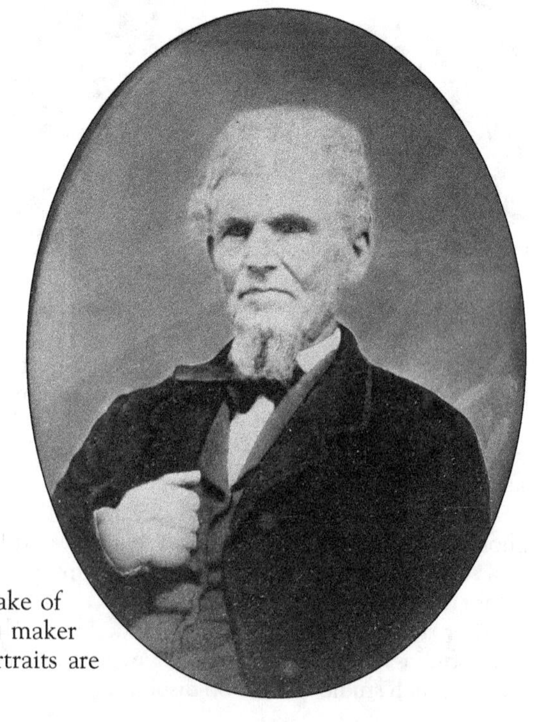

Daniel Crane Doty was the son and namesake of the town's first settler. He became a brick maker and contractor. Both Vail's and Doty's portraits are examples of early studio photography.

The two photographs on this page are from tintypes, which followed the daguerreotype. It utilized a metal plate coated with silver and required an exposure time of ten minutes. George M. Williamson is shown in the first tintype. He was a partner in the realty firm of Eaton and Williamson and resided at 1306 East Sixth (Girard) Street.

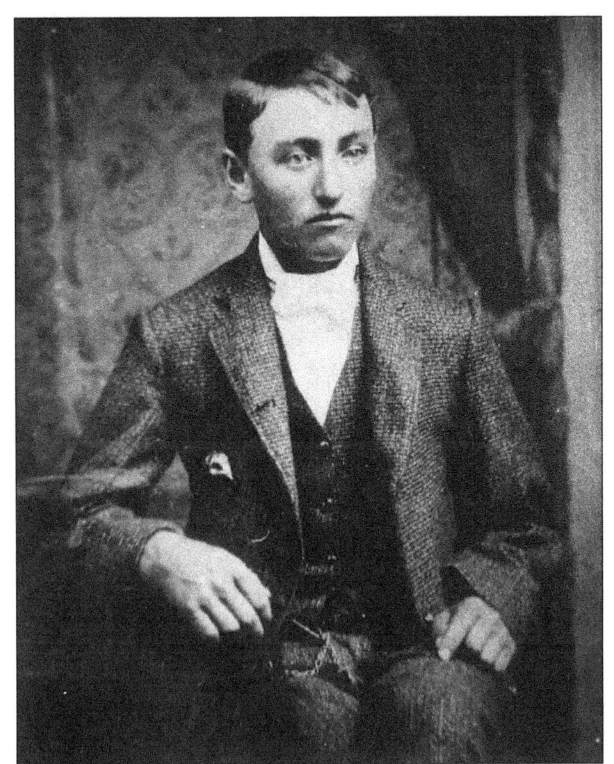

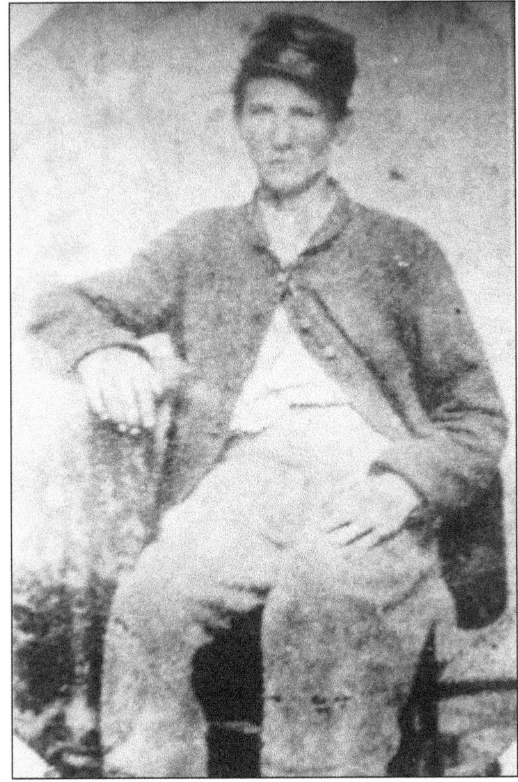

Clinton D. Orr was a Civil War veteran who was well known in Middletown and was once custodian of South School. He was the last survivor in Butler County of the Grand Army of the Republic. He headed many a Memorial Day parade. (Both tintypes by J.B. Nunneley.)

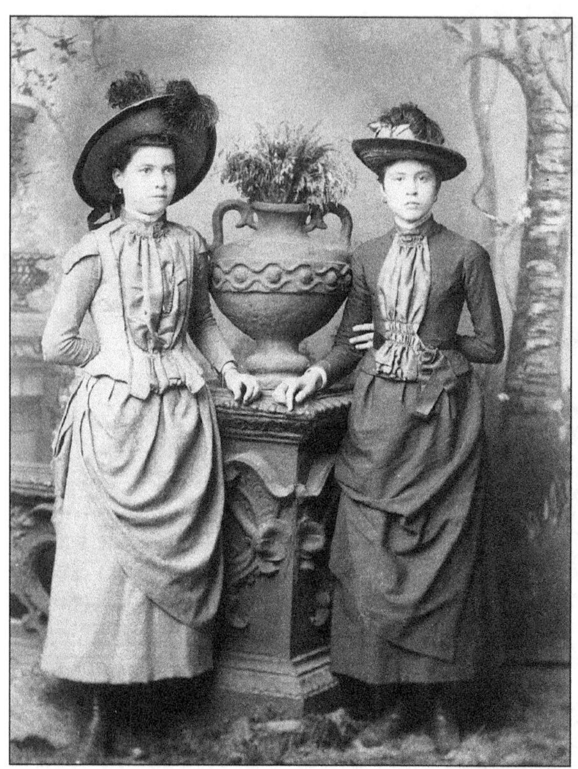

The following group of four photographs are examples of the work of local studios. The teenage girls posed at the Ferguson-Hale Studio, which advertised, "Artists Photography," and promised to preserve negatives so "duplicates can be had anytime." This photograph was on a glass negative.

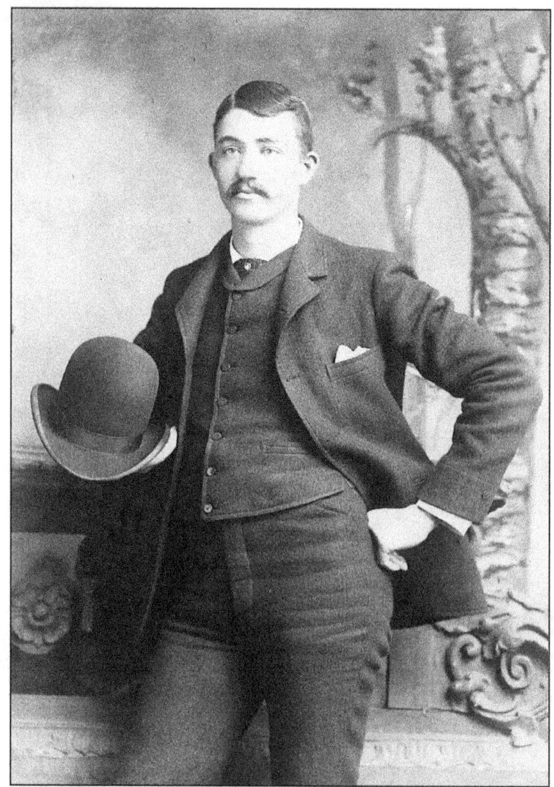

The young man, with hat in hand, had this portrait made at Conkle Brothers "Photographic Studio." It shows how a "real dude" dressed in the 1890s.

This setting was an enticement of Lawson and Matthews Studio at 27 South Main Street, illustrating how elaborate some settings were, almost overwhelming the subject.

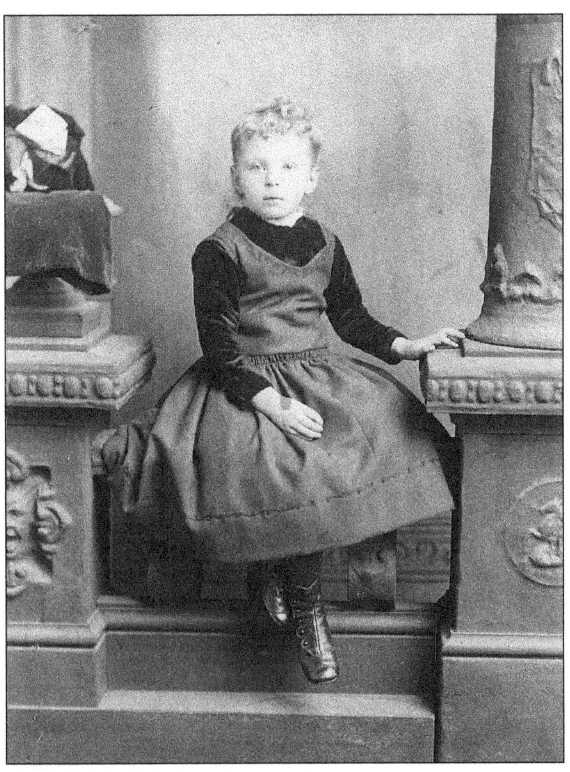

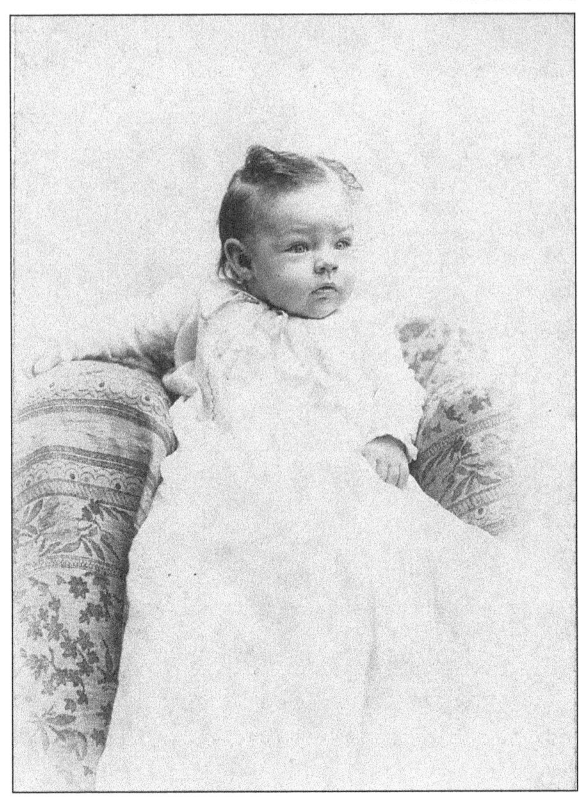

The F.S. Biddle Studio snapped this typical baby picture. Such unidentified photos as this group illustrate the importance of marking family photos with the names on the back.

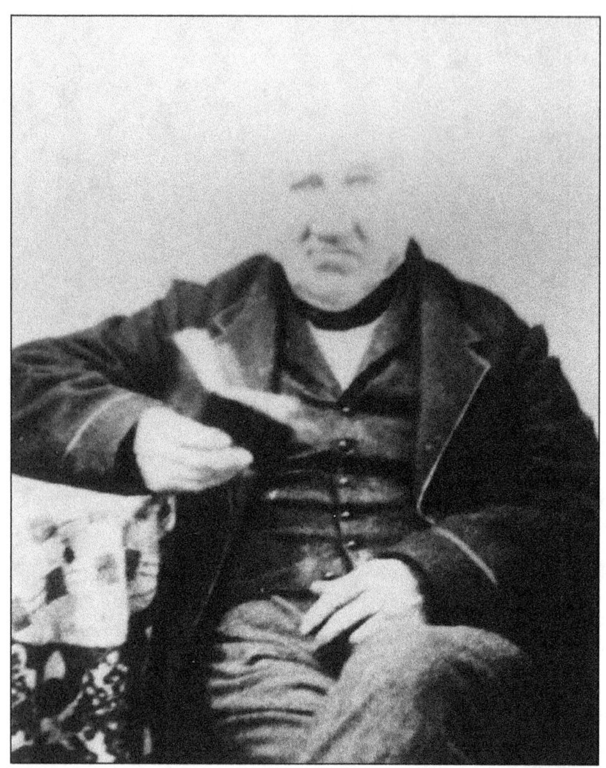

The name on the back of this photograph, made by the W.E. McKecknie Studio, corner of Main and Third (Central), is that of Arthur Lefferson (1787-1869). In 1827, he built the house at 404 South Main. It is the oldest house in the city which still stands on its original site.

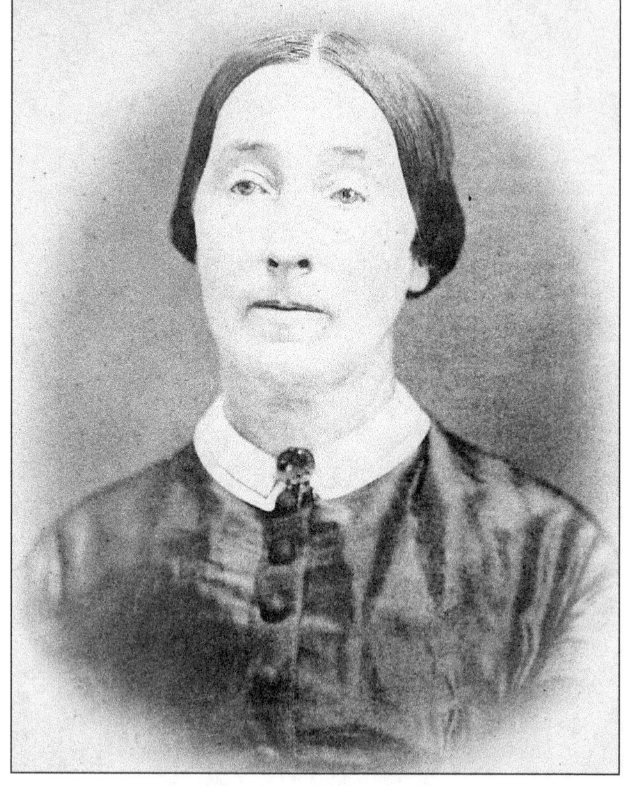

This portrait of Mrs. Louis F. Anders was made sometime in the 1870s in the studio of J.B. Nunneley, the town's first photographer. The Anders family opened a grocery store, which, after being operated by three generations of Anders, closed in 1952. Mrs. Anders helped in the store, making her one of the first women in the city to work outside the home.

This is a portrait of the William and Elizabeth Gardner family, who lived on the southeast corner of Main and Second. The original structure was later replaced by Dr. Mabel Gardner, who is seen standing in the photo. The baby is her brother, William. Dr. Gardner returned from medical school to practice here and delivered over 10,000 Middletonians.

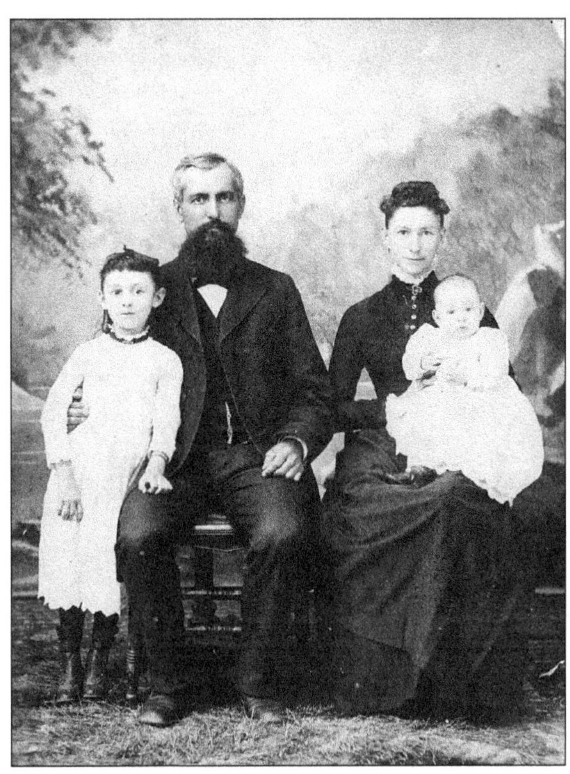

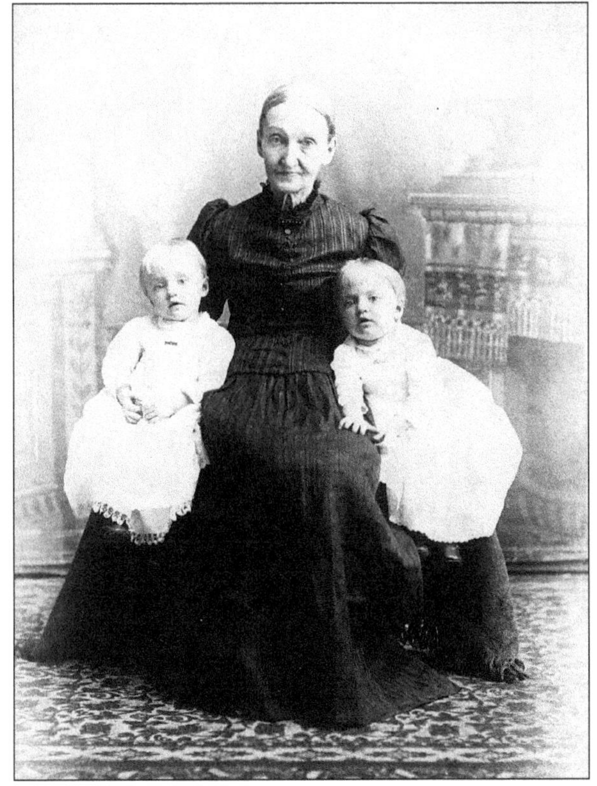

The twins in this "Lawson" photo, Myrtle and Mabel Williamson, are being held by grandmother Julia Ann Hetzler, whose family name is on Hetzler Road. Both alert ladies grew up to become local school teachers.

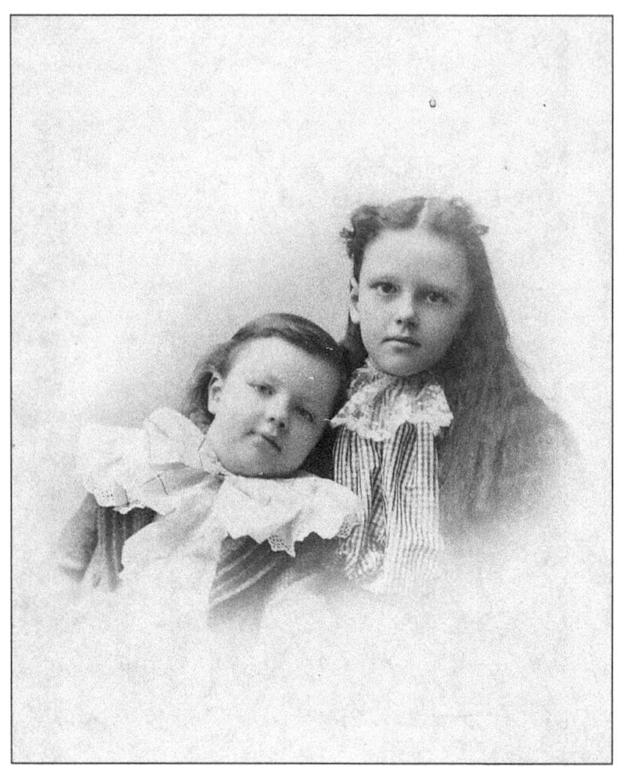

Lulu and Robert McClellan of Blue Ball, well-dressed children of the 1890s, were members of a prominent pioneer family of Scotch-Irish descent. Both grew up to become prominent musicians on the national stage. Lulu's home was in Middletown, but when on a concert tour she was a famous whistler. Later in the 20th century, another Blue Ball native, Bonnie Murray, won national recognition as a concert soloist.

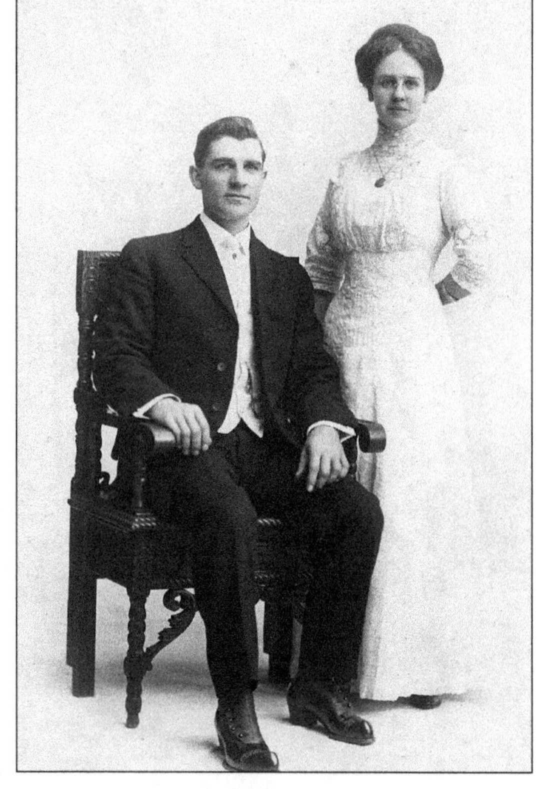

Pictured here is a studio marriage picture of Clarence E. Crauder and Mabel Mosteller, a Sharonville school teacher. Crauder was a Preble County schoolmaster in the early 1900s. The marriage took place around 1910. He is remembered in Middletown as a pioneer in the frozen foods industry with his frozen locker business on Park Street.

Rev. John B. Morton, a graduate of Princeton, was a Presbyterian minister assigned here in 1840, and leaving in 1865. While here, he operated a private academy at his home, which became the Barnitz Home (the city's oldest home). Later, he moved the home to Thornhill Lane. Besides his work in the ministry and education, he served for a time as editor of the local newspaper.

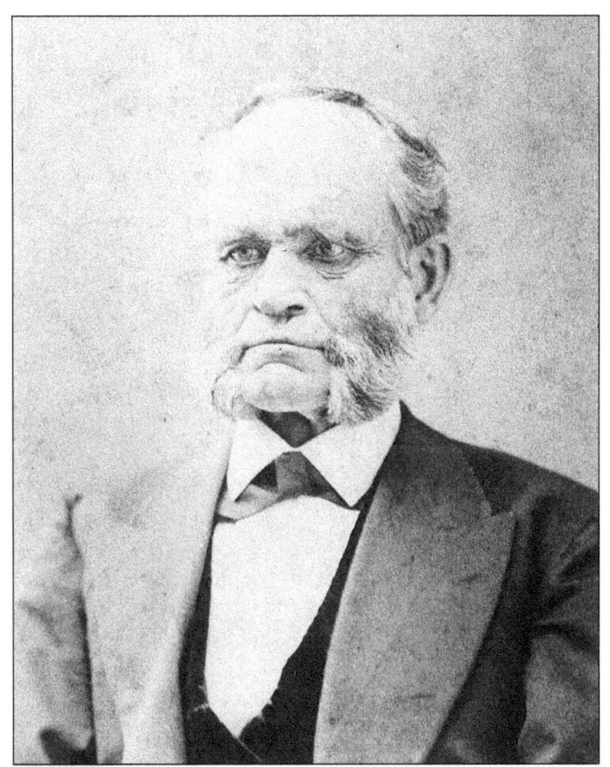

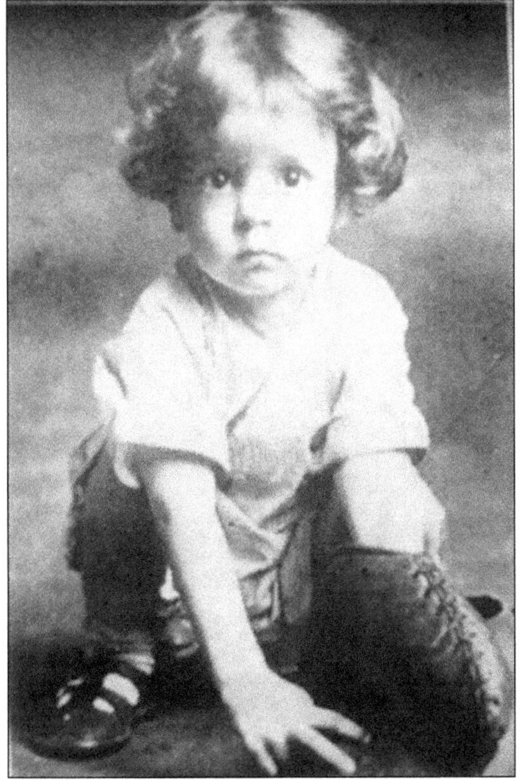

This is young Roger Burton Palmer around 1914, and his interest in football is clearly shown. He was one of the Palmer family who developed Burton and Lylburn Roads off Central Avenue, which is known as the Runnymede subdivision. The plat was filed in 1922, and the area became part of the city on July 10, 1948. At the same time, Valley View, East Side Farms, Thorn Hill, and Eldorado were annexed. Wilson School was opened in 1951 to serve the district.

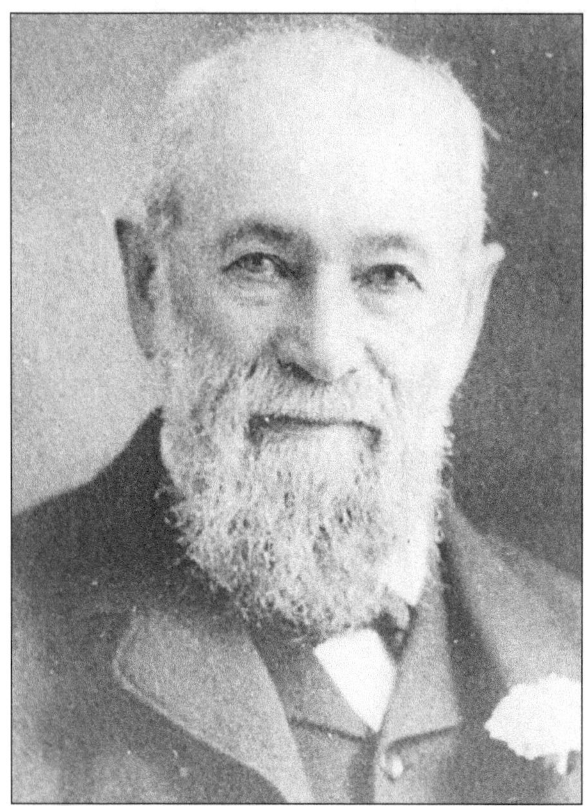

Simon Goldman, the pioneer merchant of Middletown, began as a pack peddler, then obtained a wagon, and finally a store, which became the city's first major department store, operating for 60 years. He headed the first Jewish family in town, and his legacy is Goldman Park.

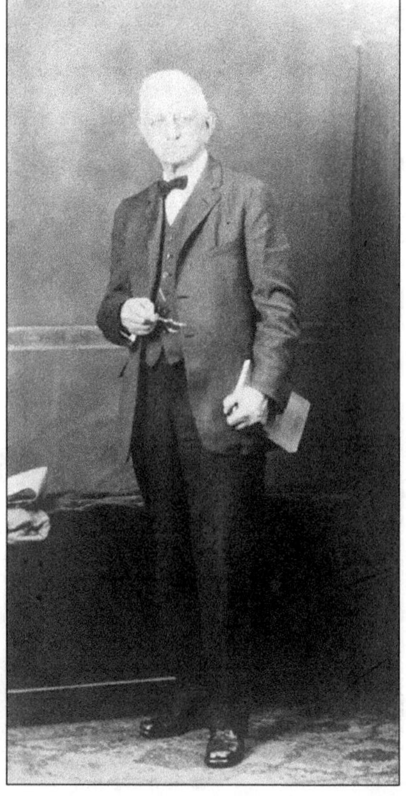

Judge William H. Todhunter, whose family name is on an area road, was born near Monroe. Admitted to the bar in 1871, he settled in Middletown, joining the established law firm of Doty and Gunckel. In 1917 he was elected Judge of the Municipal Court. He was one of the founders of the public library and a president of the school board.

Here is a young Louis B. McCallay, around 1915, in a photographic studio dressed as an engineer. The family home, later inherited by him, was at 228 South Main and is now owned by Lawrence Mulligan.

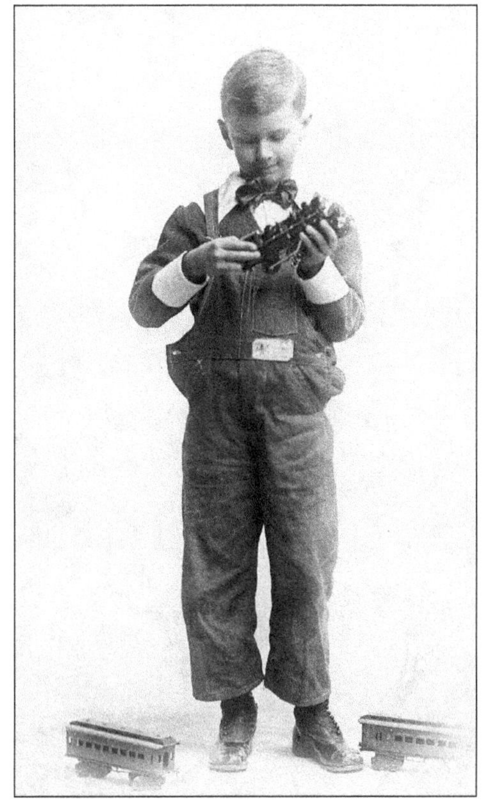

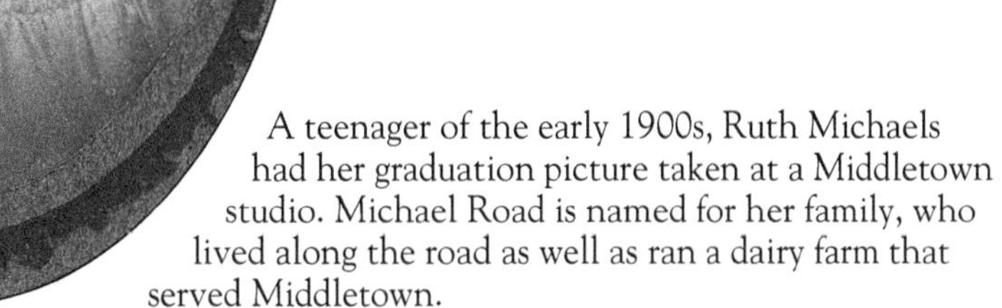

A teenager of the early 1900s, Ruth Michaels had her graduation picture taken at a Middletown studio. Michael Road is named for her family, who lived along the road as well as ran a dairy farm that served Middletown.

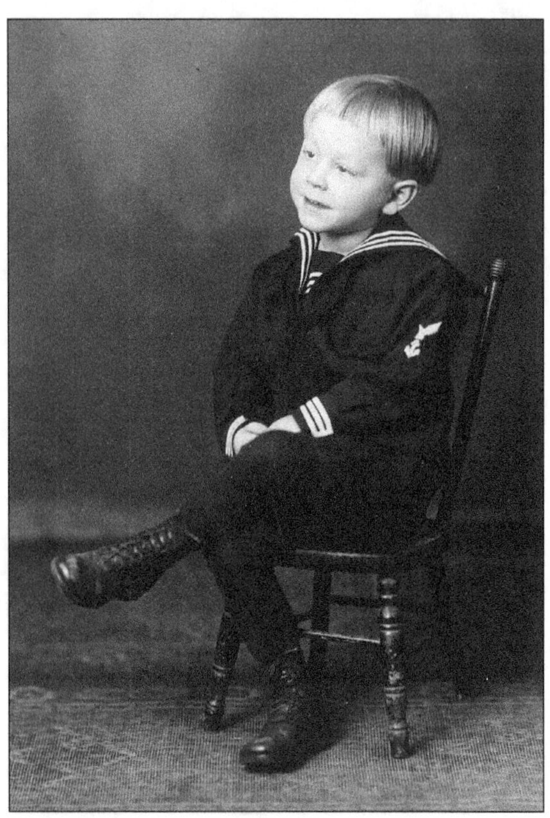

By the 1920s, photographers began to use draperies instead of elaborate scenery and props to focus on the dress and the individual. Here is master George Crout in his sailor's uniform in 1921. Such nautical outfits were in style following WW I. Thousands of such photos were taken of little boys. Crout later served in the Air Force, and became a local educator and historian.

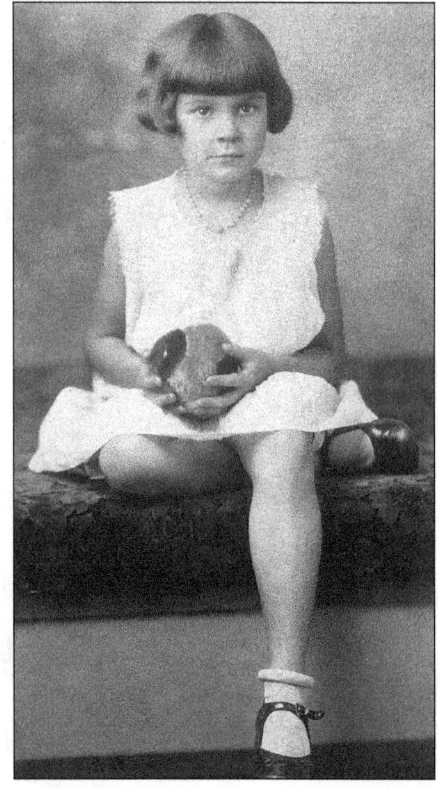

This little girl, Betty Ann Hollenbaugh, with her "Dutch" haircut, lived on Panama Street. Here, in the late 1920s, she came to the studio dressed in her best—a cotton dress with lace insertions, rolled stockings, and black, patent-leather, Mary-Jane shoes. She would later work at Aeronca and then join the Waves.

Between 1910 and 1920 some studios reached new heights with trick photography. Paper moons became a popular setting, due to such popular songs as "Moonbeams," "Shine on Harvest Moon," and others. Here two friends, Myrtle Williamson and Edna Wagner, had their picture taken.

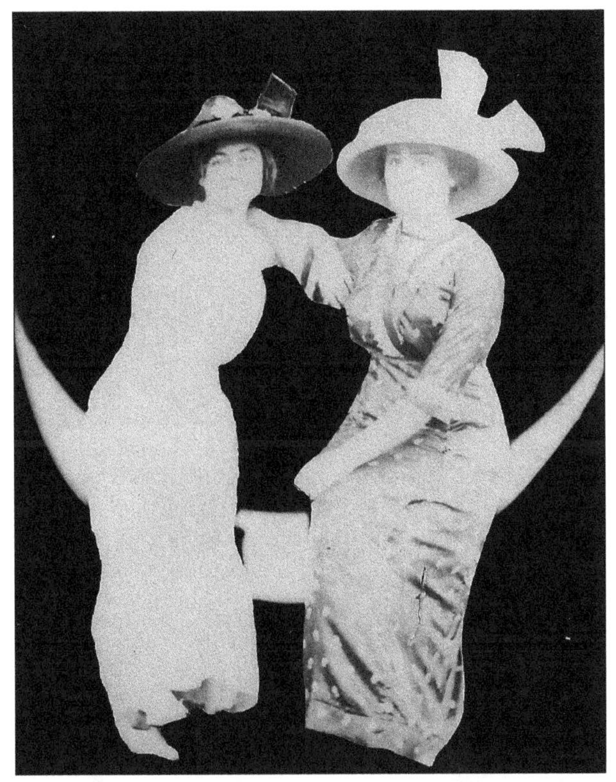

For young men the airplane was a popular prop. Here three local young men—Gingerich, Walters, and Crout—have taken off in the studio flight over scenic Middletown. Upon seeing the photo, one shocked grandmother remarked, "What will those boys do next?"

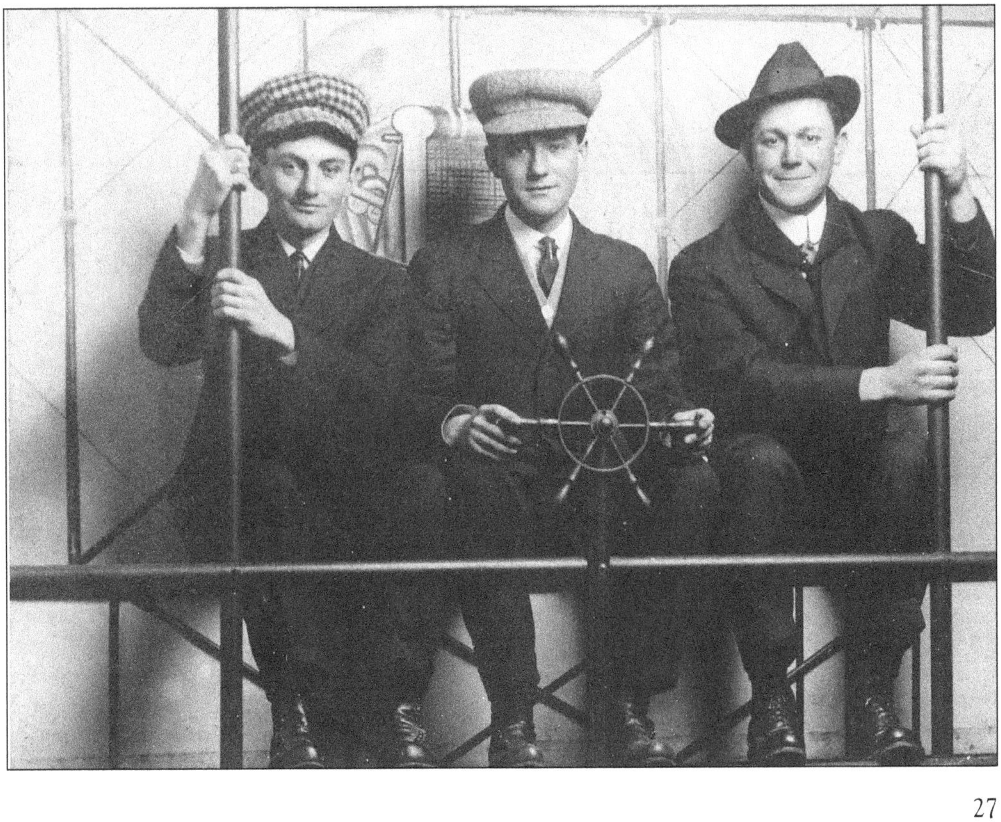

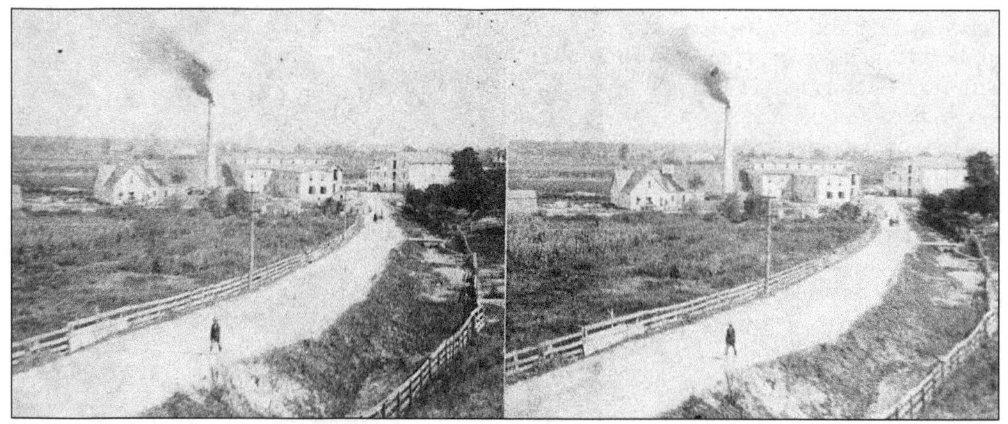

Between 1850 and 1920, stereoscopes were popular, with millions of pictures taken in three dimensions for this device, which was similar to Viewmasters of later times. It required a special camera, and usually a local photographer would buy one to go out and shoot local scenes. This photo was taken on the road leading to the Wardlow-Thomas Paper Mill.

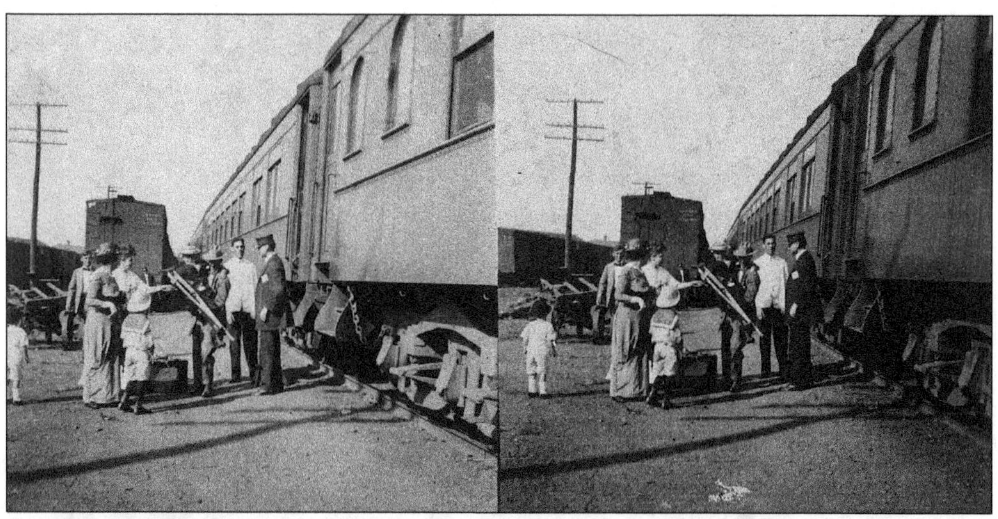

A wealthy family, the George Harveys, has a stereograph made of their arrival home on the Big Four Railroad from a Boston vacation. This stereograph was taken by son, Arthur, at 3 p.m. on August 27, 1913, as recorded in a family diary. The Harveys were involved in the local paper industry.

Three

The Nineteenth Century on Film

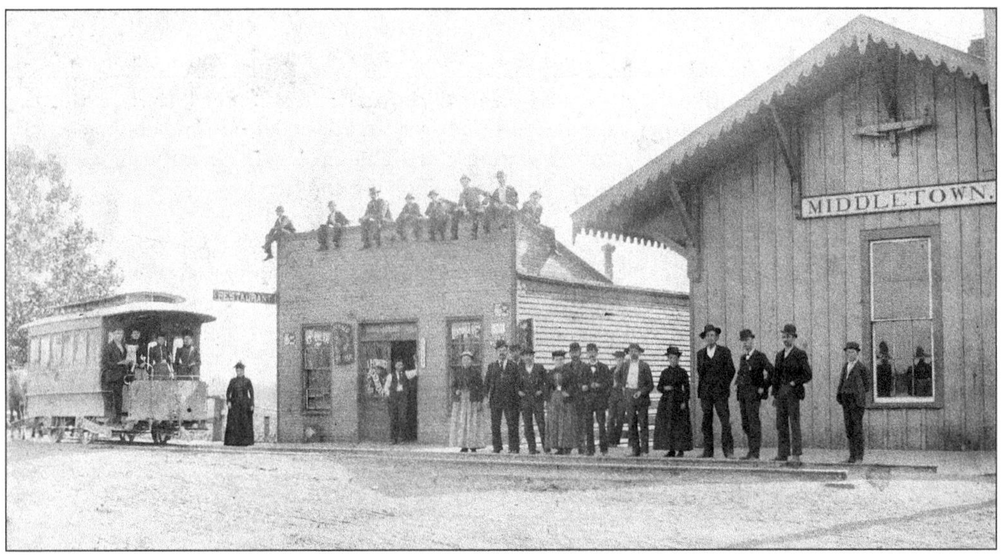

After the Civil War, professional photographers began to take their cumbersome equipment around town, and some of the views they took are reproduced in this chapter. Taken together, they provide a picture of a growing town which became a city in 1886. On this page appears a view of the Cincinnati and Springfield Railroad Station in the East End, along Charles Street. It was built with the coming of the first locomotive on July 2, 1872. The new railroad was popularly known as the "Beeline," for its route was a bit shorter than that of the Cincinnati, Hamilton, and Dayton Railroad across the river in Madison township, which arrived in 1851, with its depot known as the "Middletown Station." The two railroads aroused a lot of interest when races were held to see which line could get a locomotive through faster.

Interest in getting your "picture taken" can be shown by some of the people in this picture—some probably coming out on the waiting horsecar, which went into operation in 1879, running from one railroad station to the other. This dates the picture as being taken in the early 1880s. In 1881, the first set of scenes around town was taken. This set was known as calotypes, being produced by a more simple process on a paper negative. However, the prints were not as clear as those made on polished glass plates, over which a mixture of viscous egg albumen and iodine was poured to coat the plate.

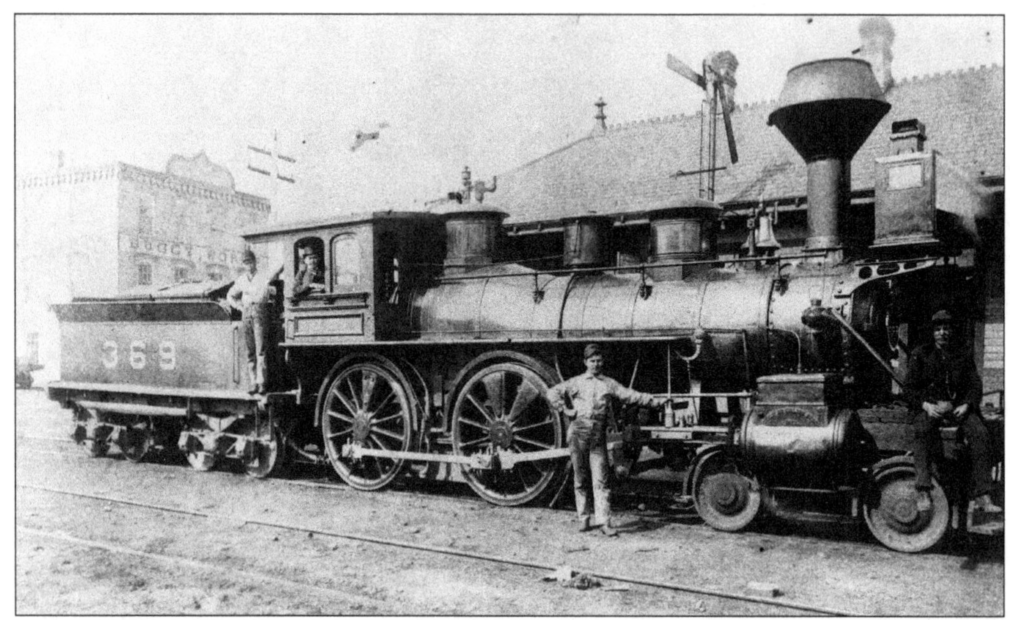

This is the type of locomotive that operated on the Beeline Railroad, later known as the Big Four, which arrived in Middletown on July 2, 1872. It was an early coal-burning engine, with a water pump that worked when the engine was in motion. There is a spark arrestor smoke stack, steam dome whistle, sand box, oil-burning headlight, and cow-catcher.

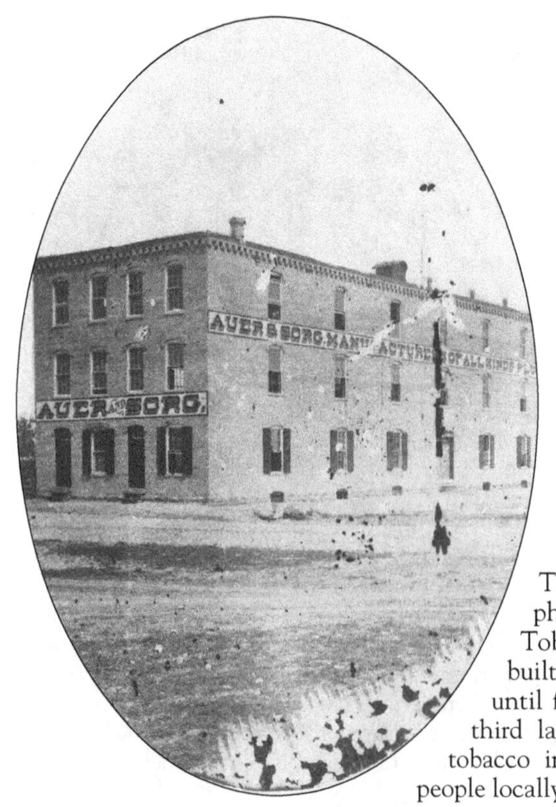

The building seen in the background of this photo is the original part of the big Sorg Tobacco factory along Charles Street. It was built in 1878 and expanded section by section until filling an entire city block. It became the third largest manufacturer of plug and smoking tobacco in the United States. It employed 1,800 people locally.

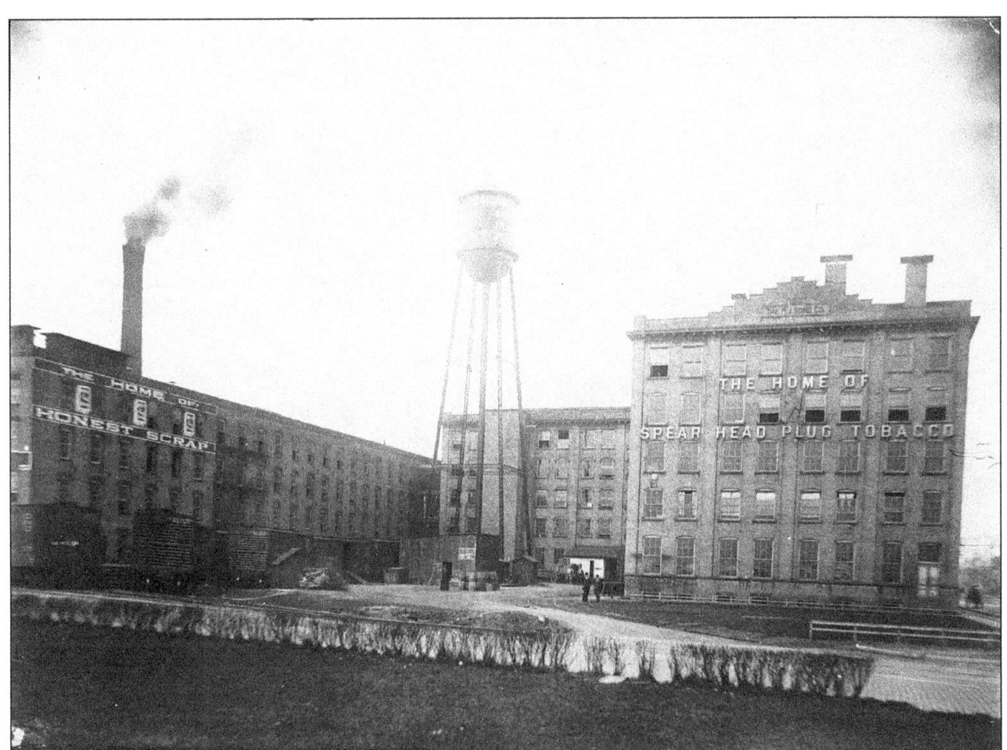

Working with Sorg were Auer and Wilson. Auer retired and Wilson purchased the original Sorg plant along the canal, forming the Wilson-McCallay firm. Sections of this plant are still standing along Girard Avenue. It also became a major producer and, along with Sorg in 1898, would become part of the national Continental Tobacco Trust, with Sorg later becoming part of P. Lorillard.

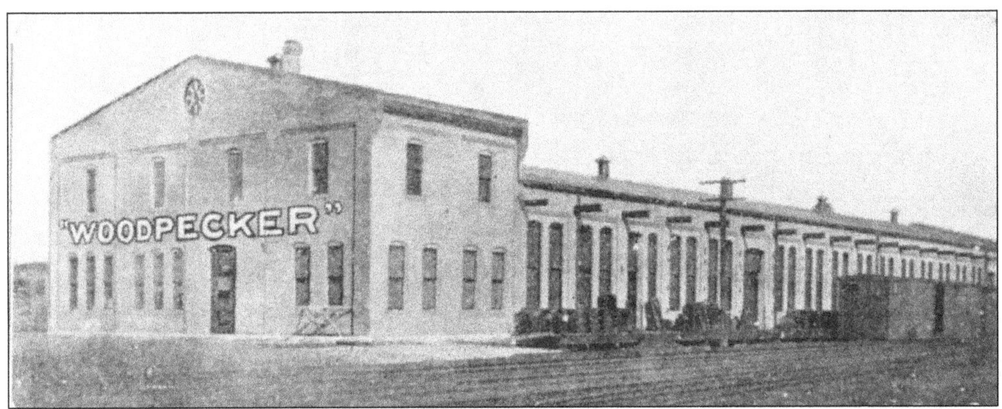

The Middletown Machine Company, along the Big Four Railroad, was formed in 1889 and reorganized when Shartle left the firm to open a new plant. It manufactured the popular "Woodpecker" and "Miami" gasoline engines, many of which are now in the hands of collectors. Barkelew Electric subsequently moved into the building.

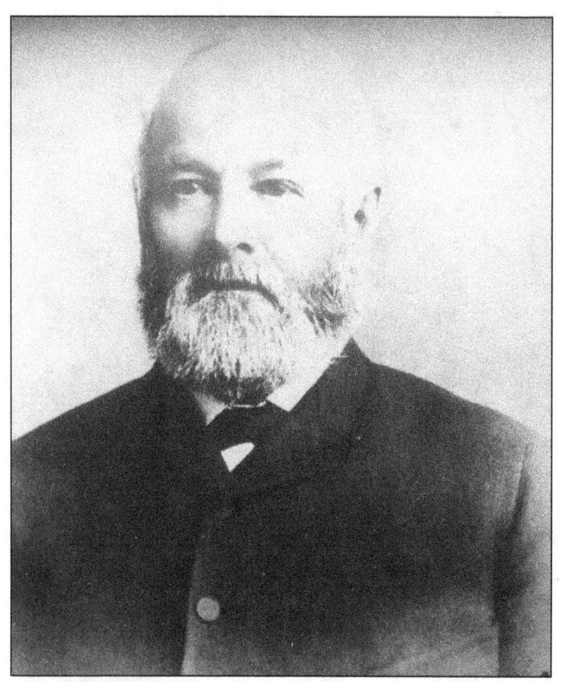

Edward Jones (1814-1892) arrived in Middletown in 1836, entered the pork-packing business—then the town's major industry. He eventually operated the largest such plant in the village. Not only were Jones's hams in demand in the East, but in Europe as well. He built a fine home along First Avenue at a site now occupied by St. John's Church.

The Poland-China hog, developed by the Shakers in cooperation with local farmers, became the nation's most prized breed. A monument in east Middletown stands on the farm where this breed was registered. It is unique, being the only known monument to a pig in the United States. Artist Fall sketched the picture of the pork house from a faded photograph.

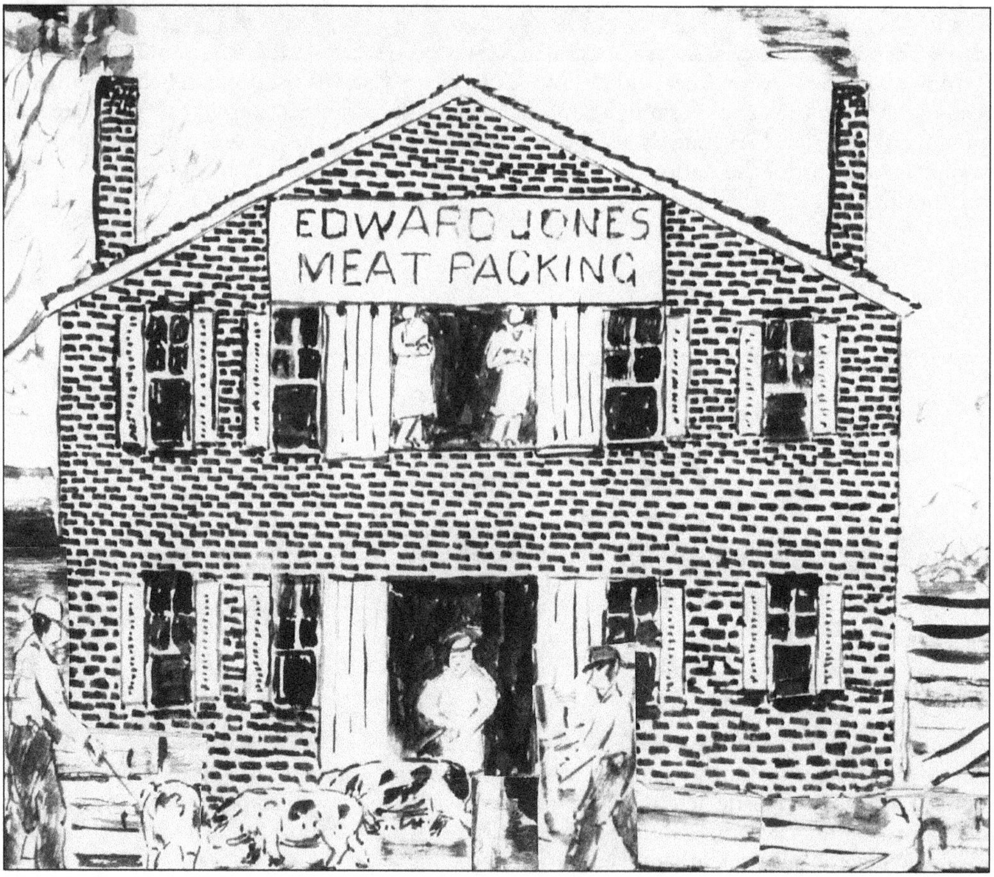

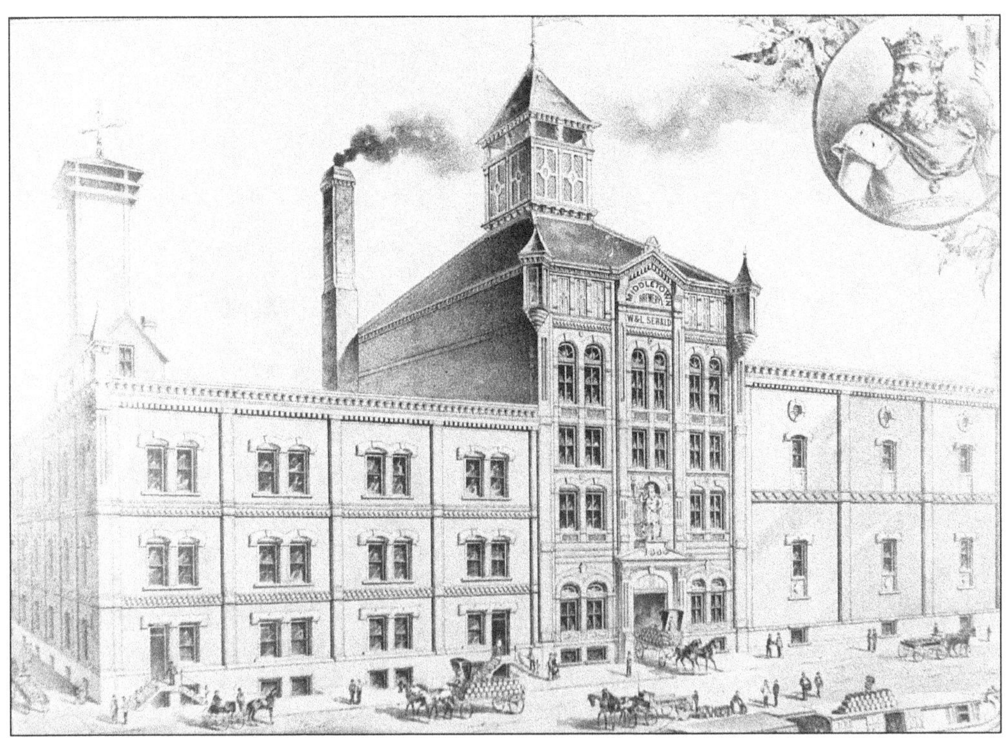

In 1866, William and Louis Sebald established a brewery along the west side of the old canal, between Central and First. It grew into a major local industry, which was closed in 1919 due to Prohibition. The canal boat *Gambrinus*, seen anchored in front, was used for beer deliveries.

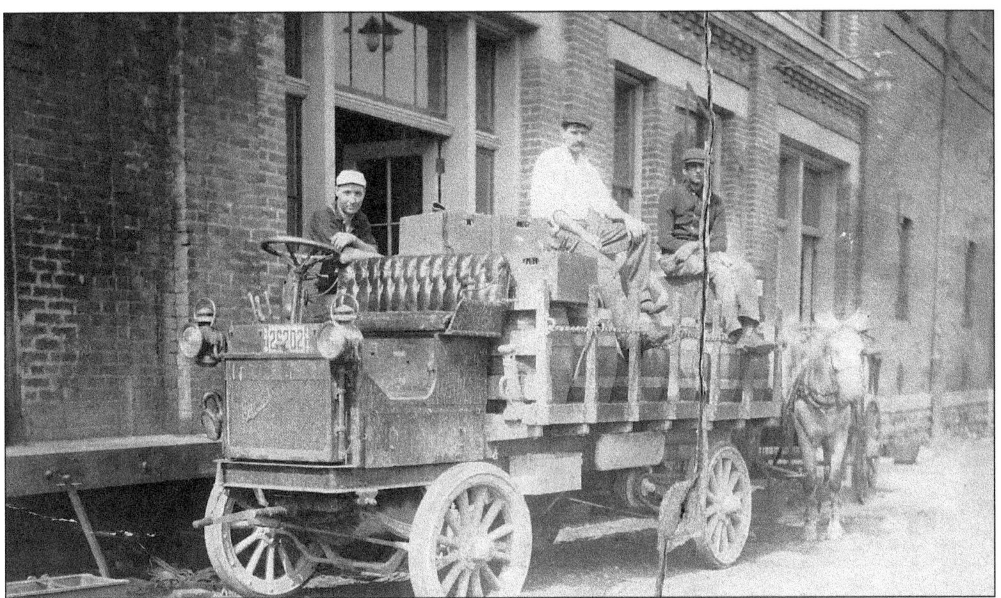

This Watson photo shows the first load of beer being taken into the new brew house in 1914, after the flood. The old gray horse behind it pulled the beer wagon, which was also used in deliveries. Although there is no indication as to the persons' locations in the picture, the following names appear on the photo: Bill Horn, Nancy Lloyd, and William Selby.

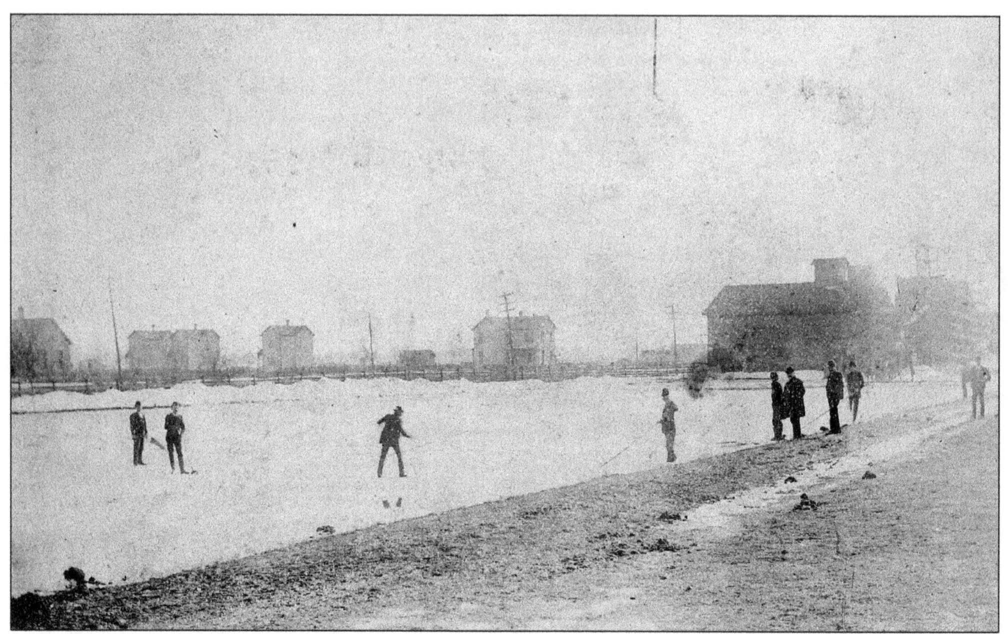

In order to cool beer, the Sebalds operated ice ponds on the grounds now occupied by McKinley and Taft Schools. They had a large pond surrounded by icehouses. However, this business ended in 1897 when the Sebalds purchased the first artificial ice-making machine in the city.

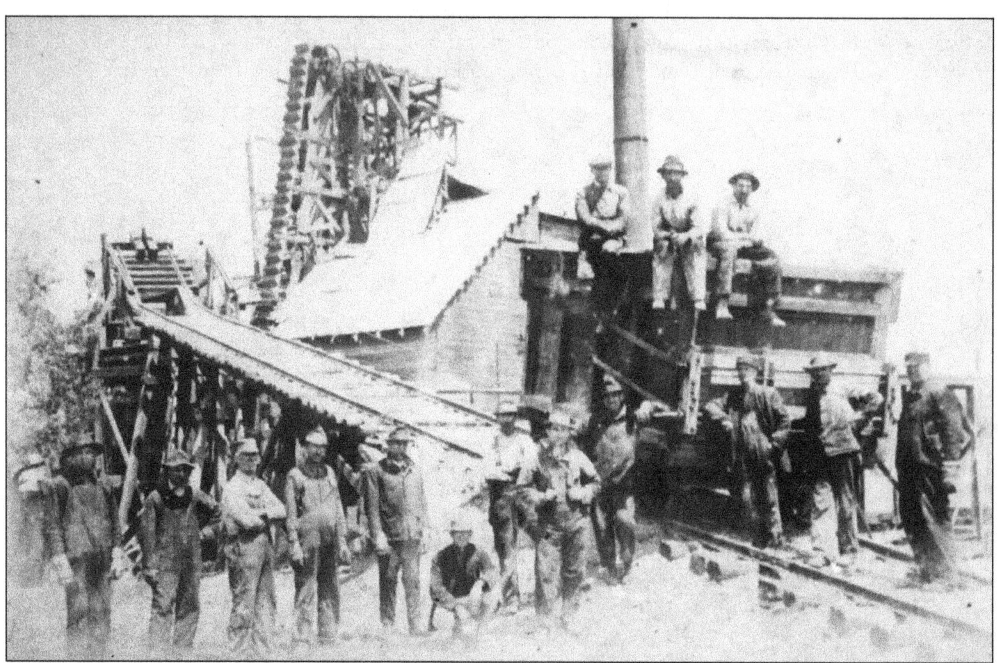

Smith Park was originally the Smith farm, then Smith erected a brickyard with kilns on part of it. When the brickyard closed, the farm was rented to Russell Stevens Sr. for a sand and gravel company, which was later taken over by his son, Russell Jr. The company then moved to Main Street. On December 3, 1940, the city purchased the 160-acre farm from William and A.D. Smith for use as a park, which is the city's largest and most used.

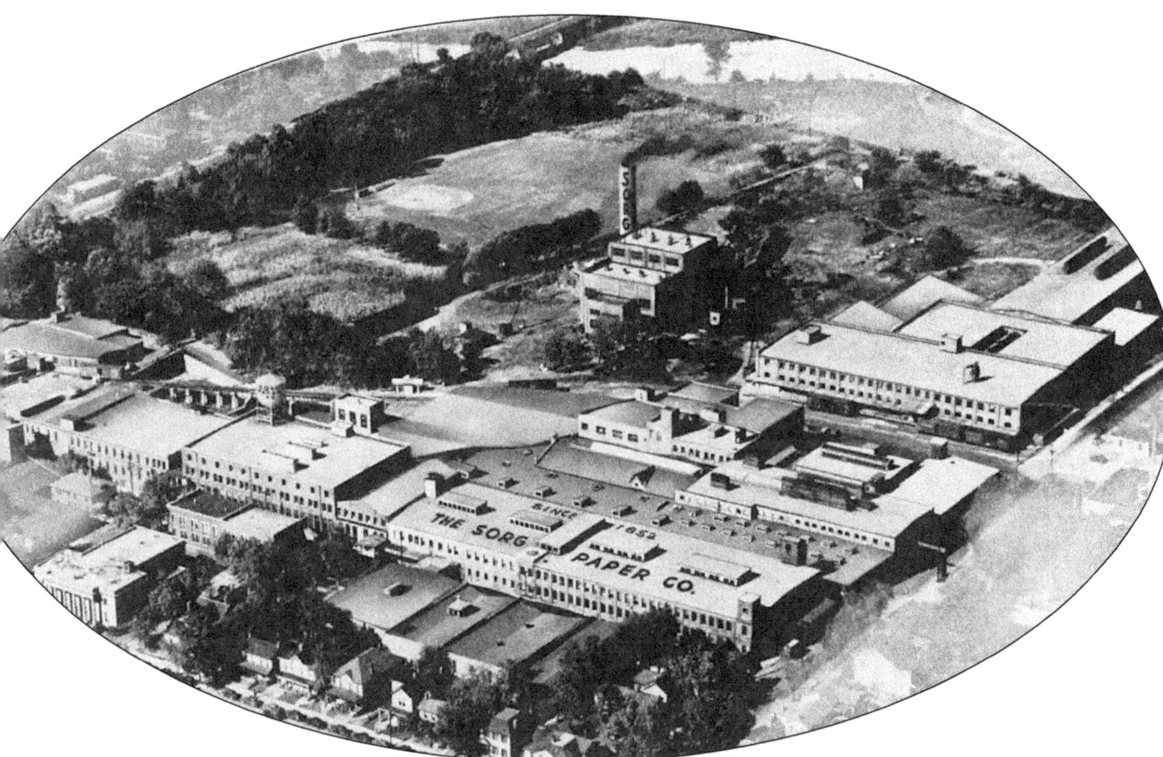

Here is an aerial view of the Sorg Paper Company. It represented a consolidation of all the old paper mills along the Hydraulic Canal. The first mill was the Erwin Paper Company, which began operation in 1852. It was purchased by Oglesby and associates, emerging as the W.B. Oglesby Paper company. Then it was merged with the Frank A. Smith Paper Company and the Paul A. Sorg Paper Company to form the Sorg Paper Company, in 1931. In 1983, it became a subsidiary of the Mosinee Paper Corporation of Wisconsin, which, in 1997, merged with Wausau Papers. A Bay West Division was established in 1989 to manufacture toweling and bath tissue. The plants have been continually updated.

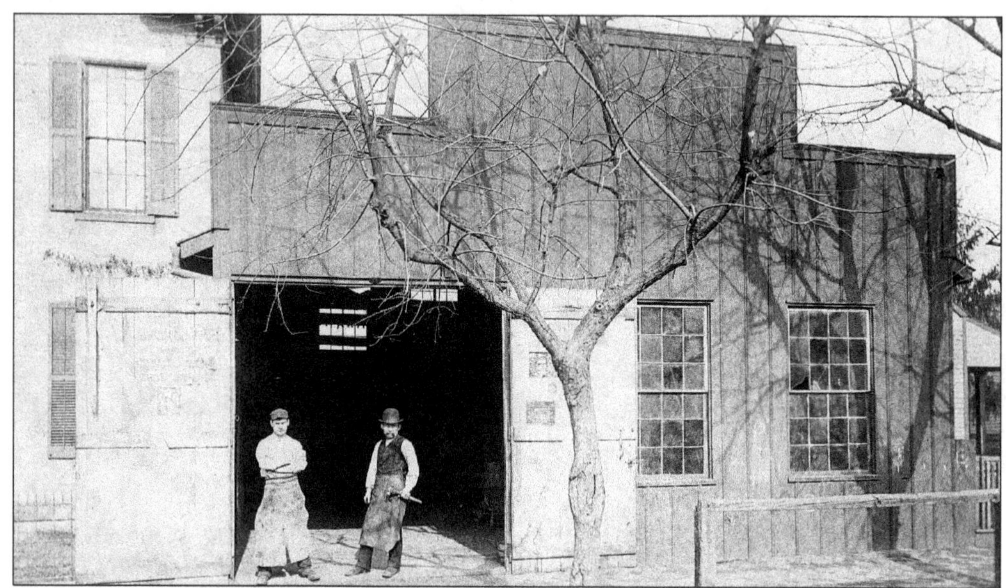

Here is the Greter blacksmith shop, which stood along South Broad Street at the present site of a church parking lot. Charles W. Greter, seen here with hammer in hand, was one of the city's last blacksmiths. They were the mechanics who worked with iron to produce hardware, which is now machine-made.

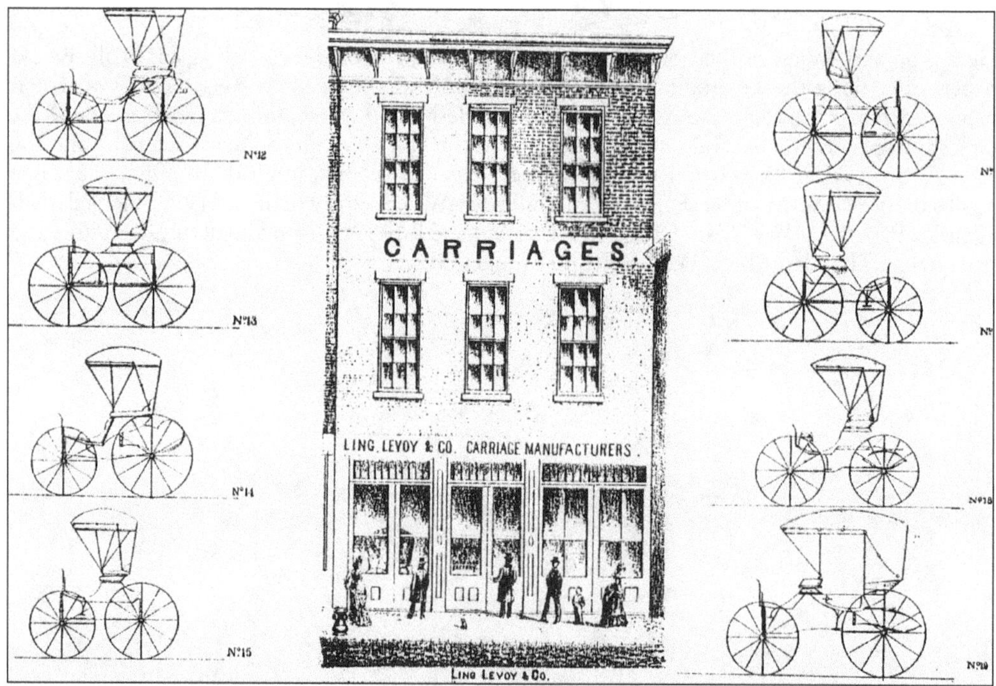

Middletown had several blacksmith shops that did work for its buggy and wagonmakers. The city was a major producer of carriages, being the third largest in the state. Ling-Van Sickle introduced mass-production techniques in making carriages. The Decatur Buggy Works was larger, however, manufacturing horse-drawn vehicles until 1908, when forced out of business by the coming of the automobile.

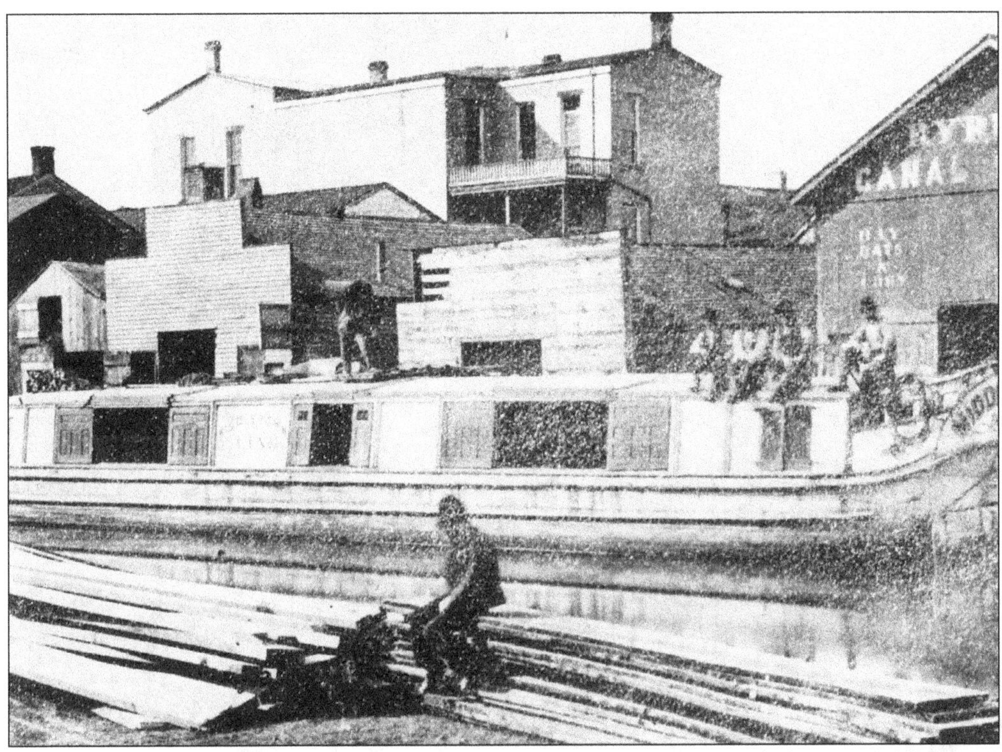

This is an 1881 calotype produced using the paper negative process. Entitled "Port Middletown," this photo was taken at the port, located at the canal just south of present Central Avenue. The tall building is the then-new City Hotel. Tolls were collected at the port and a scale was located at the site.

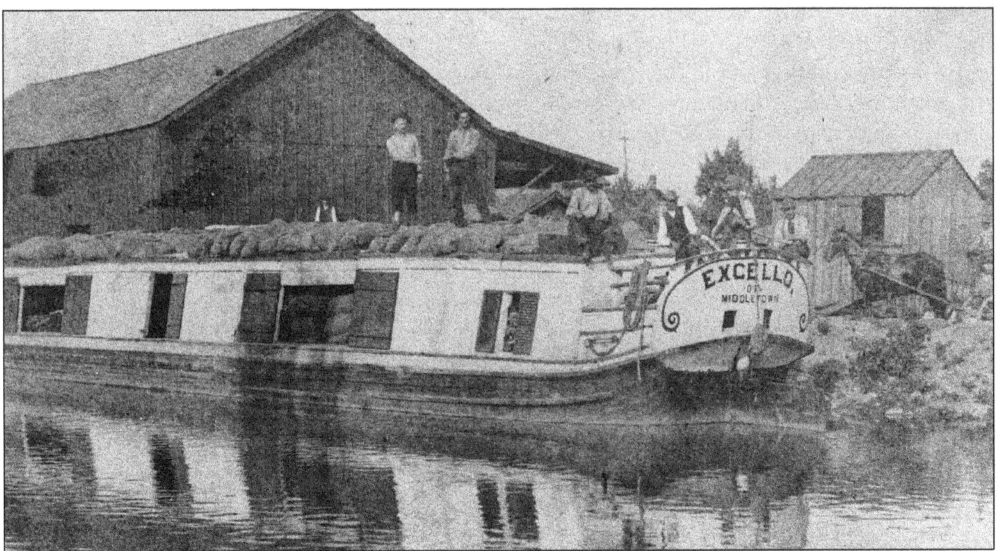

Captain Earl Witner and his crew took the last regular canal boat, the *Excello*, out of Middletown sometime in 1906. It was a freighter with a bow cabin for the crew, a stern cabin reserved for the captain's and cook's quarters, and freight compartments located between the two.

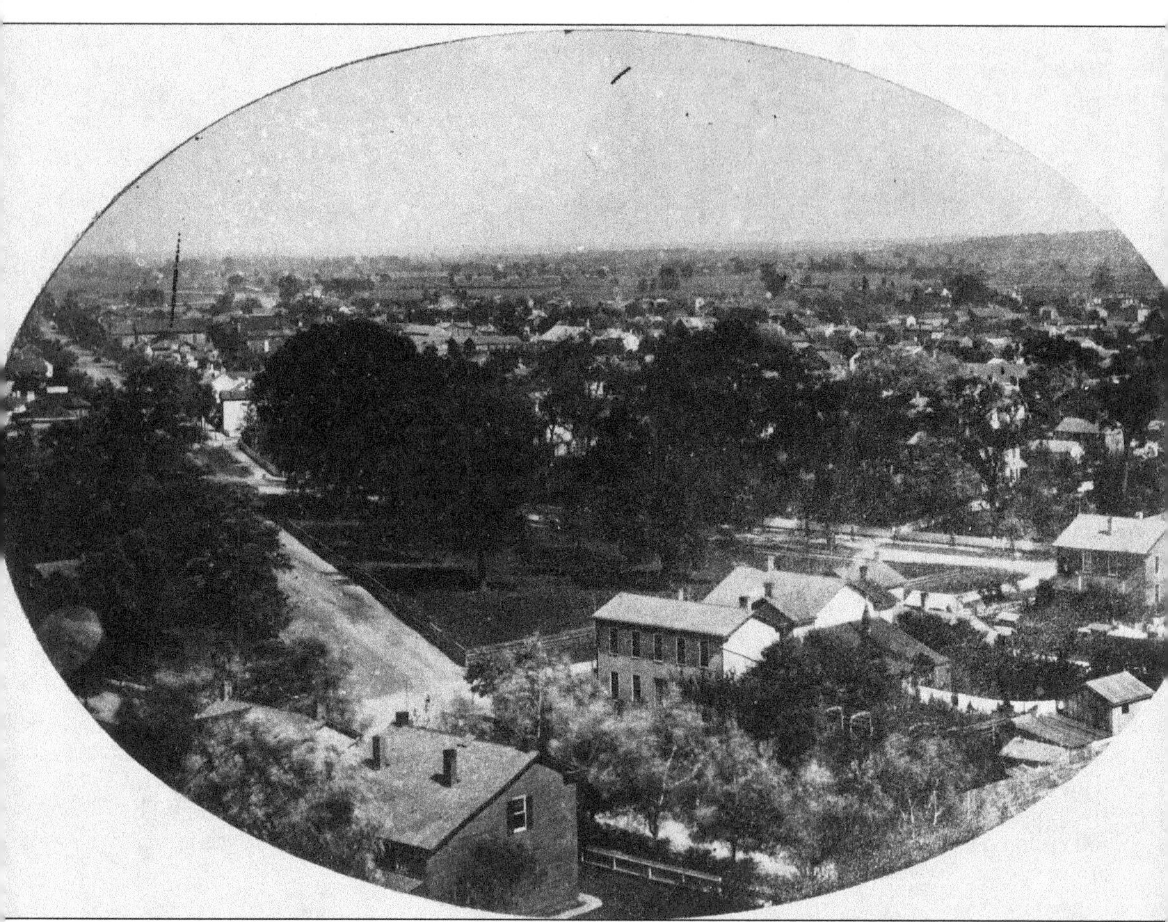

This is a "Bird's-Eye View," as such shots were called, being taken from the top of a high building—in this case the old South School tower. Entitled "flat iron," it refers to the shape of the land resembling an old flat iron, bounded by Girard, Vanderveer, and Broad. The photo was taken in 1881. A little later this land, after being drained, became the location of Burk's Grocery. Seen here are Van Sickles's big double-house and the Benjamin Harwitz home at the point. Harwitz was a noted attorney in charge of the negotiations that brought the American Rolling Mill Company (Armco) to Middletown. A tall elm on the site was purported to be the oldest tree in the city.

Coming from Cincinnati to Middletown in 1869, Paul J. Sorg, along with Wilson and Auer, built a tobacco factory along the canal. His firm would grow into the city's largest employer, and he would become its leading citizen in the last quarter of the nineteenth century.

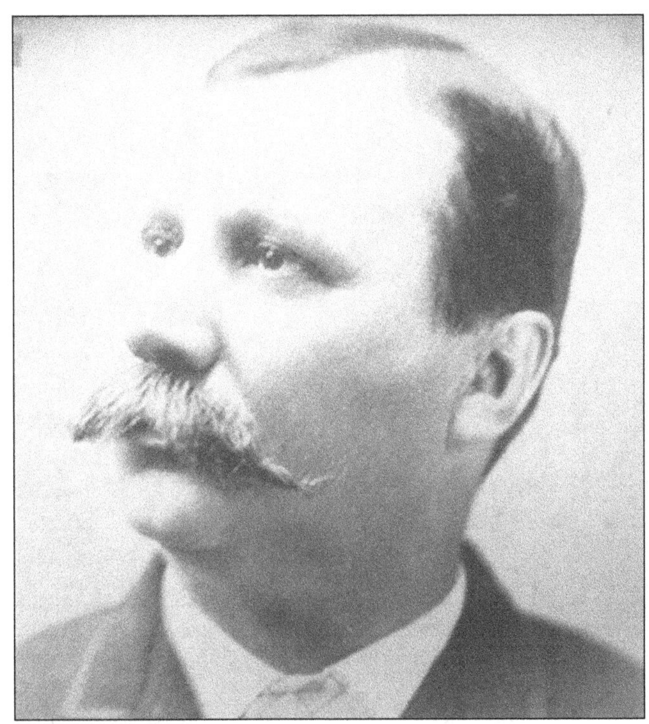

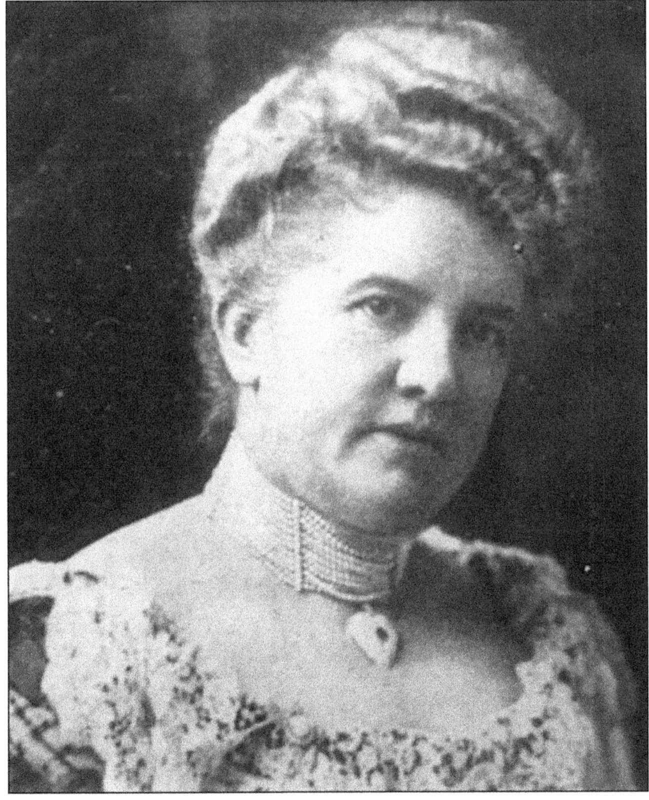

In 1876, Sorg married Susan Jennie Gruver and they had two children—Paul and Ada. The Sorgs became the city's richest family and "Jennie," as she preferred to be called, was the leader of local society—a gracious hostess who usually greeted guests bedecked with her beautiful diamonds.

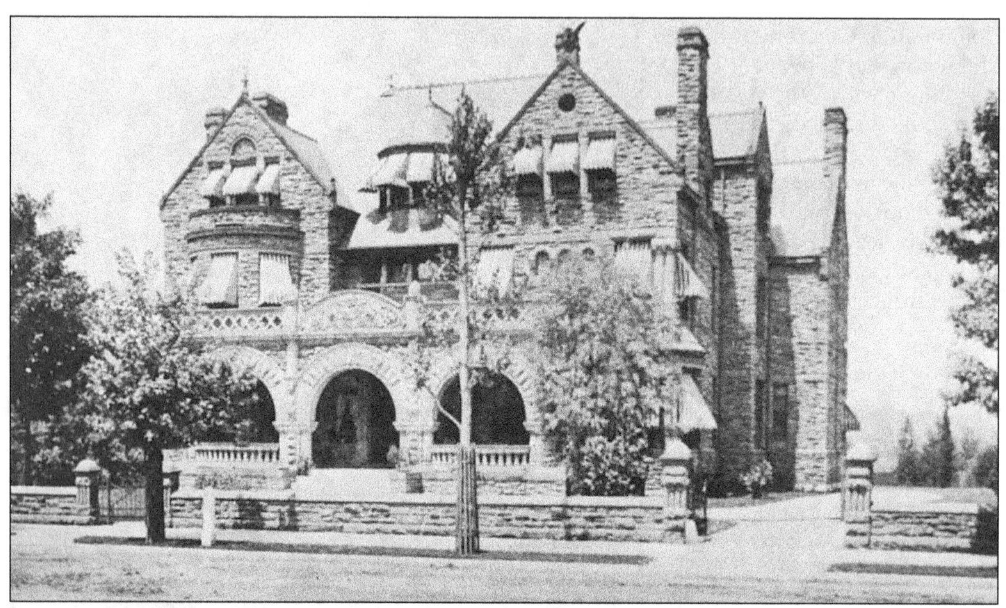

The Sorg Mansion, as it became known, was built between 1887 and 1888 in the Romanesque style and was designed by architects Samuel Hanneford, Pretzinger, and Musselman. The 35-room house likely cost $1 million, which meant little to a family with assets of over $50 million, including a bank. Sorg ranked among the 4,000 richest men in America.

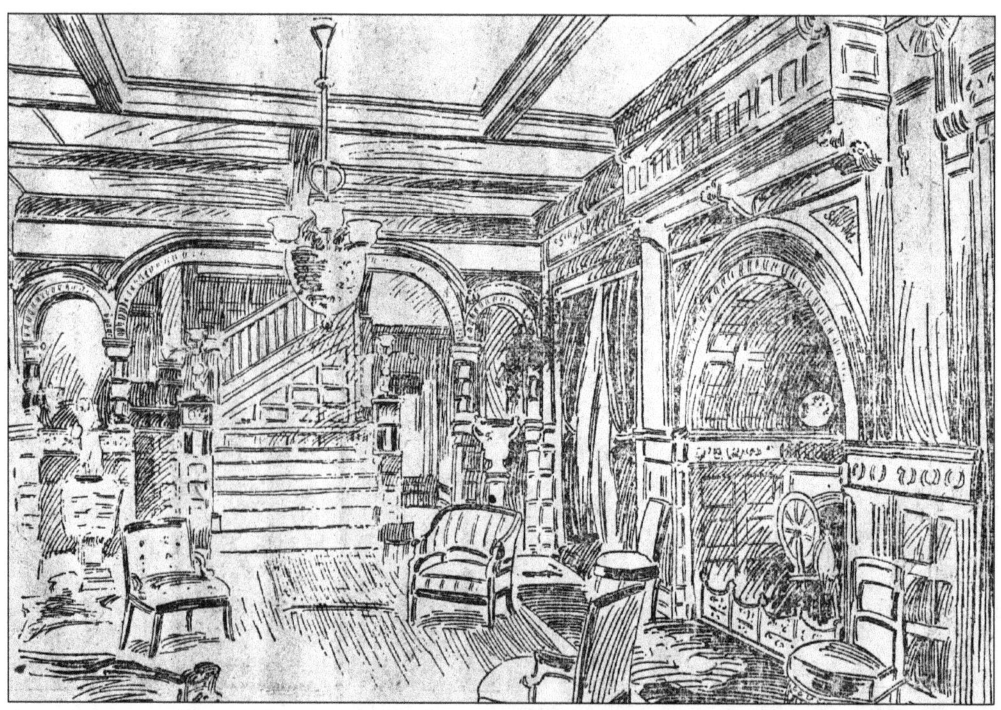

A newspaper etching of the main hall, where Sorg guests entered, is shown here. When a party was held, a red carpet reached to the curb for guests as they alighted from their fine carriages. The house was adorned with fine, hand-carved woods, jeweled chandeliers, a stained-glass window, and some wall coverings of gold cloth.

Sorg's Opera House opened on September 12, 1891. It is in the Romanesque style, utilizing imported Italian red sandstone. Now owned by Harry A. Finkelman and the Commercial Realty Co., it is lovingly watched over by "Friends of the Sorg," who present regular programs on its stage, including operas.

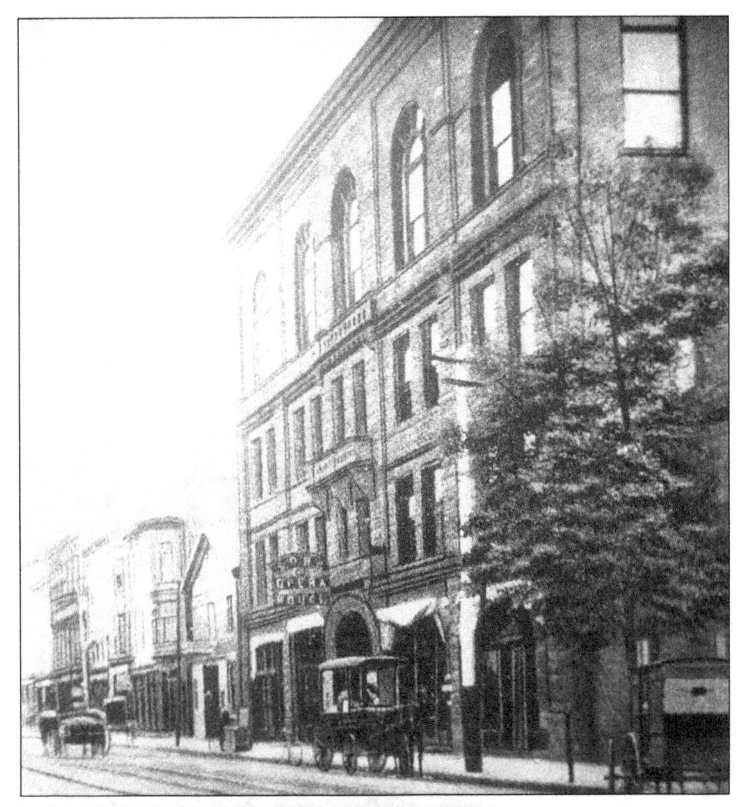

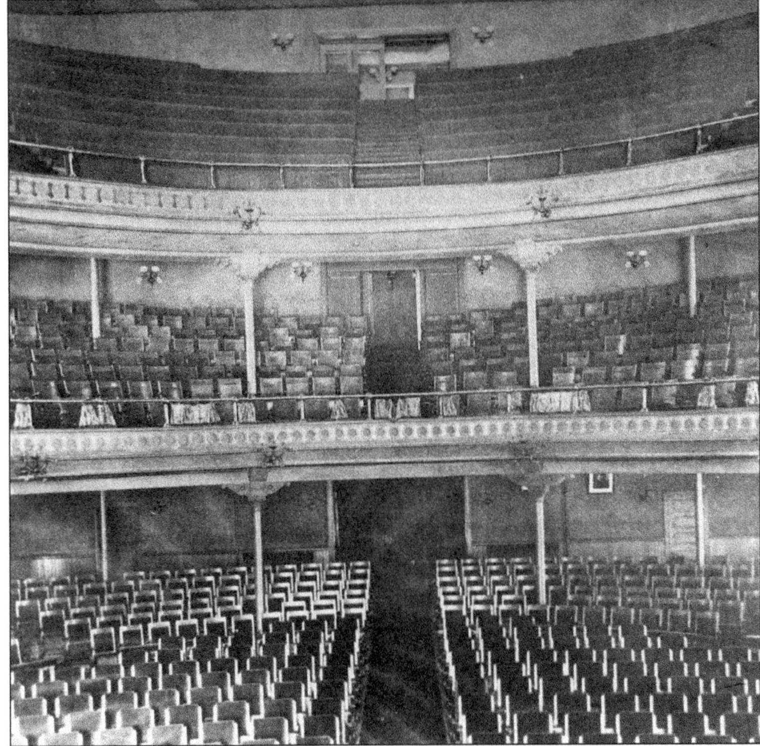

The interior was lighted by 1,200 electric light bulbs—a wonder of its time. Its unique backstage was designed to handle large sets using a "fly tower" and "Chinese Windlass." It had two balconies and it became the cultural center of southwestern Ohio, with patrons coming from all directions on the traction line.

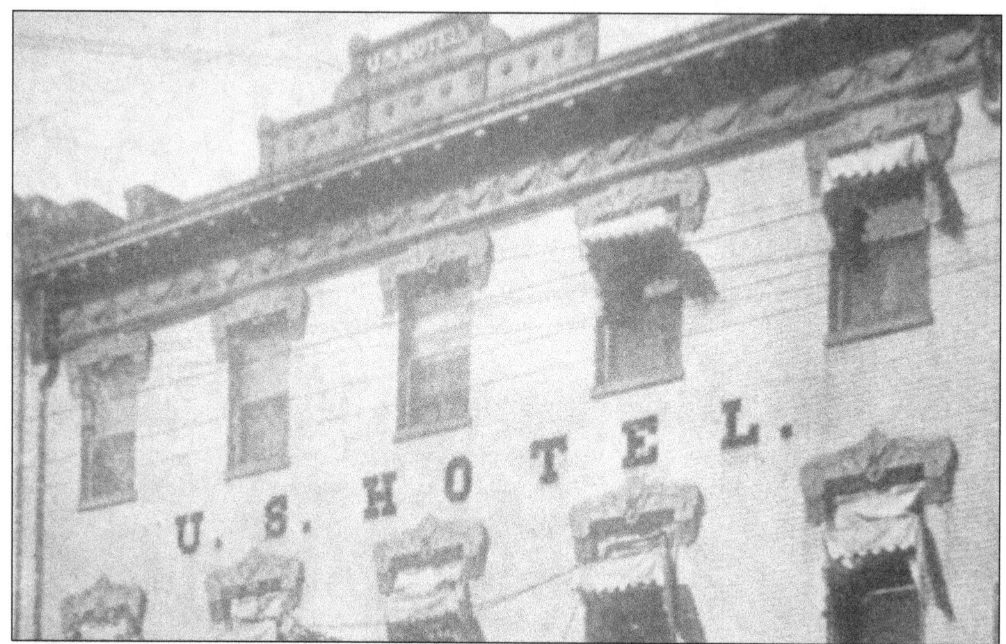

Sorg also purchased the United States Hotel, which he refurbished, opening it to community activities. Great balls were held in its "Hall of Mirrors." Its dining room served the finest cuisine. The 76-room facility hosted the great parties of the period.

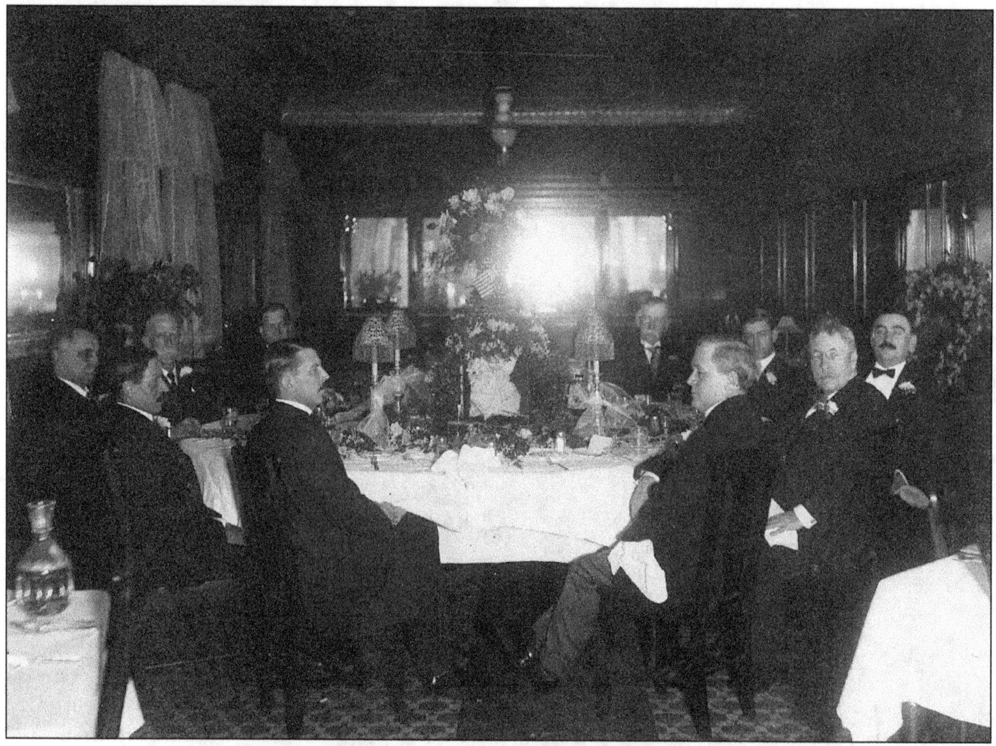

This banquet was held at the U.S. Hotel in 1890. Left to right, starting at the water vessel, are: John Boyd, Paul A. Sorg, C.B. Niederlander, George Phipps, and Tony Walburg.

Born in Middletown in 1825, Ferdinand Vanderveer graduated from a Cincinnati college, then studied law and was admitted to the bar. At age 21 he was in the army and enlisted for the Mexican War, from which he returned to practice law. As an officer he then enlisted in the Civil War, where he had a distinguished record and rose to the rank of general.

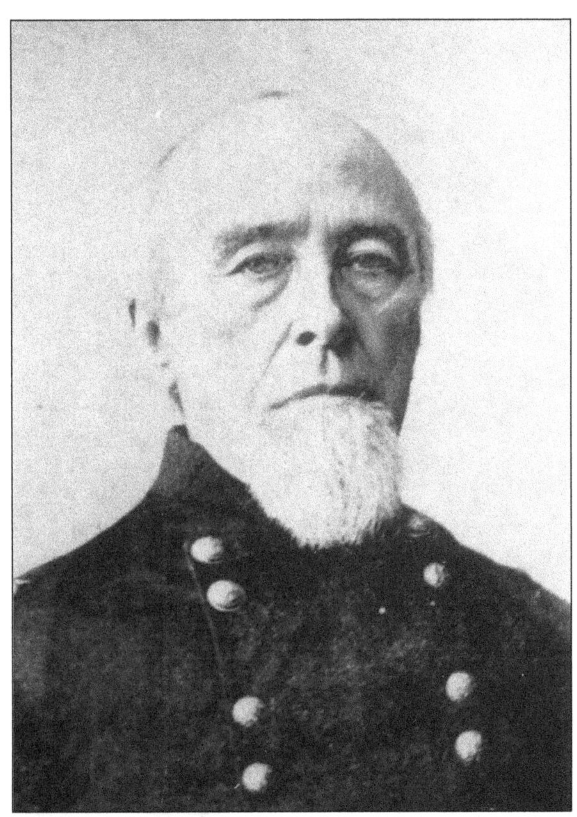

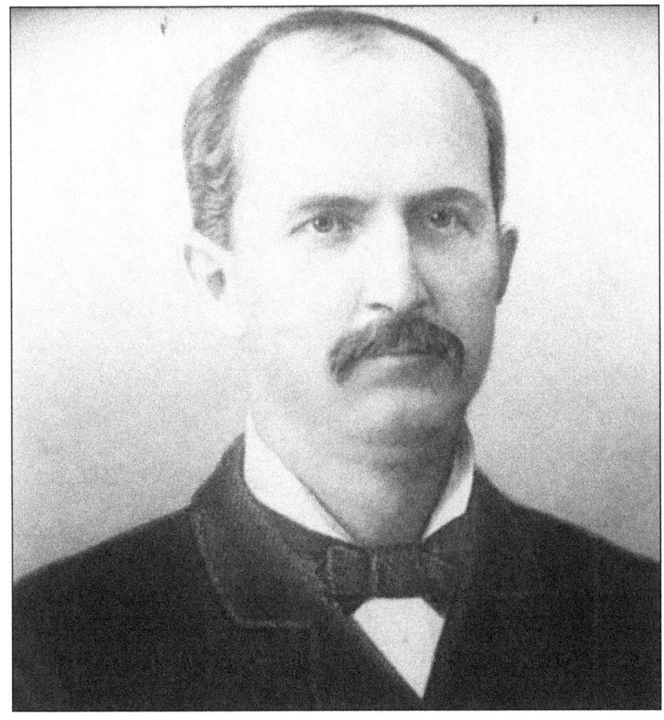

James E. Campbell, born in Middletown in 1843, studied to be a teacher and then a lawyer. In 1889 he was nominated for Governor of Ohio and elected by a majority of 11,000. He set aside the first Labor Day and introduced the Australian secret ballot system. Later James Cox was elected Governor. He was born in Jacksonburg, but moved to Middletown where he lived for several years—working first as a newspaper reporter, then as Secretary to Congressman Paul J. Sorg.

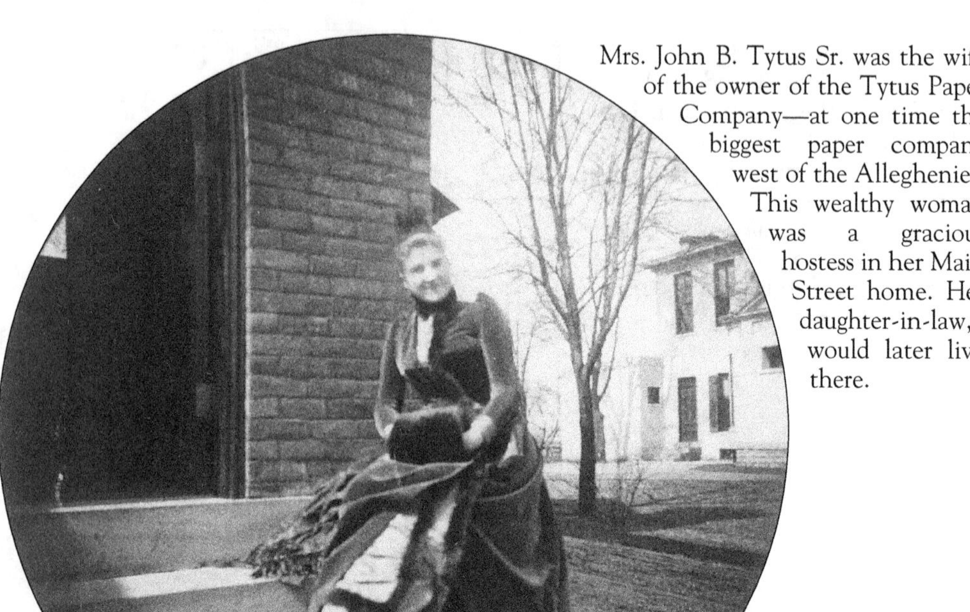

Mrs. John B. Tytus Sr. was the wife of the owner of the Tytus Paper Company—at one time the biggest paper company west of the Alleghenies. This wealthy woman was a gracious hostess in her Main Street home. Her daughter-in-law, would later live there.

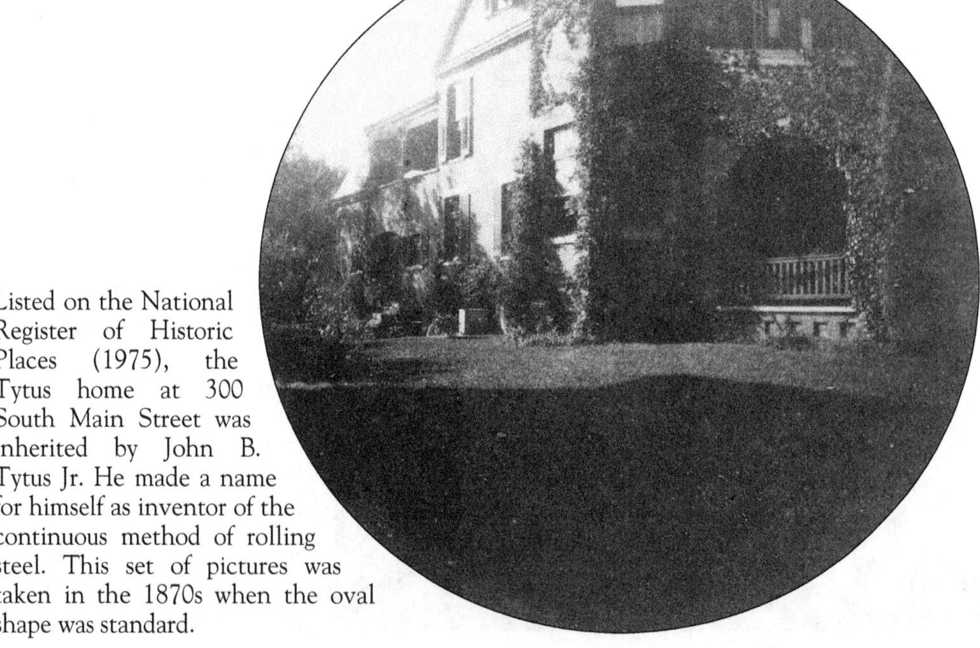

Listed on the National Register of Historic Places (1975), the Tytus home at 300 South Main Street was inherited by John B. Tytus Jr. He made a name for himself as inventor of the continuous method of rolling steel. This set of pictures was taken in the 1870s when the oval shape was standard.

This is an interior shot of the Tytus home taken in an upstairs bedroom, which at the time was heated by a fireplace.

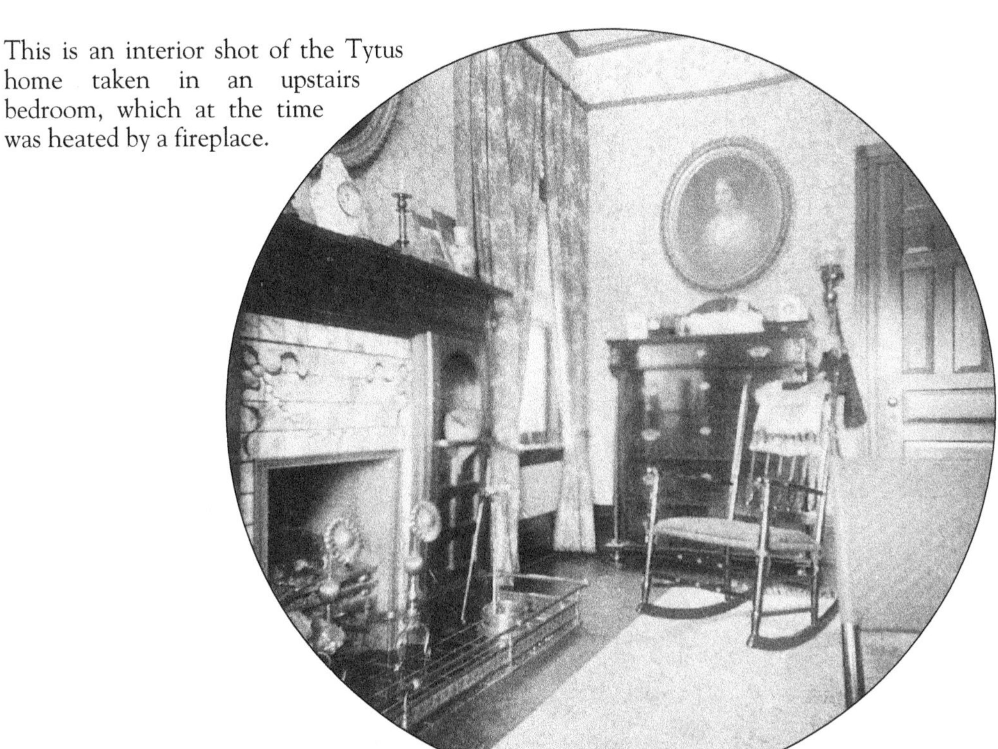

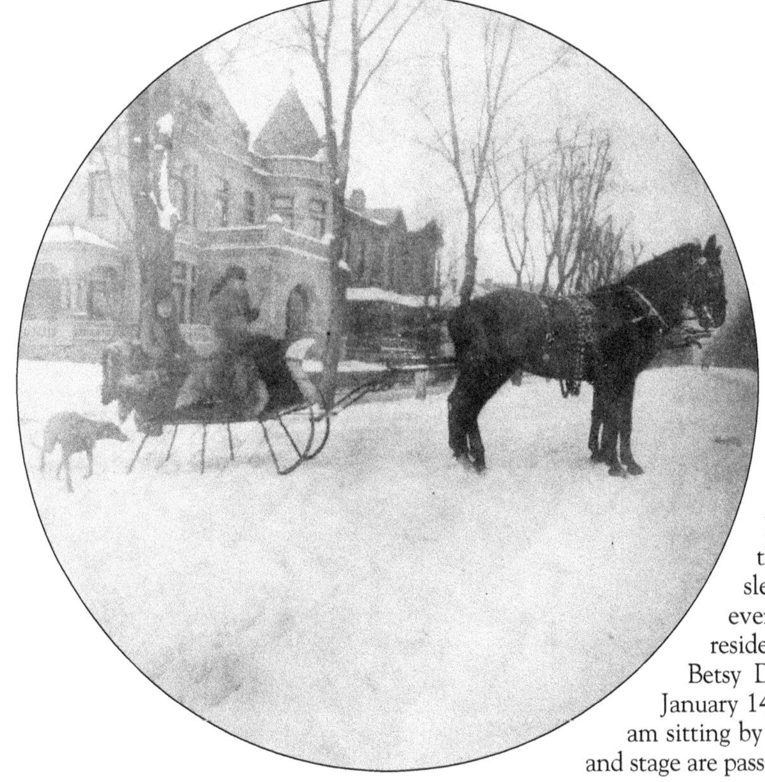

This picture was taken along Main Street sometime in the 1870s. Sleighing in the winter had long been popular in Middletown. Families liked to show off their fine horses and sleighs—and there were even races. A much earlier resident along the street, Betsy Doty, in a letter dated January 14, 1816, had written, "I am sitting by the fireside while sleds and stage are passing."

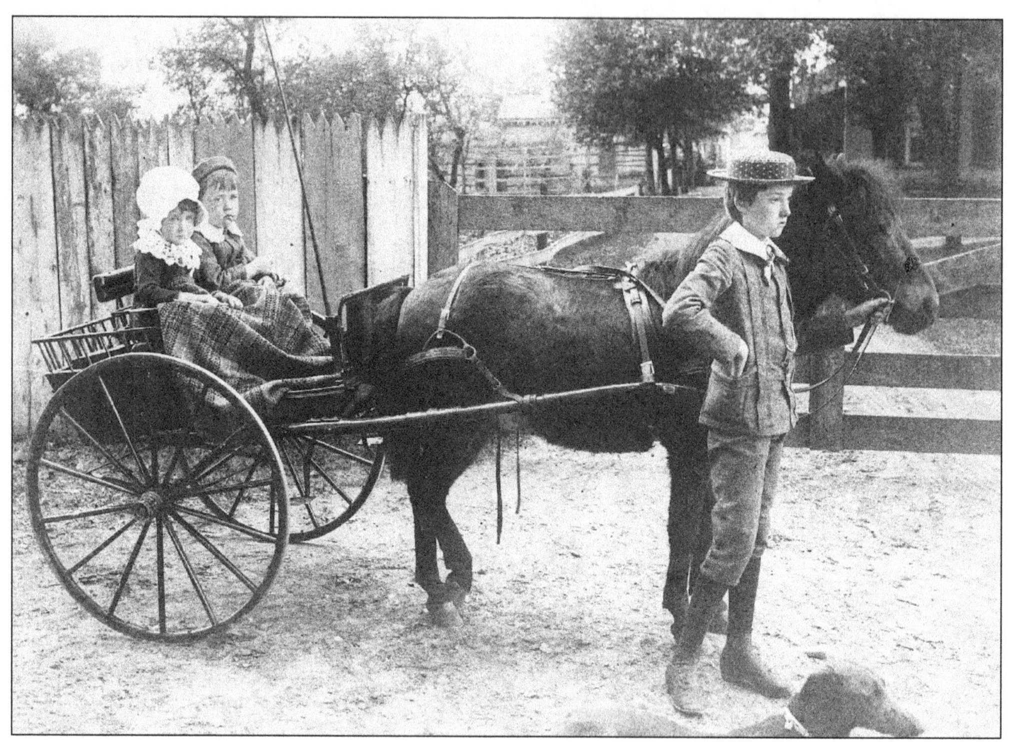

This glass plate photo shows young John B. Tytus Jr., pony, and dog with Lillian and Worthington Stuart in the pony cart. It was taken by Charles Phipps. The old S.V. Curtis home is in the background. The street was East Sixth, now Girard.

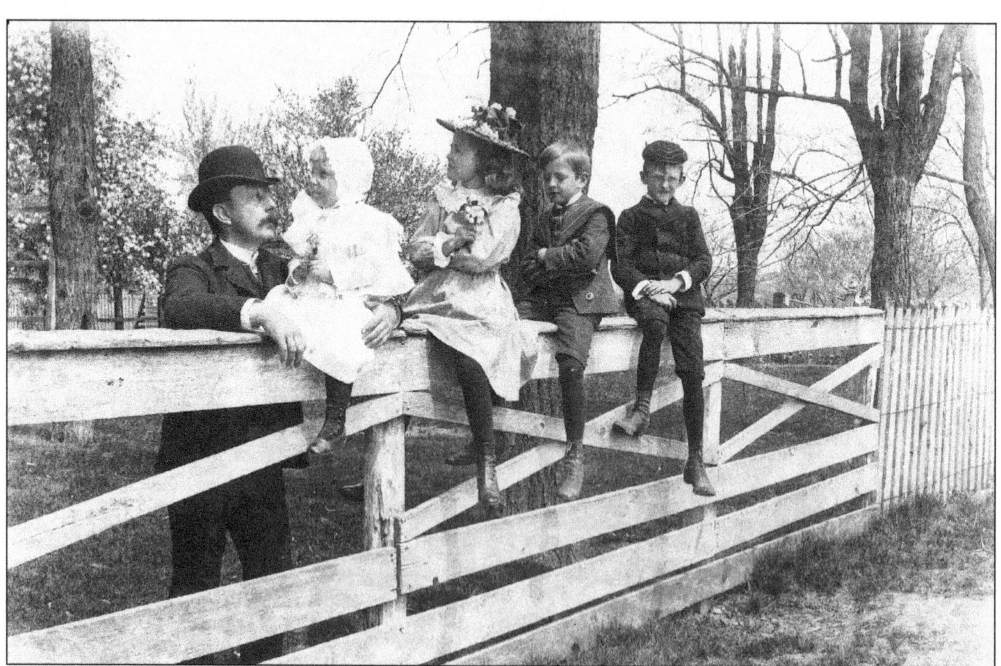

This is from a group of glass plates showing life at Engle's Corner (Main Street and Oxford State Road) sometime in the 1890s. The children are Engle and Harding cousins.

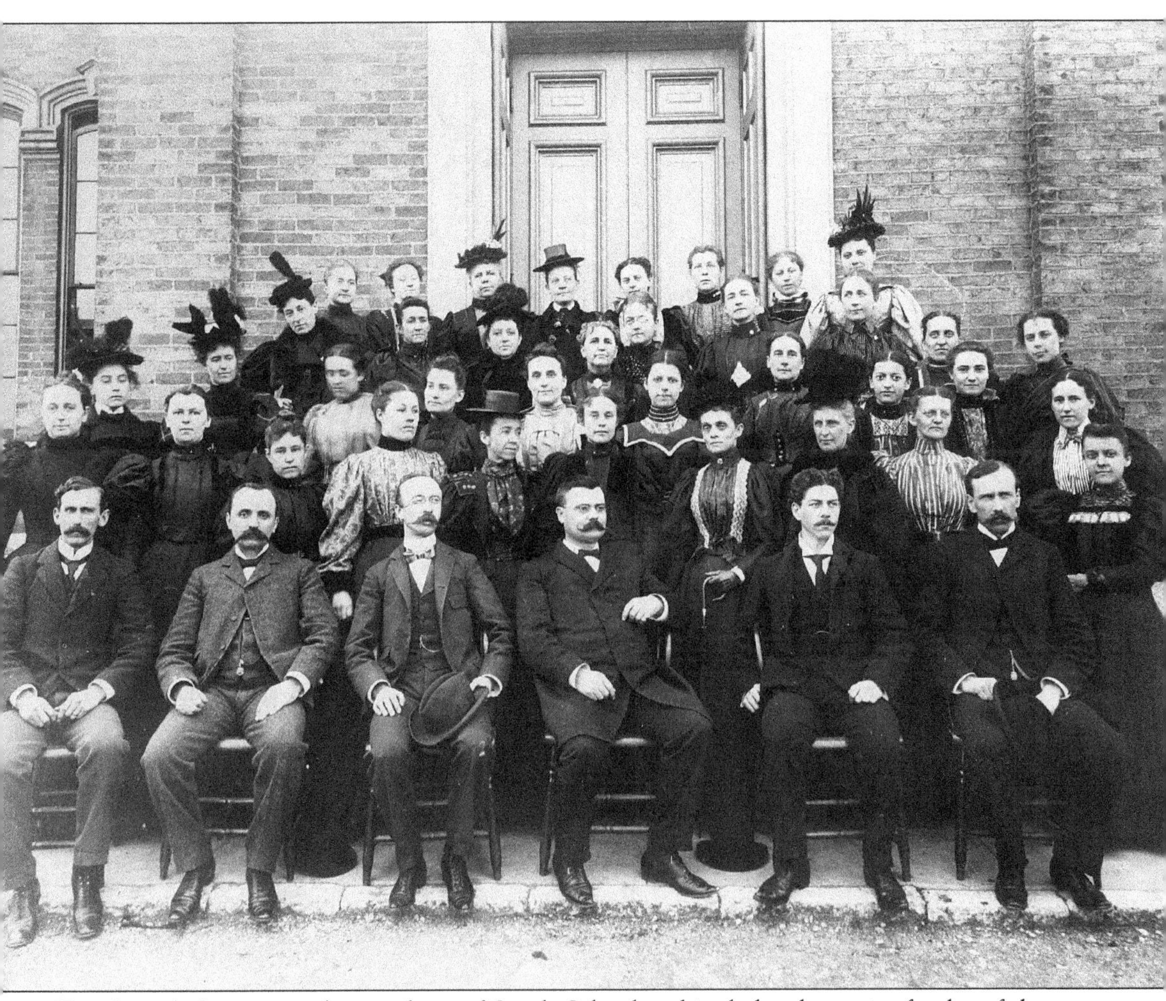

This formal photo was taken in front of South School and includes the entire faculty of the Middletown School System from 1897. The administrative staff is seated in the front row. Front left to right are: Ira King and E.M. Jefferies, elementary principals; Charles Stanage, music supervisor; J.H. Rowland, superintendent; C.B. Palmer, elementary principal; and Principal Miller of the high school. At the time, there were three elementary buildings, North, South, and Central, with the high school at South on the third floor. In 1897 there were 40 high school students. All of the principals taught part time.

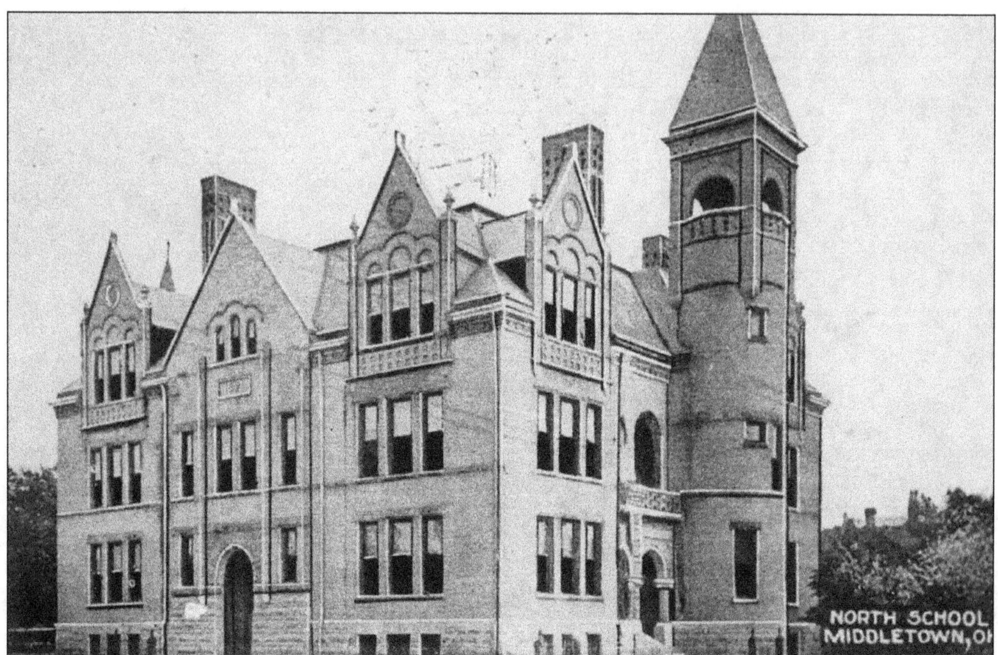

This school, known as North School, was the third building on the site now occupied by the YMCA at Main and Manchester. It was built in 1891 and closed in 1952. Before it was there, on that location stood a four-room brick building constructed in 1854, preceded by the village's first school—a one-room schoolhouse which was built in 1815. In 1988, a large, gray, granite monument was erected here commemorating the historic site.

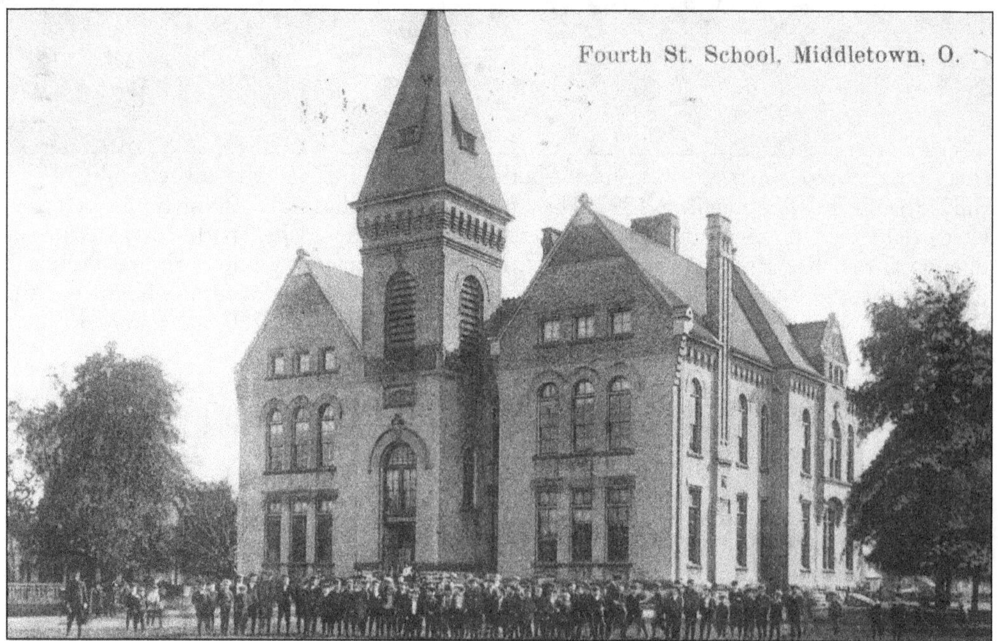

Central School was completed on September 13, 1887. It was known as the East School or Fourth Street School. It had eight rooms, with a four-room addition in 1904. When old Sherman School opened it became Central School. It was replaced by a new building in 1958.

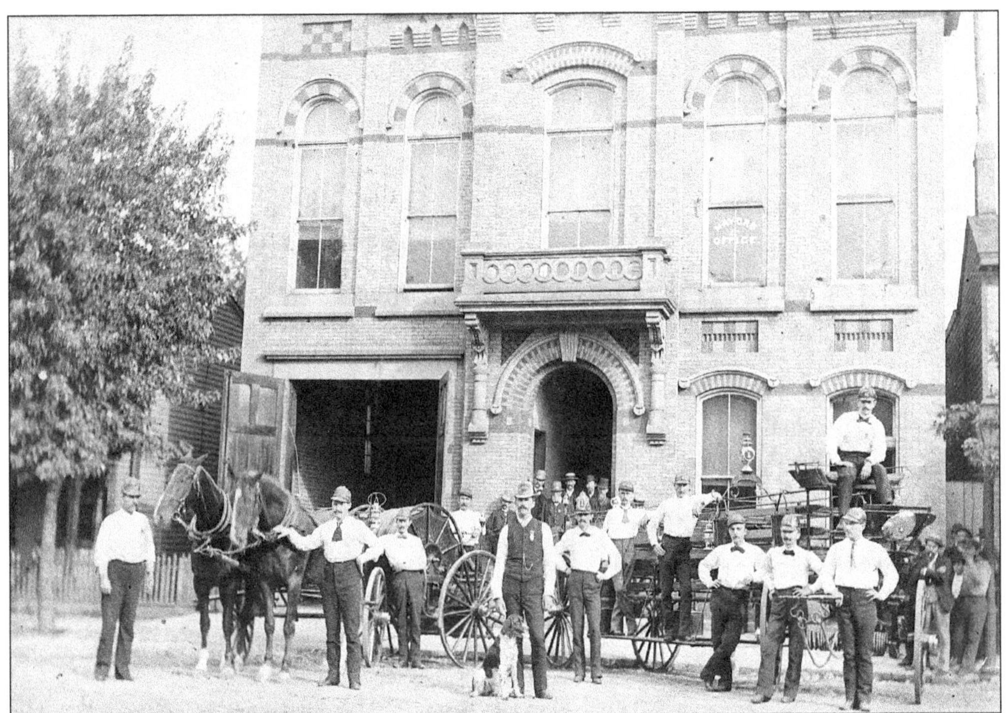

The volunteer fire department proved unsatisfactory as all its members had other jobs. In 1871, the town council decided to appoint a paid chief with firemen paid for runs. In the 19th century, horse-drawn vehicles were used, as shown here around 1885 in front of the new city building, which had opened in 1880.

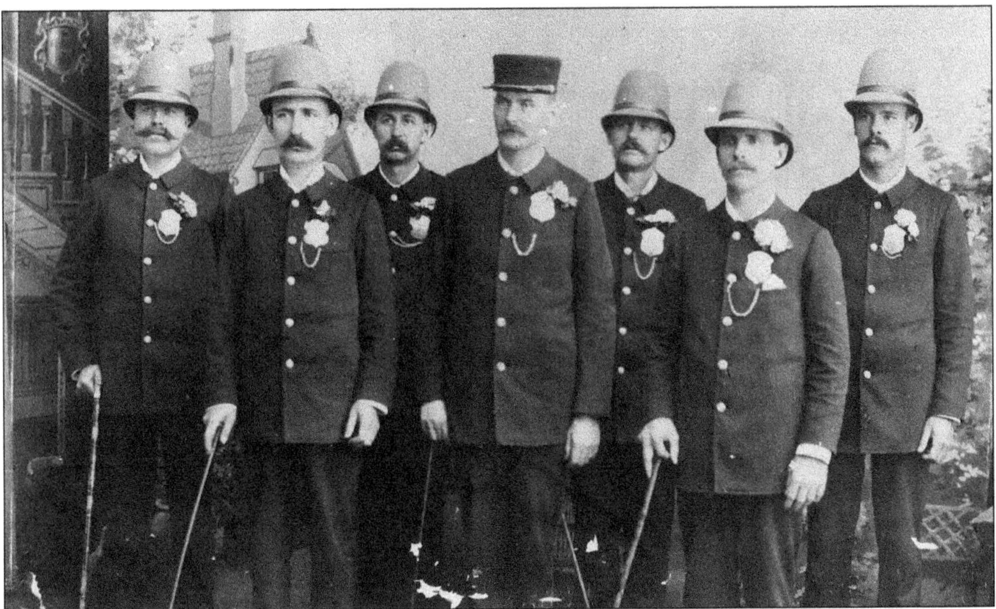

In 1871, the city authorized the mayor to swear in a police force of four men. In 1882, a police department was legally established by ordinance with a chief, assistant, and two patrolmen—all paid from city funds. Here is the force in 1885.

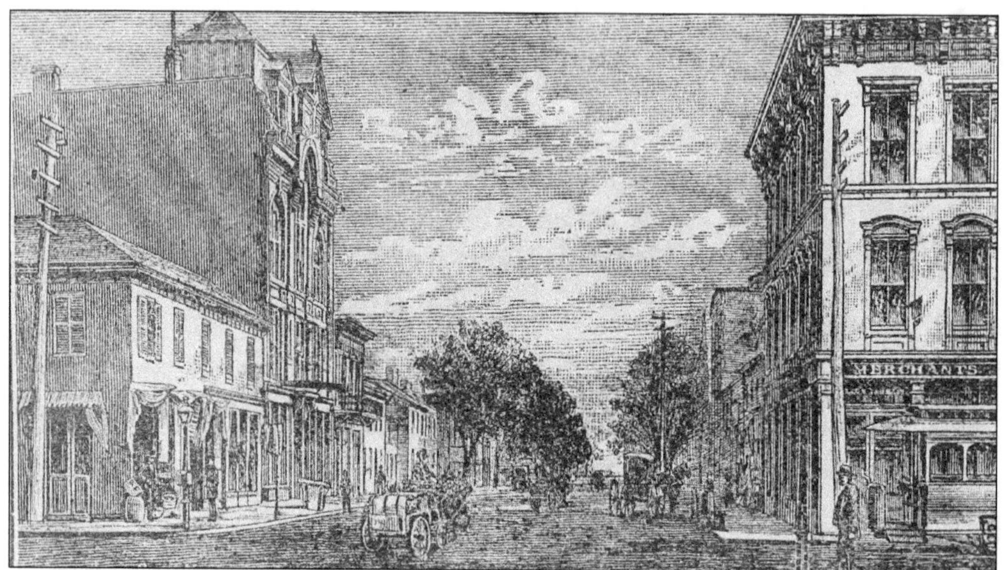

Henry Howe returned to Middletown in 1887 with his son, Frank, who took this picture of North Street for use in making an engraving. The buildings on the right (east) have been replaced largely by the Cinergy Building, with the old Masonic Temple and two others remaining on the west side. There were 7,000 people in town at that time.

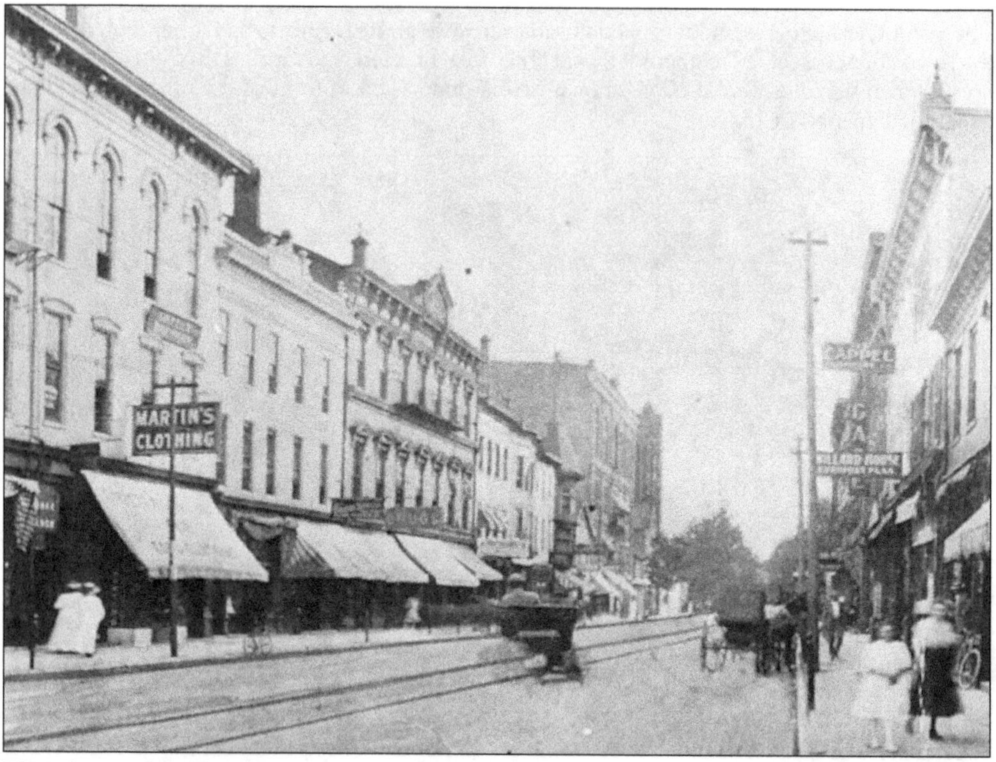

This photo of South Main Street is a section of a panoramic view taken by a special camera just after 1900, as shown by the lone automobile. With this auto the story moves into the 20th century.

Four

A Camera Record from 1900 to 1950

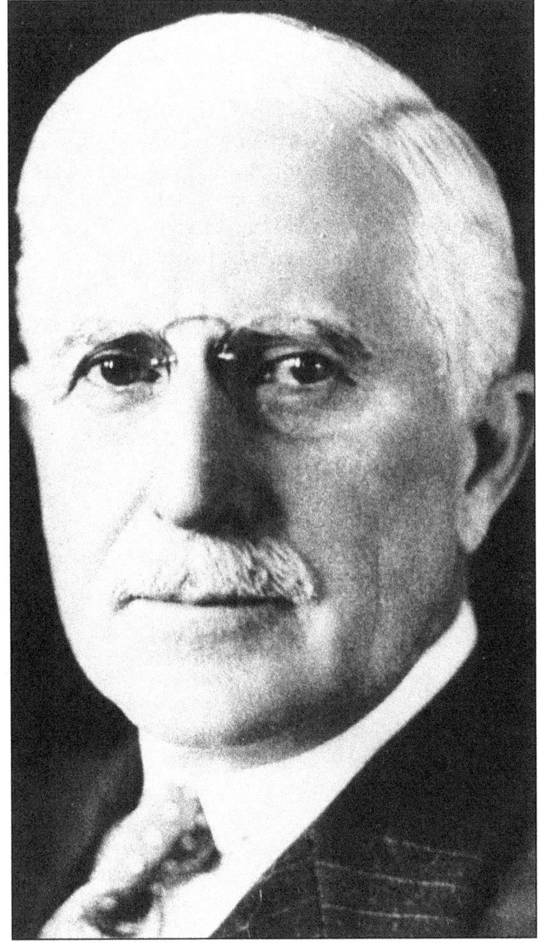

The twentieth century began with photographic images being made on polished glass plates, but flexible safety film was rapidly replacing it. Eastman Kodak led the world in photo technology during the first half of the century. In 1888, George Eastman came out with a camera designed for amateurs. One of his first such cameras contained pre-loaded film for one hundred pictures. When the film had all been used, it went back to Kodak for processing, along with the camera. Kodak advertised the service with the slogan, "You Push the Button, We Do the Rest." Thus photography soon became a hobby, and before long many were snapping pictures—so the pictures in this chapter are from many sources. One such amateur, after taking some professional training, was hired by Armco steel as the company's first full-time photographer. Thomas Portsmouth chronicled almost a half century of Armco history along with that of the city. Most of his work was done outdoors, but he had a studio at Armco where he took this photograph of George M. Verity, long-time president of the company. Verity, a great industrialist as well as local leader, dominated the years between 1900 and his death in 1942.

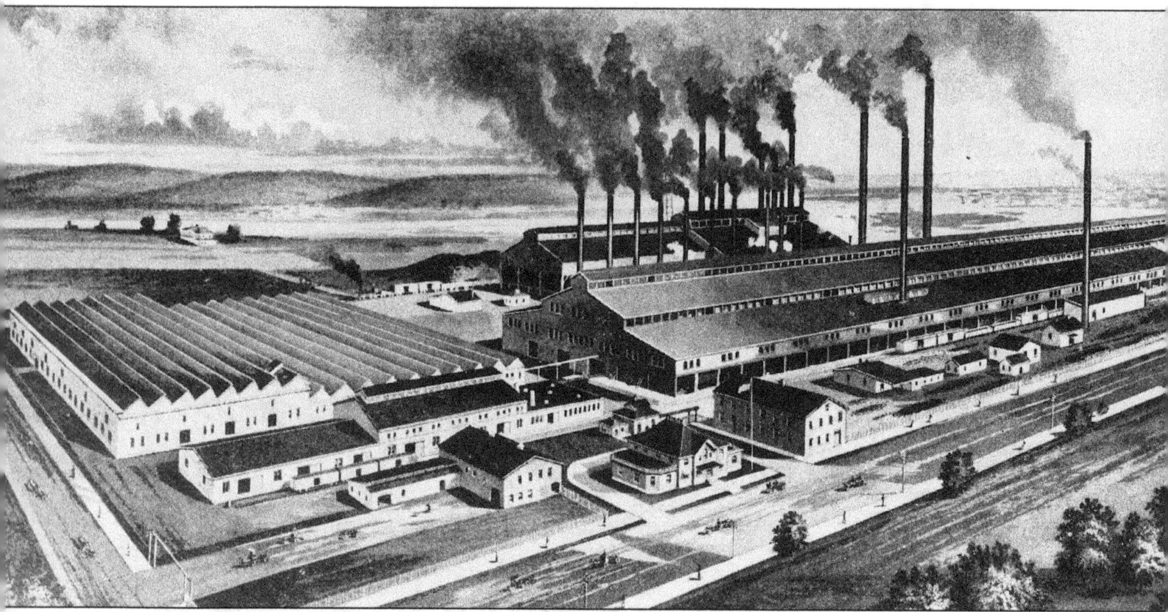

On May 29, 1900, Middletown's Industrial Commission signed an agreement with George M. Verity for the removal of his American Steel Roofing plant to the city, where it would begin operations as the American Rolling Mill Company—Armco—which had been incorporated as such on December 27, 1899. The first heat was tapped on February 7, 1901, and the first sheet of steel was made. This steel was converted into building materials. Steel sheets went through the galvanizing works and corrugating machines to emerge as roofing.

The little mill grew into an international corporation. Between 1900 and 1930, the city's population grew from 9,215 to 29,992. Other steel-fabricating plants clustered around Armco, and Middletown became a steel city.

Since most local residents were employed, Armco had to attract new workers, hopefully with some steel-making skills. Some came from European steel mills and others from the south, where Birmingham was a major steel center. Many African Americans, such as Lige Moss (left) and Lonny Matthews, found work at Armco.

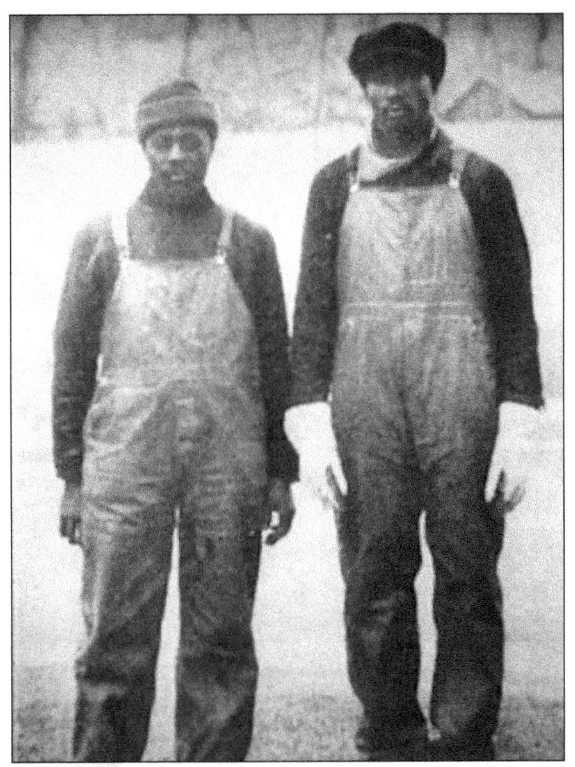

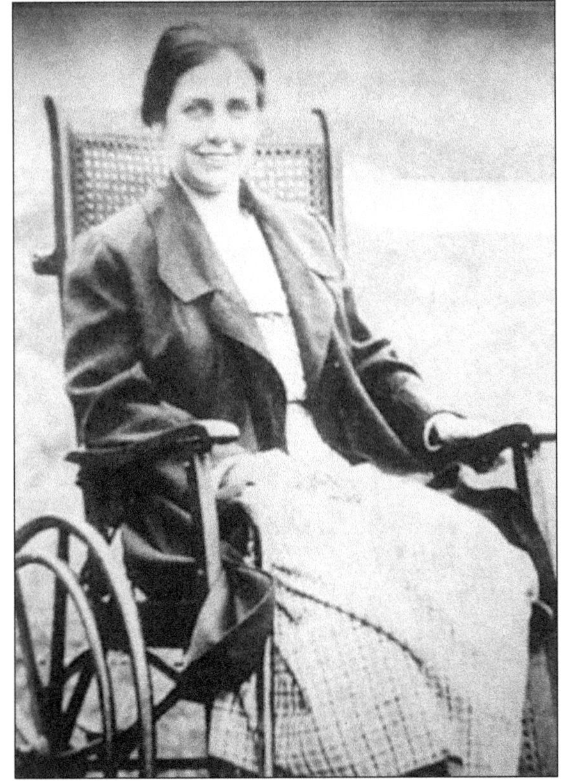

Armco offices and support facilities required the service of women, whom Verity referred to as "Armco Girls." One remembered for her indomitable spirit was Ida Collins, whose wheelchair was seen in many local parades.

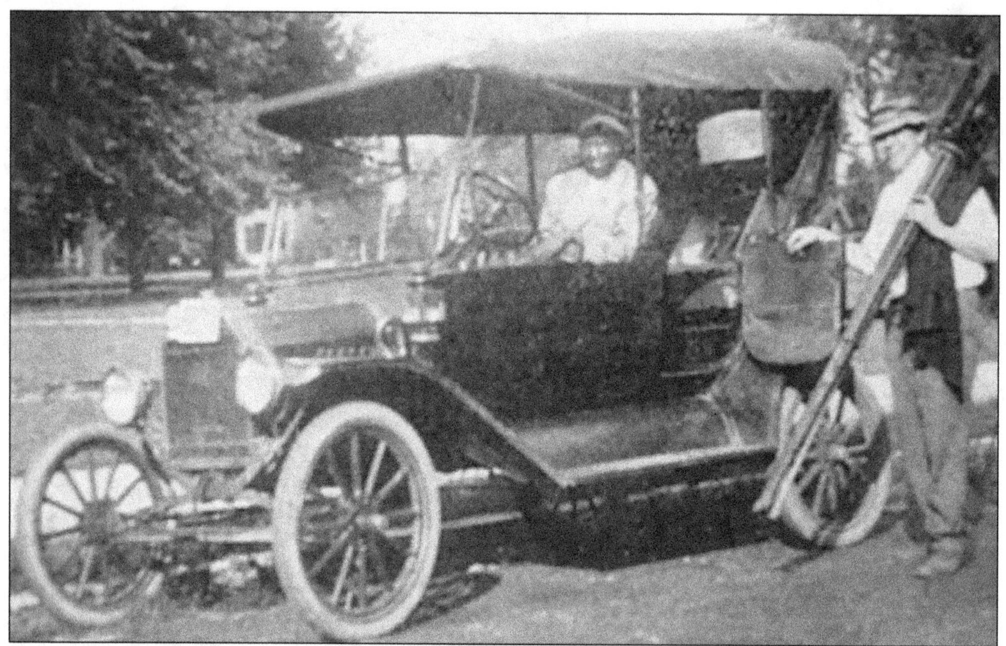

Tom Portsmouth began his career as an Armco photographer early in the century. Portsmouth is shown with equipment, his car, and trusted assistant Bob Stark. Verity's picture, which heads this chapter, was taken at Portsmouth's Armco Studio.

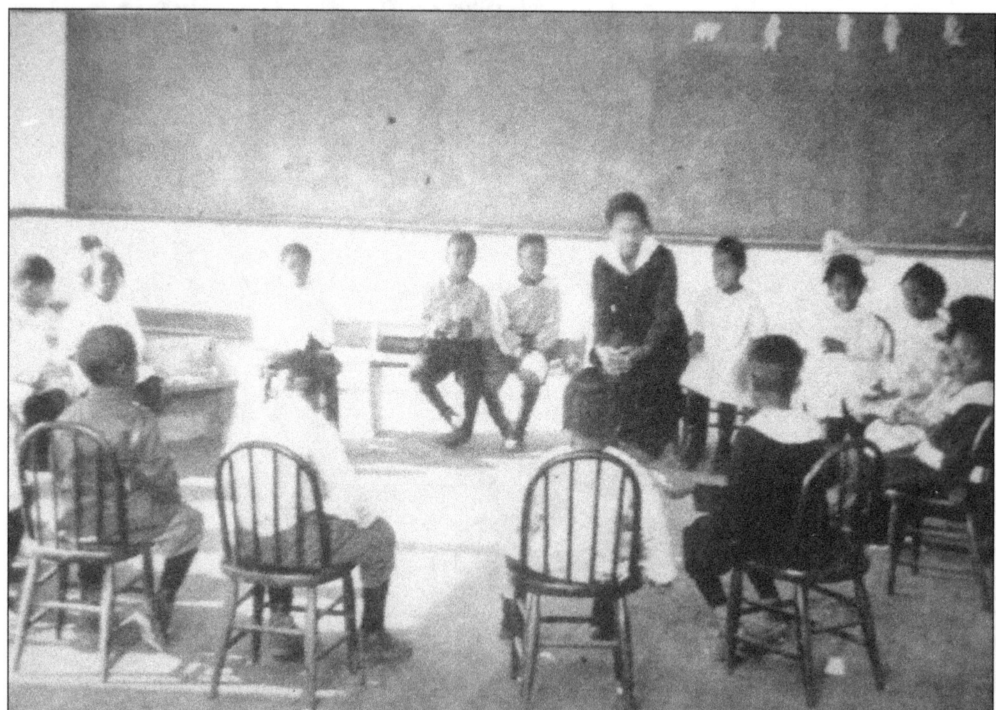

Armco built a modern school—Booker T. Washington—in a neighborhood where many of its Black workers had settled. This Portsmouth photo shows Miss Durant and her kindergarten class at the school—the city's first public kindergarten.

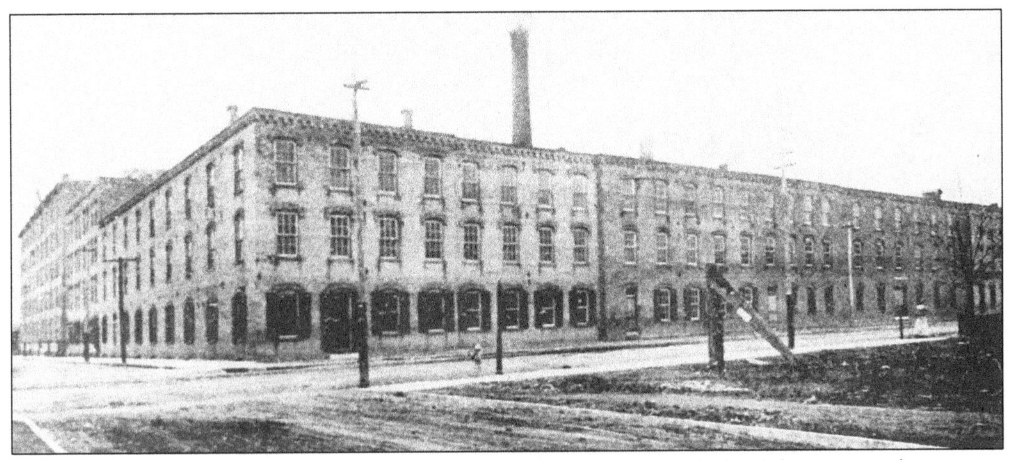

The local tobacco plant was still a major industry during the first half of the twentieth century. It covered a full block in East End. Purchased by the American Tobacco Company, it was broken off the trust as P. Lorillard Company, but was closed in 1951. At its peak, it employed 1,500 people. The building was demolished in 1958.

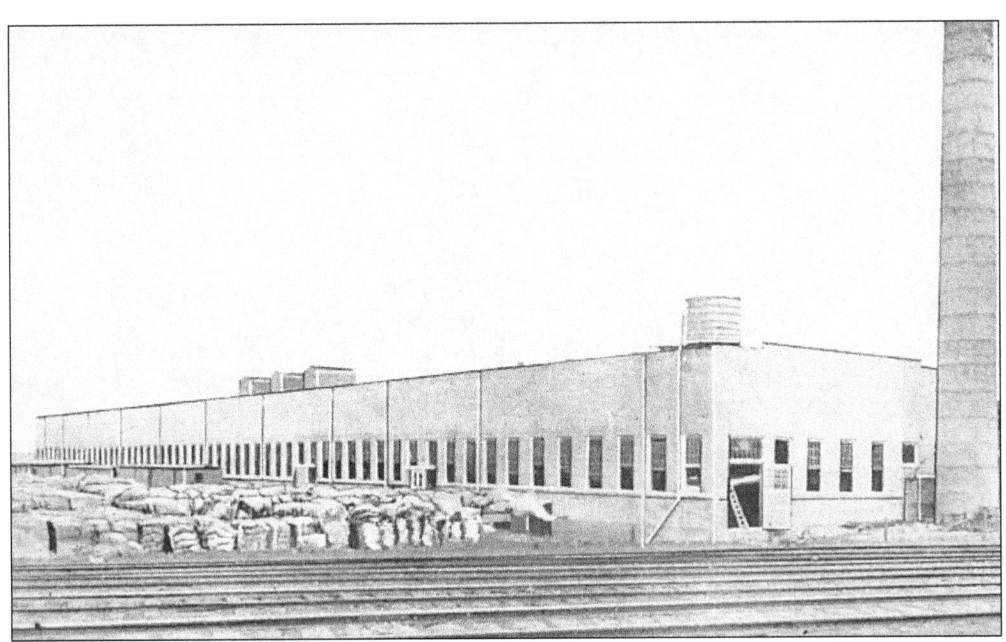

Pictured here is the Gardner-Harvey Paper Company as it appeared in 1910. It began operations in 1900, but was an outgrowth of the old Tytus-Gardner Company. It experienced great growth and later merged as a division of Diamond International. In 1982 it became part of the Jefferson-Smurfit Company. At the time of writing, another merger was in progress, which would result in the plant's becoming Smurfit-Stone Container Corp.

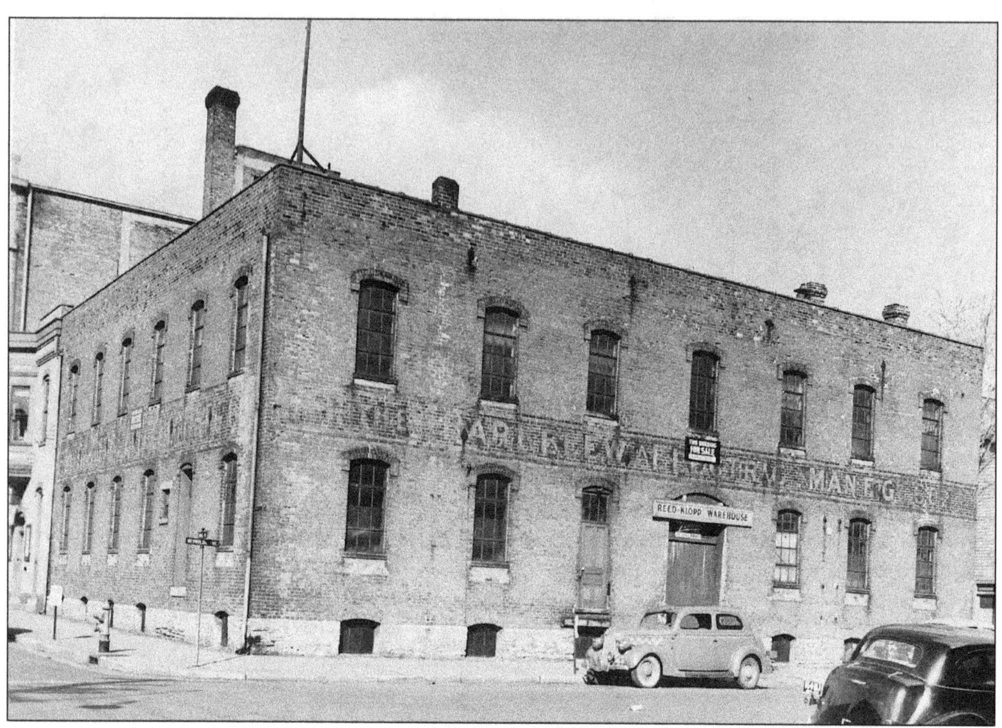

This concern began in 1900 as the Barkelew Electric Manufacturing Company at the northeast corner of Canal and Reynolds. In 1928 it moved to Columbia Avenue at the railroad. Noted for its electrical switches, it is now Square D at 1500 South University Boulevard, part of the Paris-based Groupe Schneider.

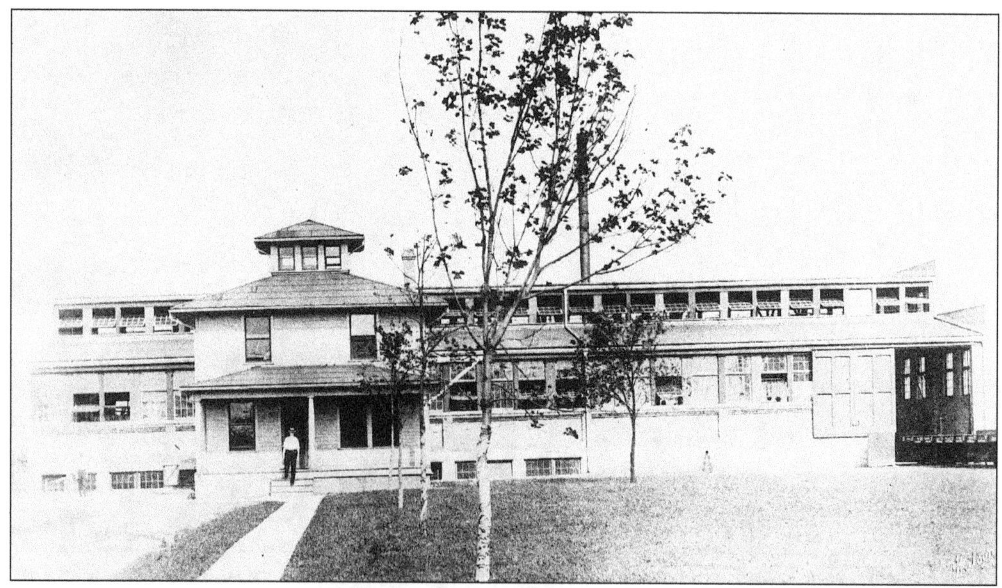

In 1900, Charles W. Shartle started a small machine shop, and by 1906 he was able to build a new plant along Clark Street. In 1926, it became a division of Black-Clawson, the world's largest maker of pulp and paper-mill machinery. Merged in 1997 with Thermo Fibertek, the company is now known as Thermo Black Clawson.

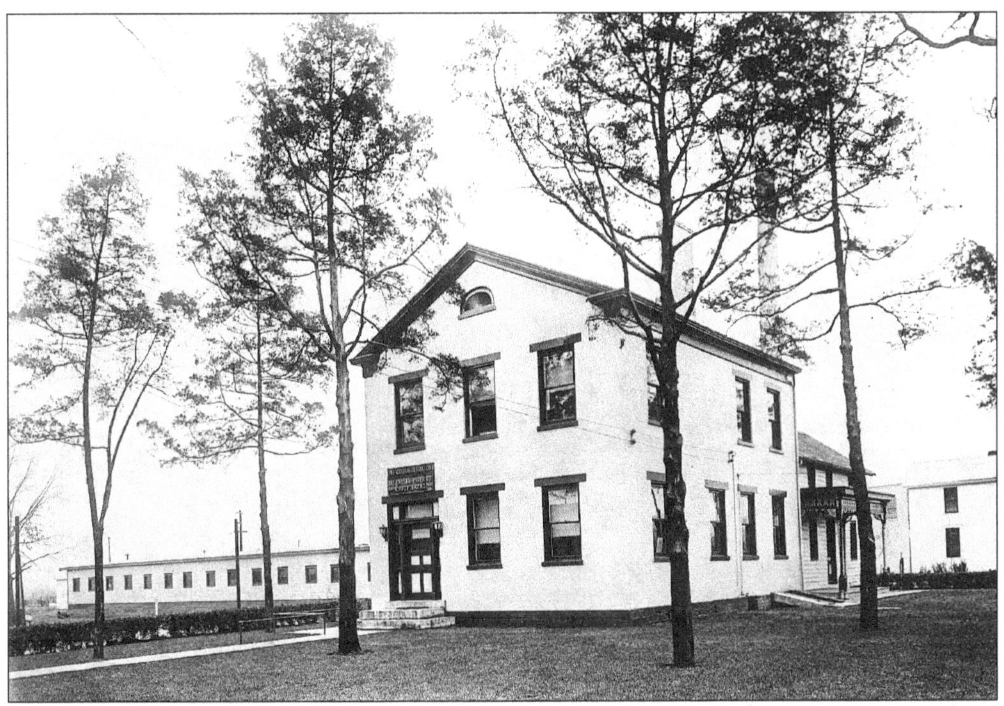

Crystal Tissue is now controlled by the Akers family, who operates a group of related firms. It began as a gristmill along a Miami-Erie Canal lock, and in 1886 was converted to a paper mill, which began to specialize in tissue paper production. Before 1930, this was its office building.

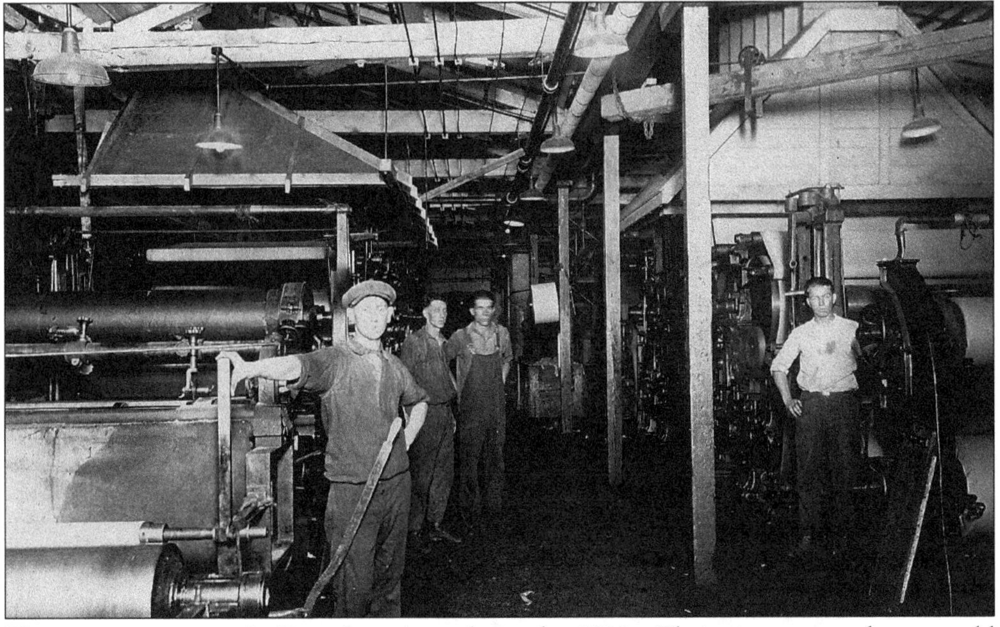

This is a picture inside Crystal at Amanda in the 1920s. Their tissue paper has a world market, with many specialty varieties including colorful Christmas wrappings. Crystal now has expanded with additional facilities in Monroe, Ohio, and Maysville, Kentucky, as well as offices in major cities.

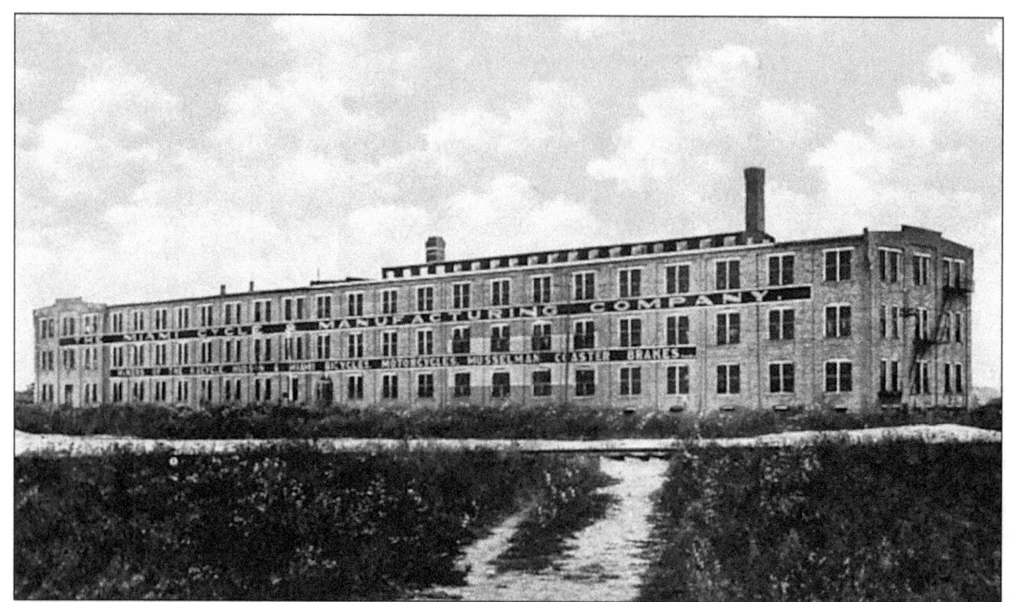

At the beginning of the century, the Miami Cycle and Manufacturing Company along Grand Avenue was a major industry. In 1910 it had over 1,000 employees producing 100,000 bicycles and 10,000 motorcycles a year. The building, later used by Miami-Carey, was destroyed by fire on March 11, 1972.

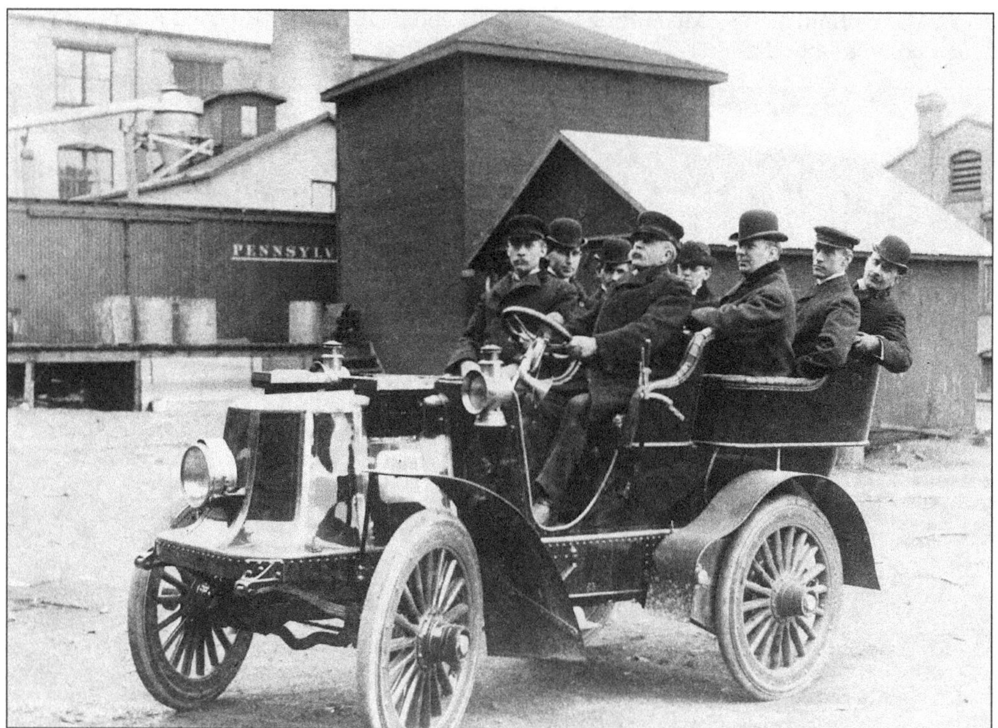

Hoping to compete in the developing automobile market, the company tried to build cars. Here is the "Miami," which was known locally as the "Ramapaugh." Other autos made here in other factories were the "Middletown" and the "Washington."

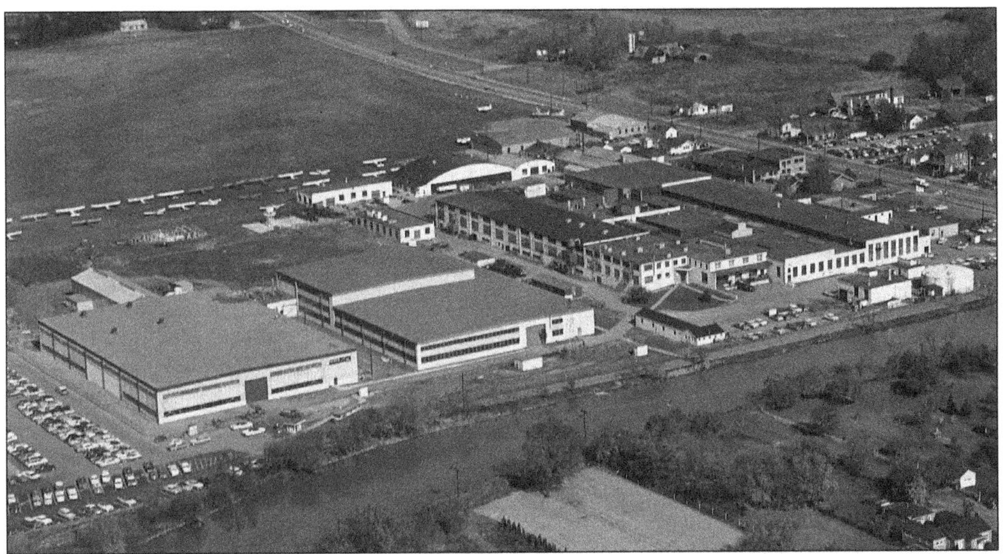

Beginning as the Aeronautical Corporation of America in Cincinnati, the company came to Middletown where, in June 1940, it began production of the light-weight Aeronca as the T series, "Champion" and "Chief." The company now manufactures airplane component parts as part of Fleet Aerospace Corporation of Canada.

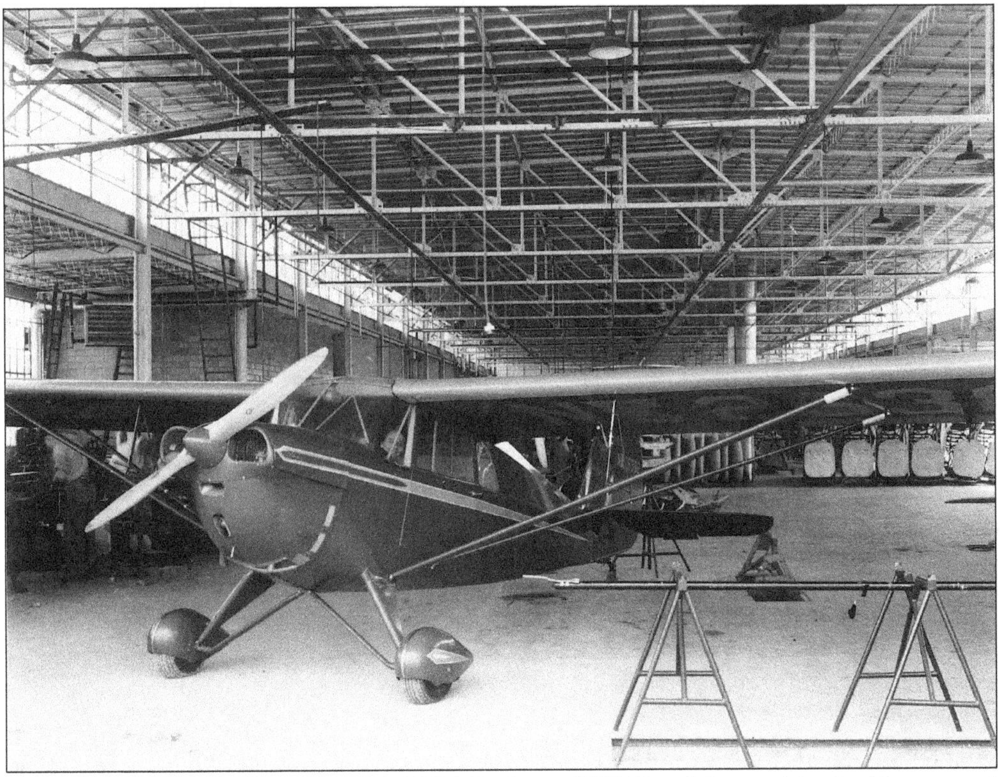

From 1929 to 1951, Aeronca produced 17,408 planes. WW II and the resulting build-up caused the company to produce nearly 2,500 aircraft for use as trainers, gliders, and liaison duty. During its hey-day the plant employed 1,800 workers.

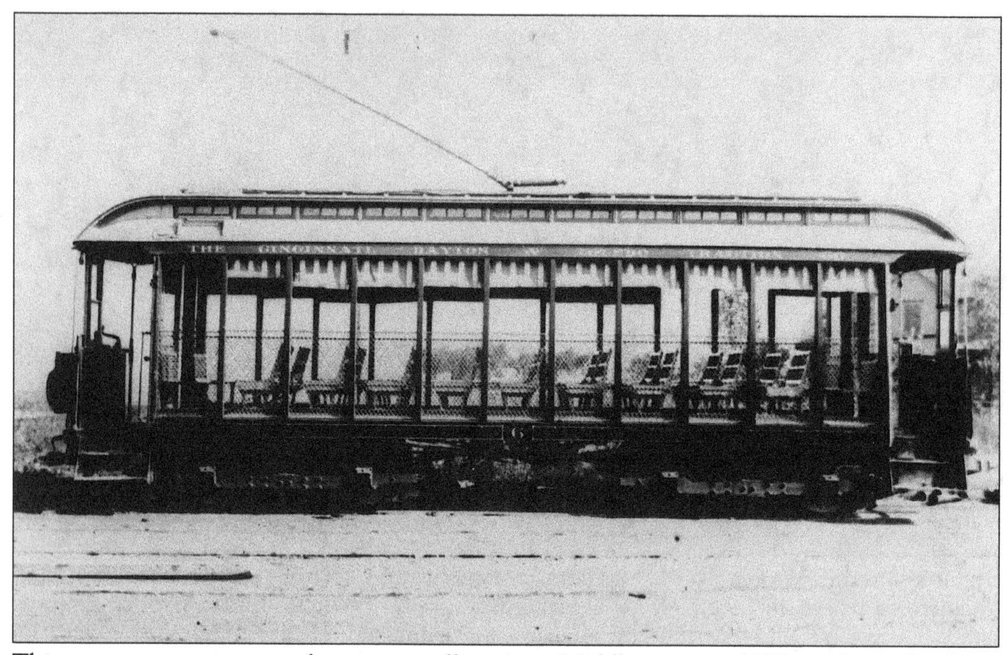

This summer traction car first came rolling into Middletown in 1897, with tracks down Tytus Avenue and Main Street to Engles Corner. Ohio trolley lines were merged forming the Cincinnati and Lake Erie Line, which ceased operation locally on April 13, 1939.

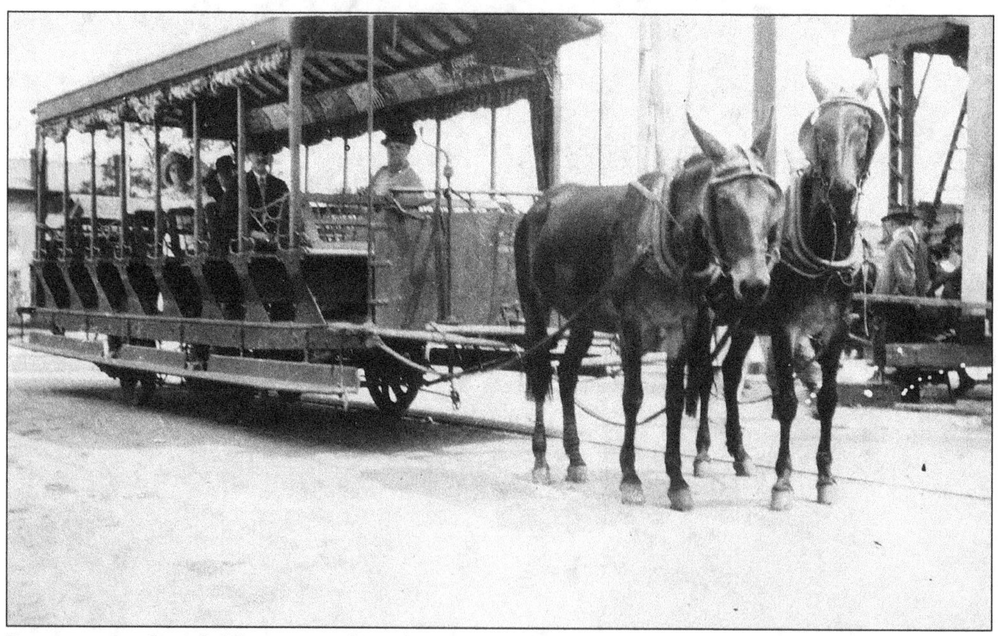

Beginning as the Middletown and Madison Street Railway Company in 1879, it connected the C.H. and D. railroad station at West Middletown with the Big Four railroad depot. After the 1913 flood it no longer crossed the river, but continued along Third Street (Central Avenue) until May 4, 1918—the last horsecar line in the United States.

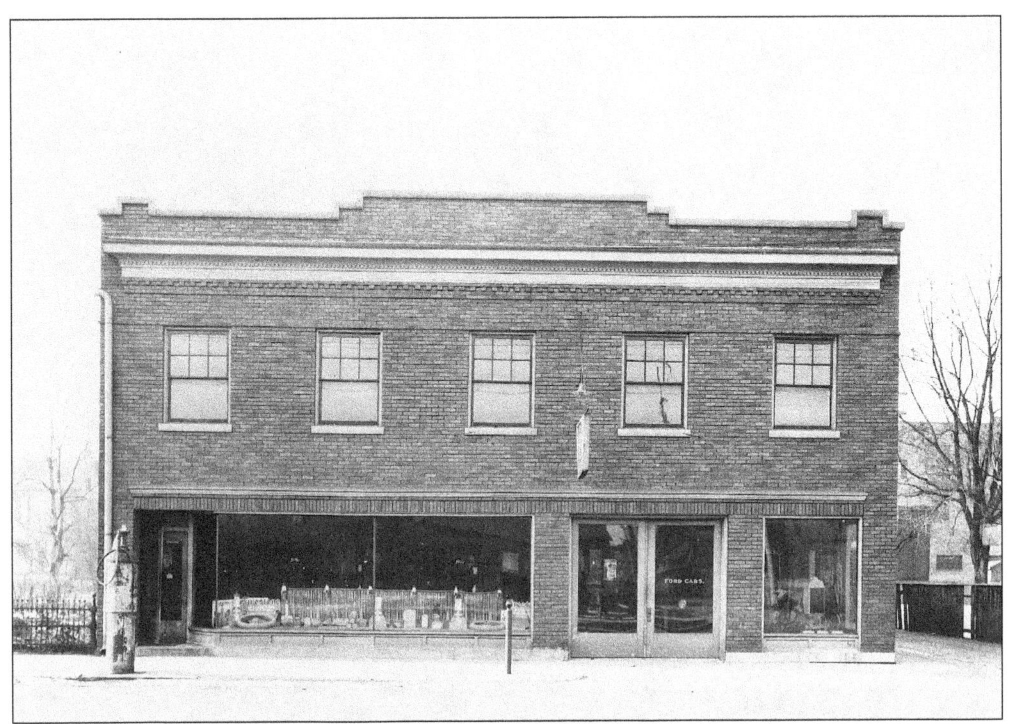

In 1911, Dan E. Snider was given the Ford Agency, and began it with one car. He expanded, and by 1920 was able to erect this building, still standing, on North Main. Within another ten years he employed 27 people and was selling more cars than any other local dealer.

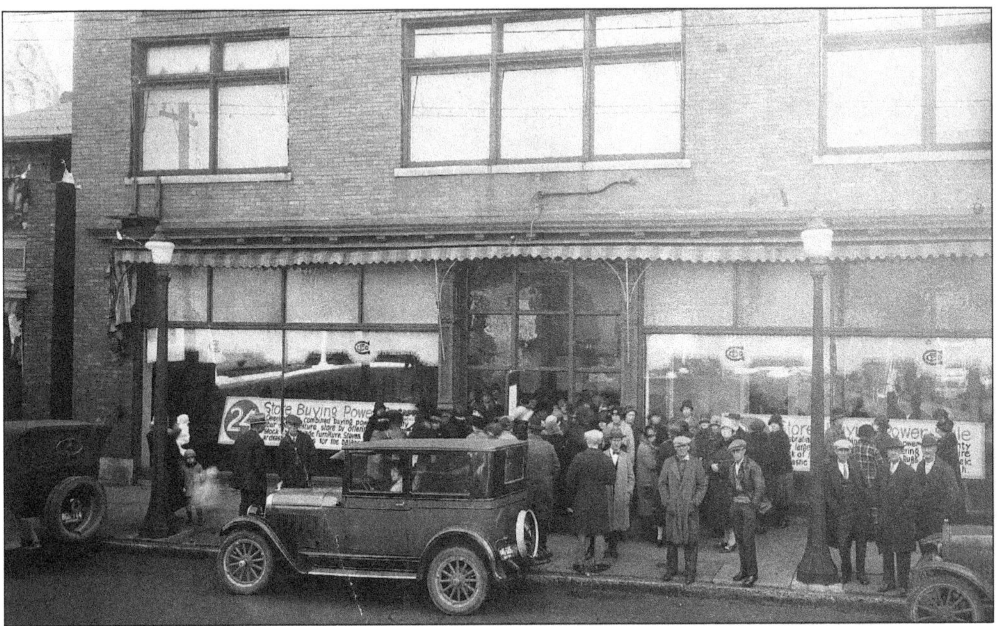

Cars park in front of Cappel's as patrons rush into the city's premier furniture store for bargains. Cappel's was located on North Main, just south of Snider's garage and North School. At one time Cappel's operated an additional store on South Main Street.

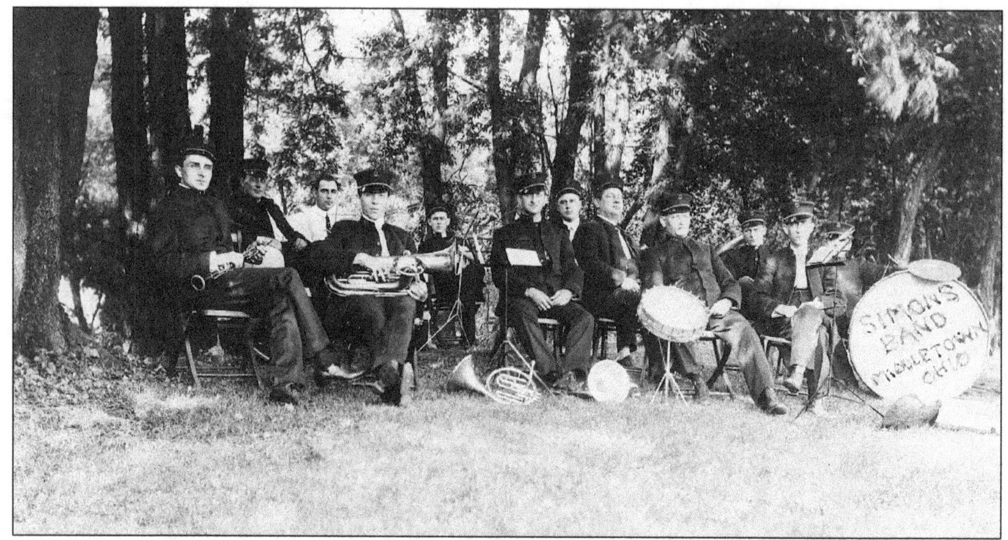

Frank Simon, seated in the middle of the picture behind the music stand, was born in 1889, and as a youth directed his own band. In 1912 he joined the Cincinnati Symphony. In 1914 he became first cornet player for Sousa's Band. In 1921 he left the band to form the famous Armco Band of national radio fame.

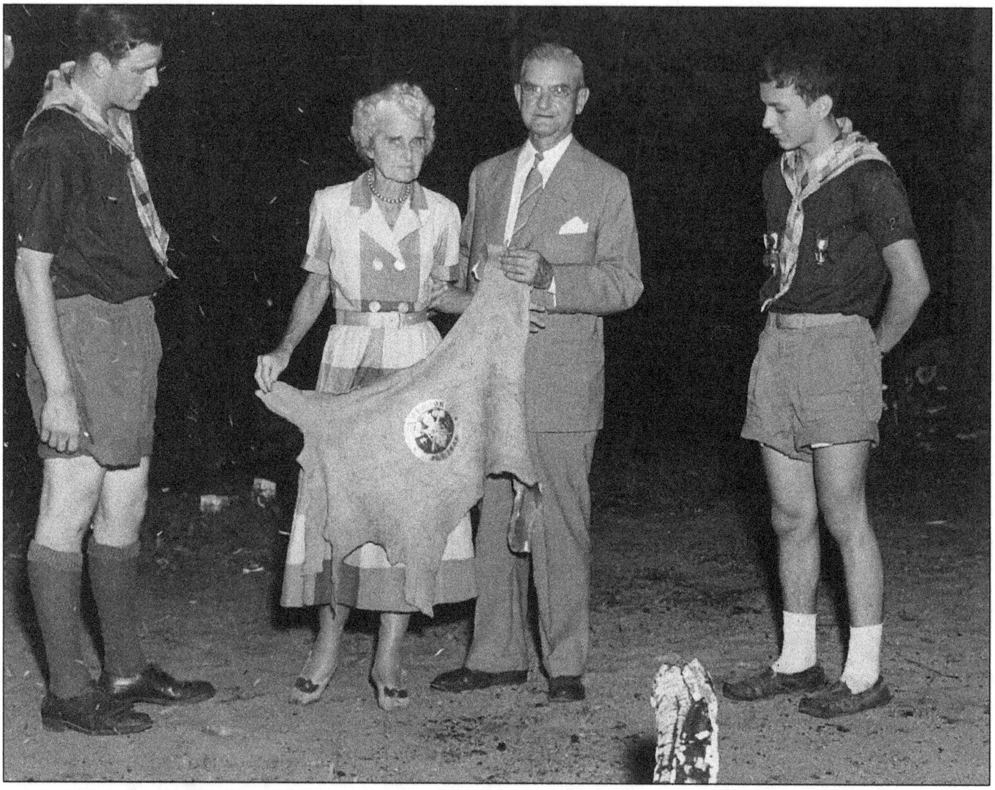

Mr. and Mrs. Charles R. Hook are shown at a special ceremony at Camp Hook. This 267-acre camp near Carlisle was given to the scouts by Hook. It has since been deeded to the Five Rivers Metro Parks of Montgomery County.

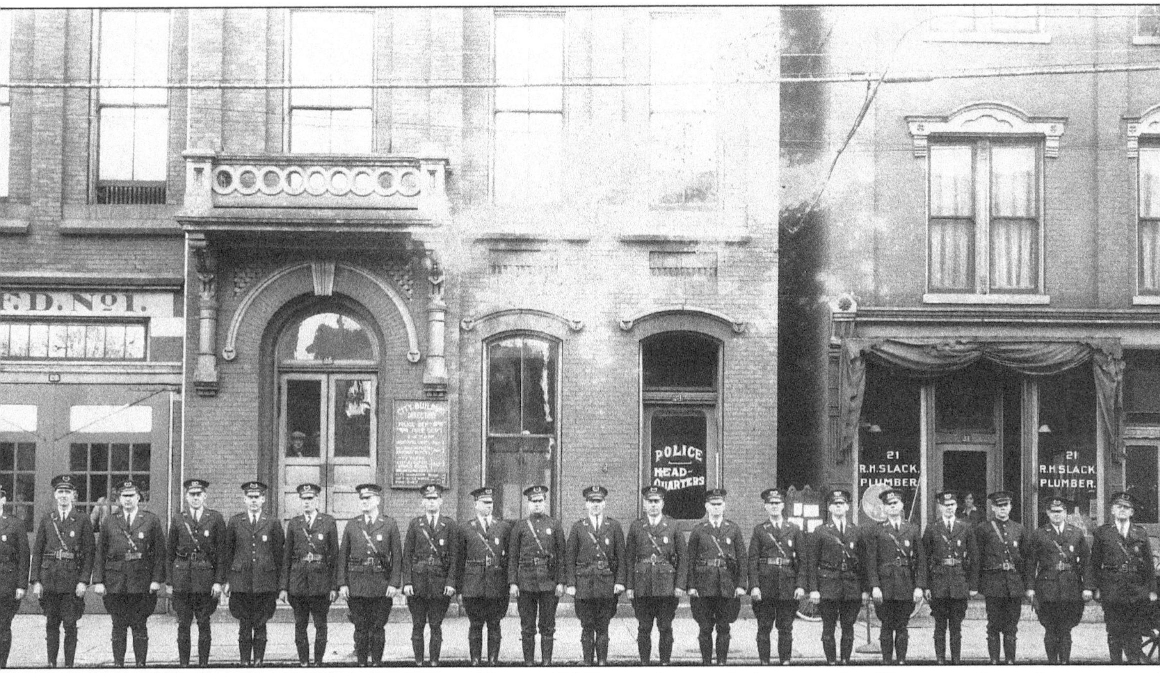

Here is Middletown's "Thin Blue Line," in 1927, in front of the city building on Broad Street. Four of these officers—Harold Roth, Ebert Crout, George McChesney, and Henry Brinkmeyer—would be killed in the line of duty. Everett Keister would be shot leading to early retirement. One, Charles Skeen, would be killed in 1926. Another, Daniel Sandlin, who joined the force a little later, would be killed in 1930. All are honored at the Firefighters-Police Officers Memorial at Woodside Cemetery, and the fallen police officers are also honored at the National Law Enforcement Officers' Memorial, Washington, D.C., where their names are engraved in a marble wall.

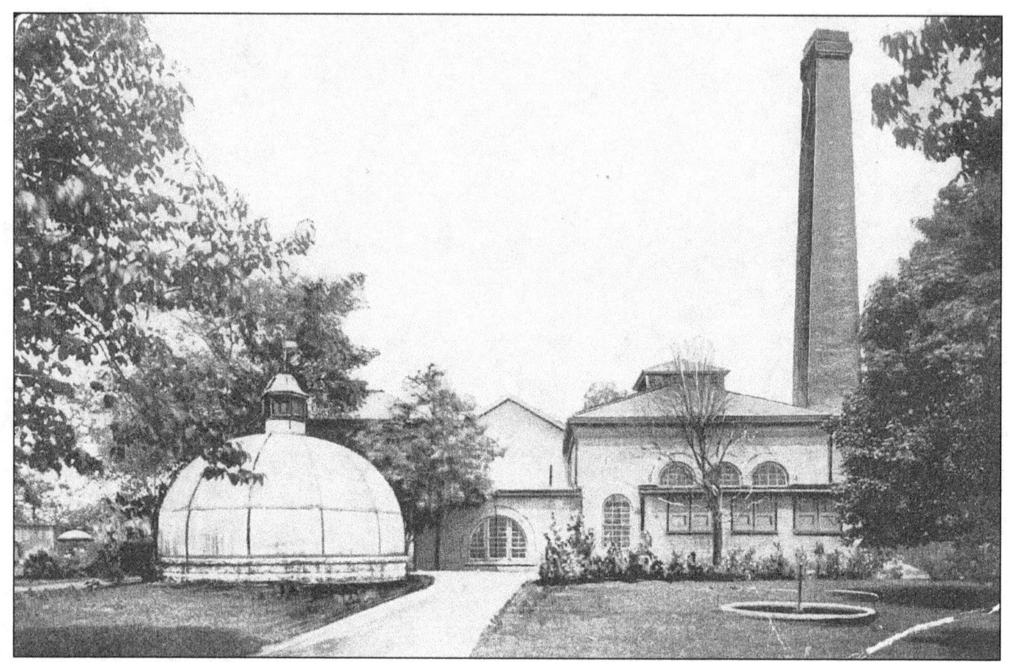

The City Water Works, which began operation on April 25, 1875, grew rapidly as the town expanded. By 1900, it stood near its present site in what was called the Water Works Park.

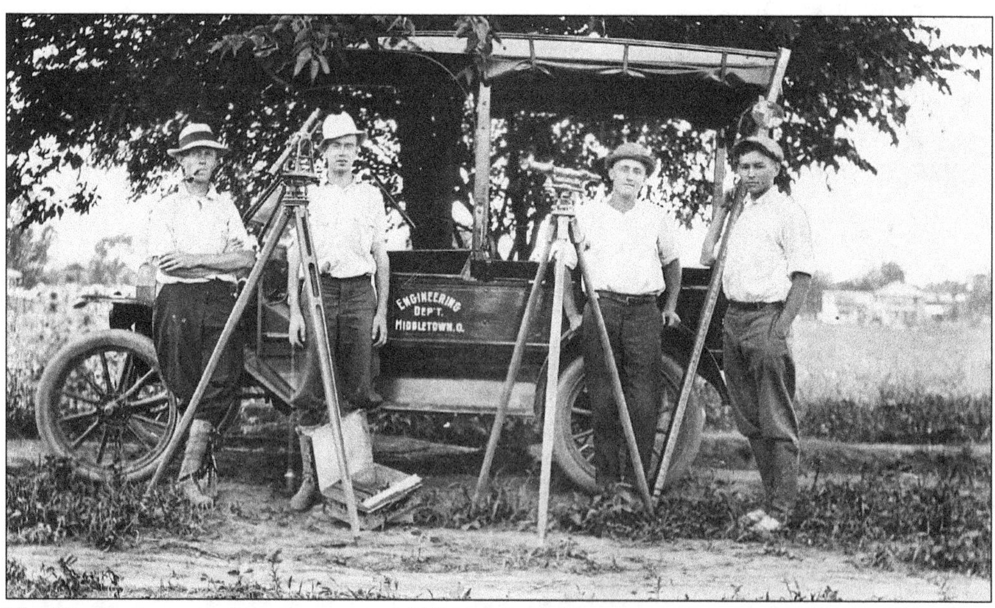

The City Engineering Department, in 1915, had the following men on its staff: Bill Conklin, Tom Palmer, Roy Lamb, and Arthur Borger. They appear here with their surveying equipment.

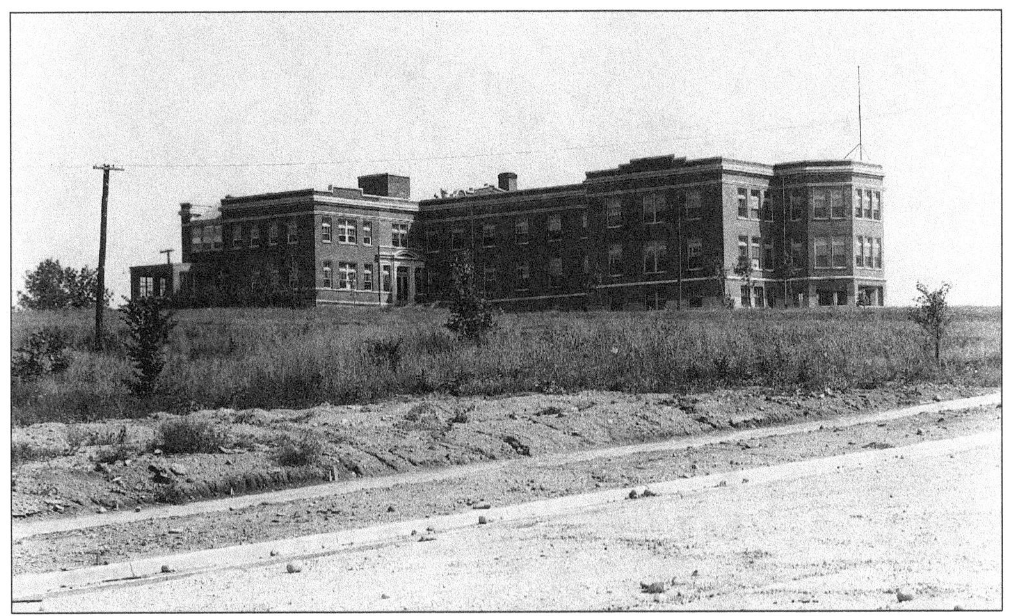

Incorporated in 1915 on a non-profit basis, Middletown Hospital construction was slowed due to WW I, but it opened in March 1917. By 1923, an addition adding 58 more beds was completed. The addition is shown in this photograph.

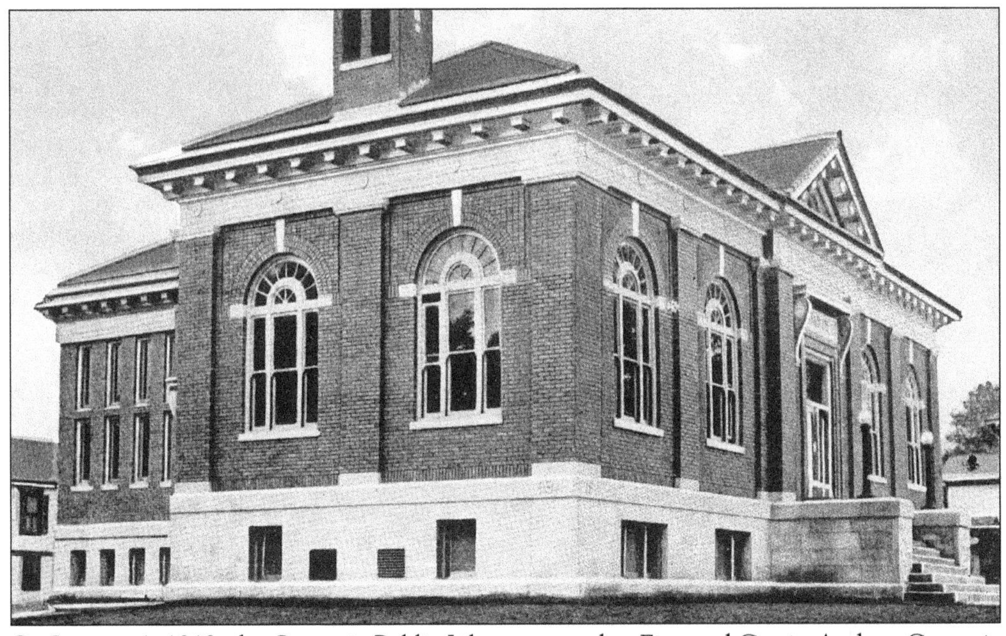

On January 1, 1913, the Carnegie Public Library opened at First and Curtis. Andrew Carnegie had donated $25,000 for the building, and the city pledged to spend at least $2,500 for library purposes. This is an early photo of the library.

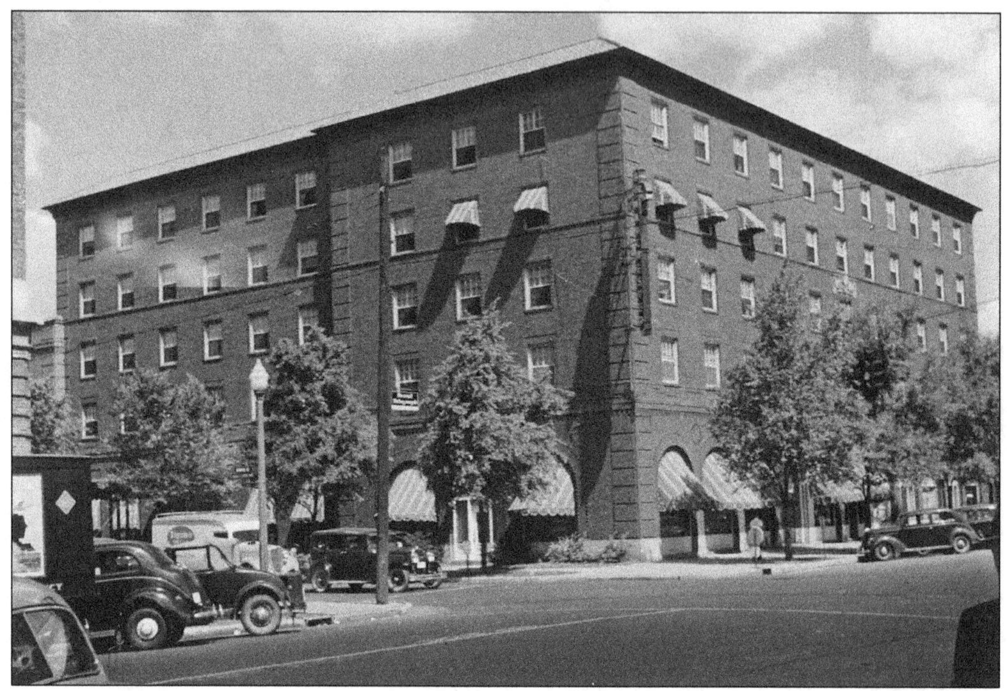

The Manchester Hotel, named for the English Duke of Manchester, was constructed by the Middletown Hotel Company, which sold $265,000 in stock. It was dedicated on November 3, 1922. This photo was taken by W.H. Alford.

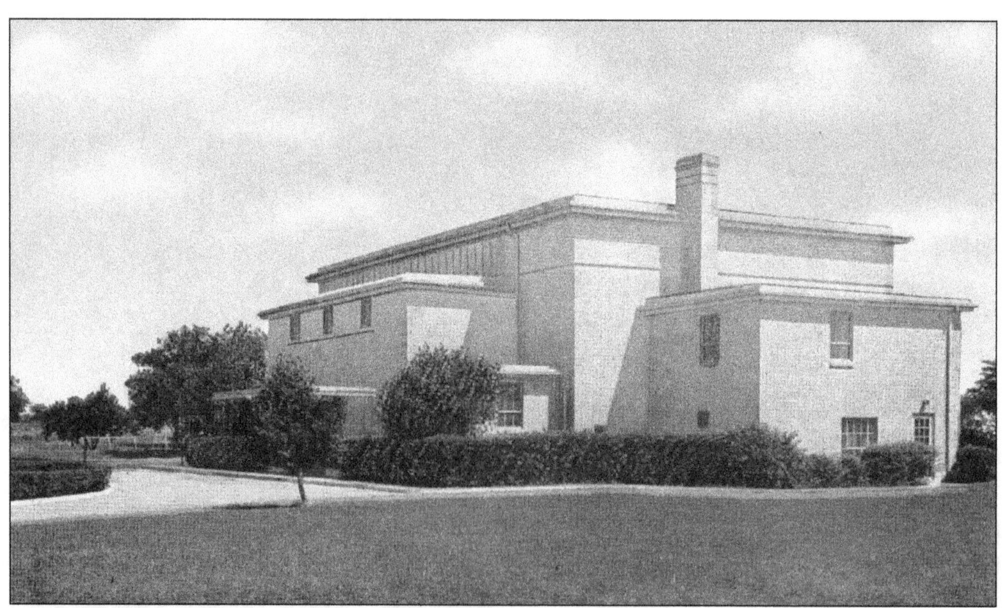

The Armco Colored Center, now the Middletown Community Center, off Verity Parkway at 800 Lafayette Avenue, is a modern facility, after extensive renovation. It was opened on October 17, 1942, with former Armco President George M. Verity giving the dedicatory speech. It was sponsored by the Colored Community Association.

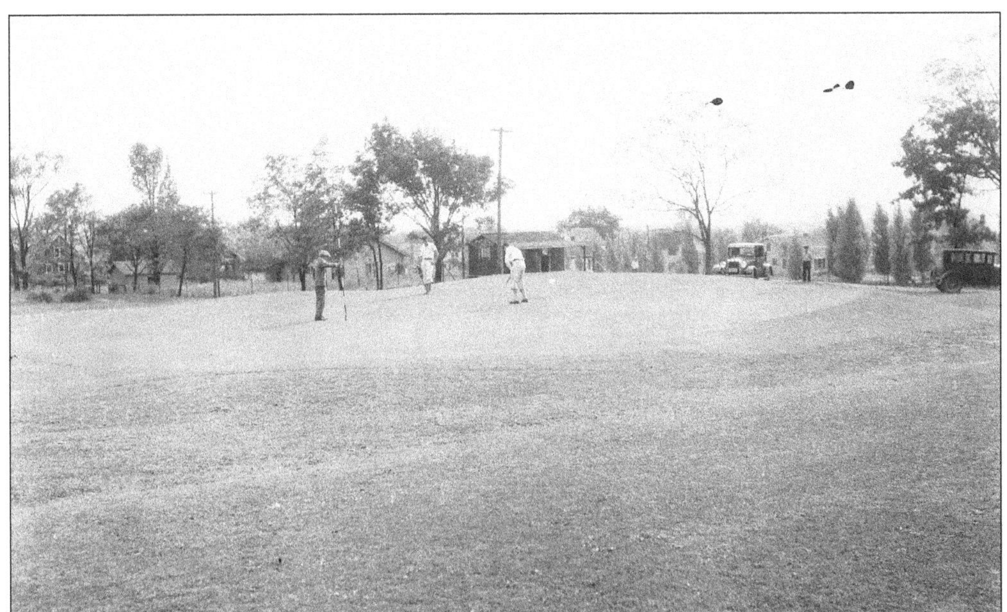

The Wildwood Golf Club was organized in 1922, utilizing 162 acres of land adjacent to old Armco Park. This early picture of the club was snapped by Portsmouth. A complete history, available at the library, has been written by Ruby M. Weidner.

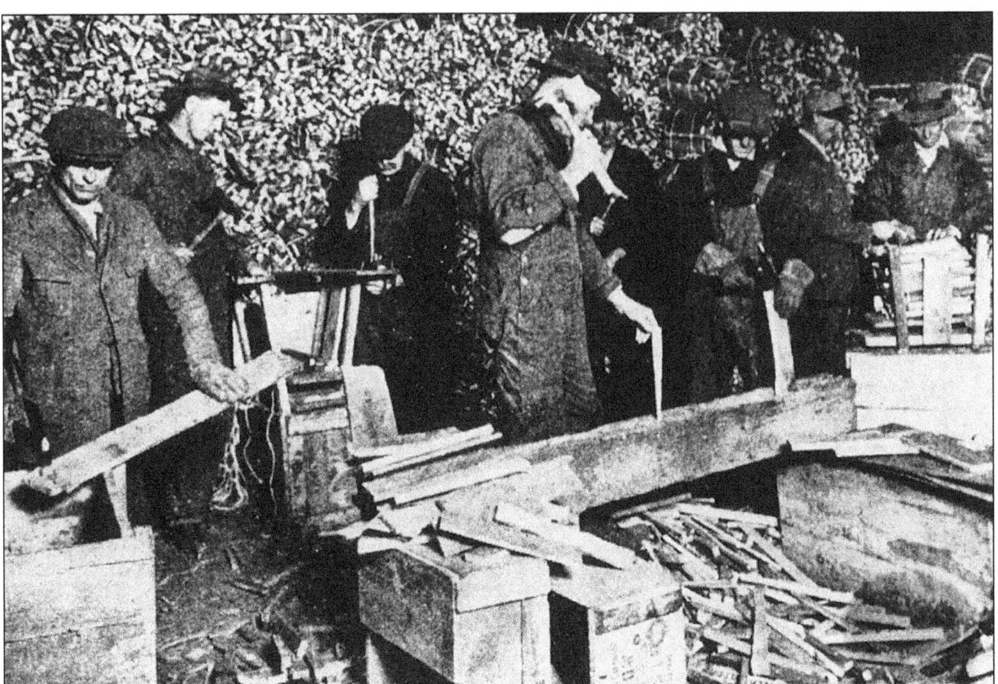

The Depression of 1929 hit Middletown, a steel city, hard, lessening the demand for Armco's product. Many men were out of work, but the tobacco company, P. Lorillard, was running full shifts. P. Lorillard donated wooden tobacco boxes, which were cut into kindling and sold throughout the town, but there were always more men than there was work.

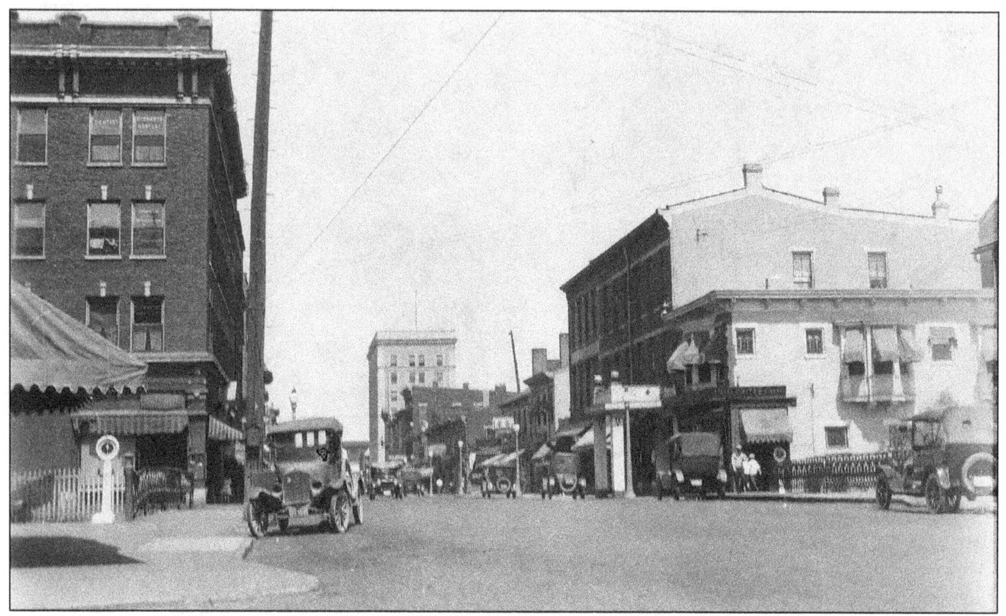

The following pictures were taken in the mid-1920s, when the old downtown provided access to over 150 businesses—both stores and services. Here, looking west at Verity and Central, is the Castell Building with Revelos's Elite confectionary at the southeast corner and the Gordon Theater across the street.

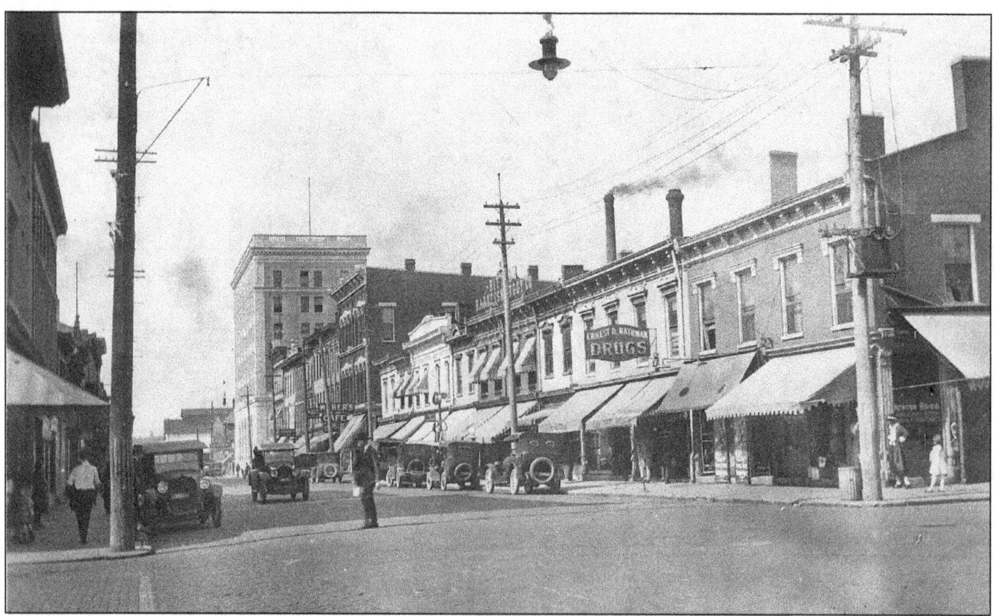

Down the next block, looking west from Broad, note Ernest Rathman's Drug Store. The view is of the north side of the street with the new First and Merchants National Bank in the background.

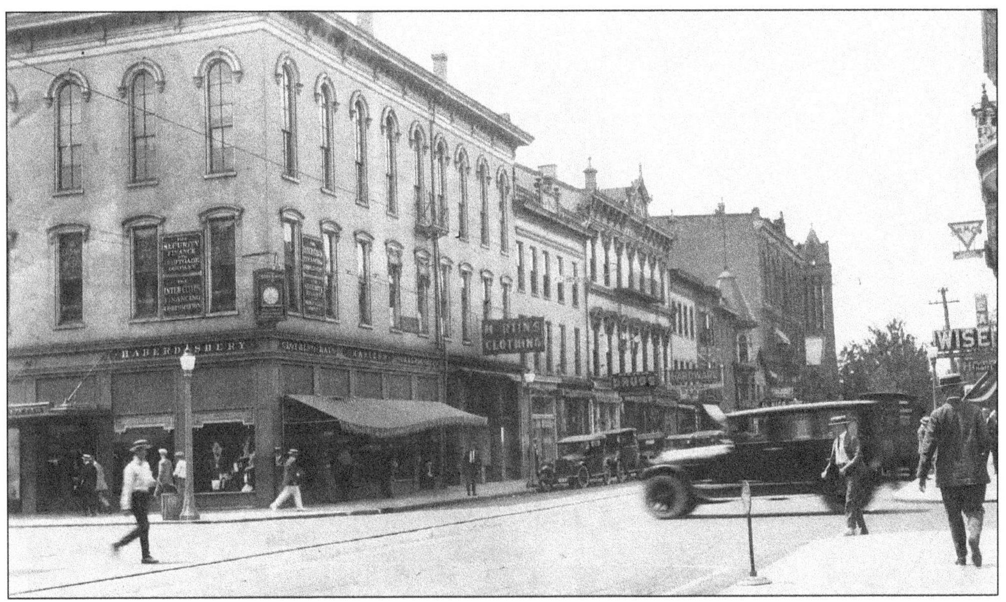

This view is looking south on Main Street to the Sorg Opera House with the old Presbyterian church at the far corner. Martin's Clothing store is on the near corner.

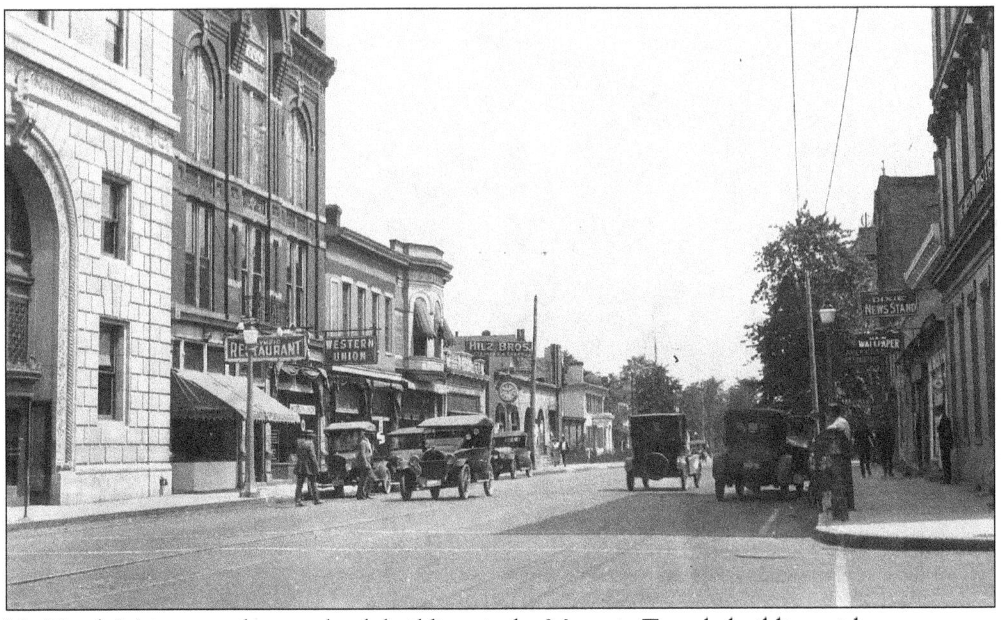

Up North Main, past the new bank building, is the Masonic Temple building with a restaurant on the first floor and a busy Western Union office next door.

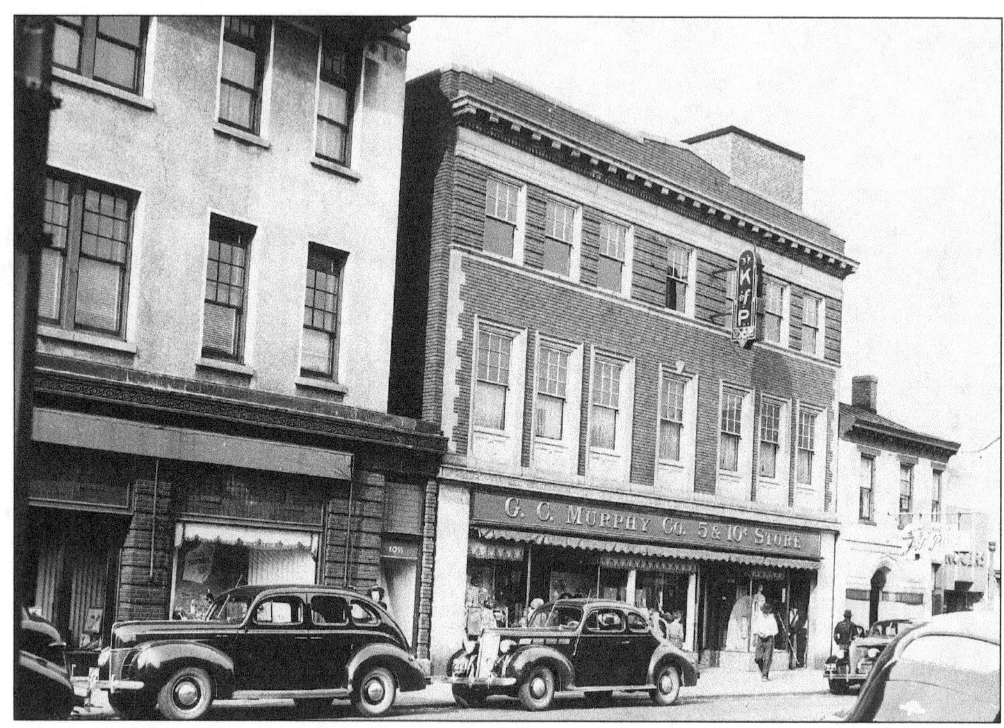

At this time the Ross store was the city's leading department store, making the southwest corner of Central and Broad the busiest one in town. Along Broad was the Ortman-Stewart Bus stop and depot. Next to the Ross store was G.C. Murphy's popular five- and ten-cent store.

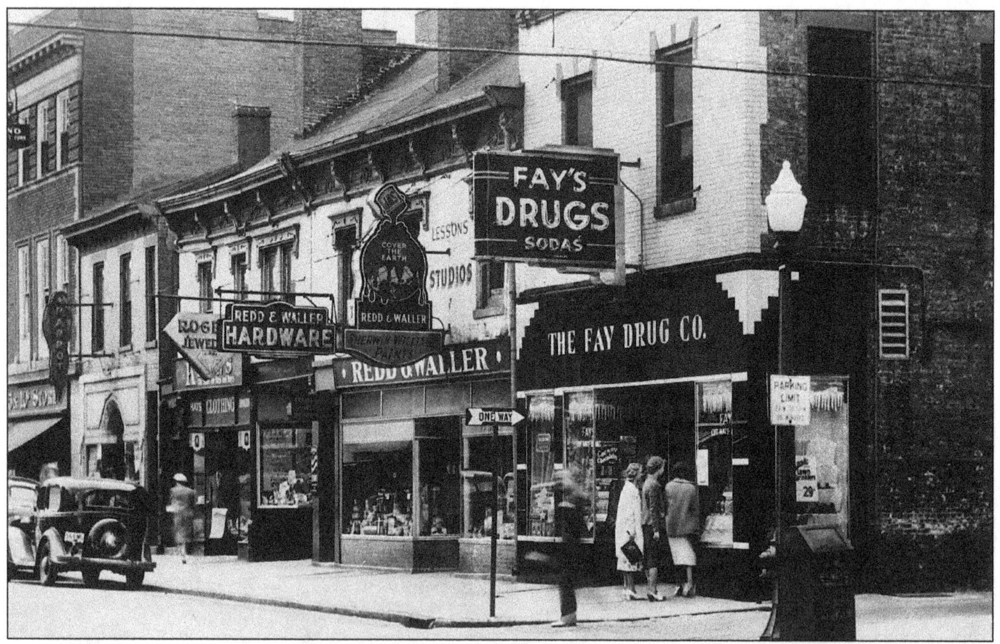

Continuing west on the south side of Central, between Broad and the Alley, were the Parrot (a clothing store), Roger's Jewelry Store, Redd and Waller Hardware, and the popular Fay's Drug Store with its soda fountain.

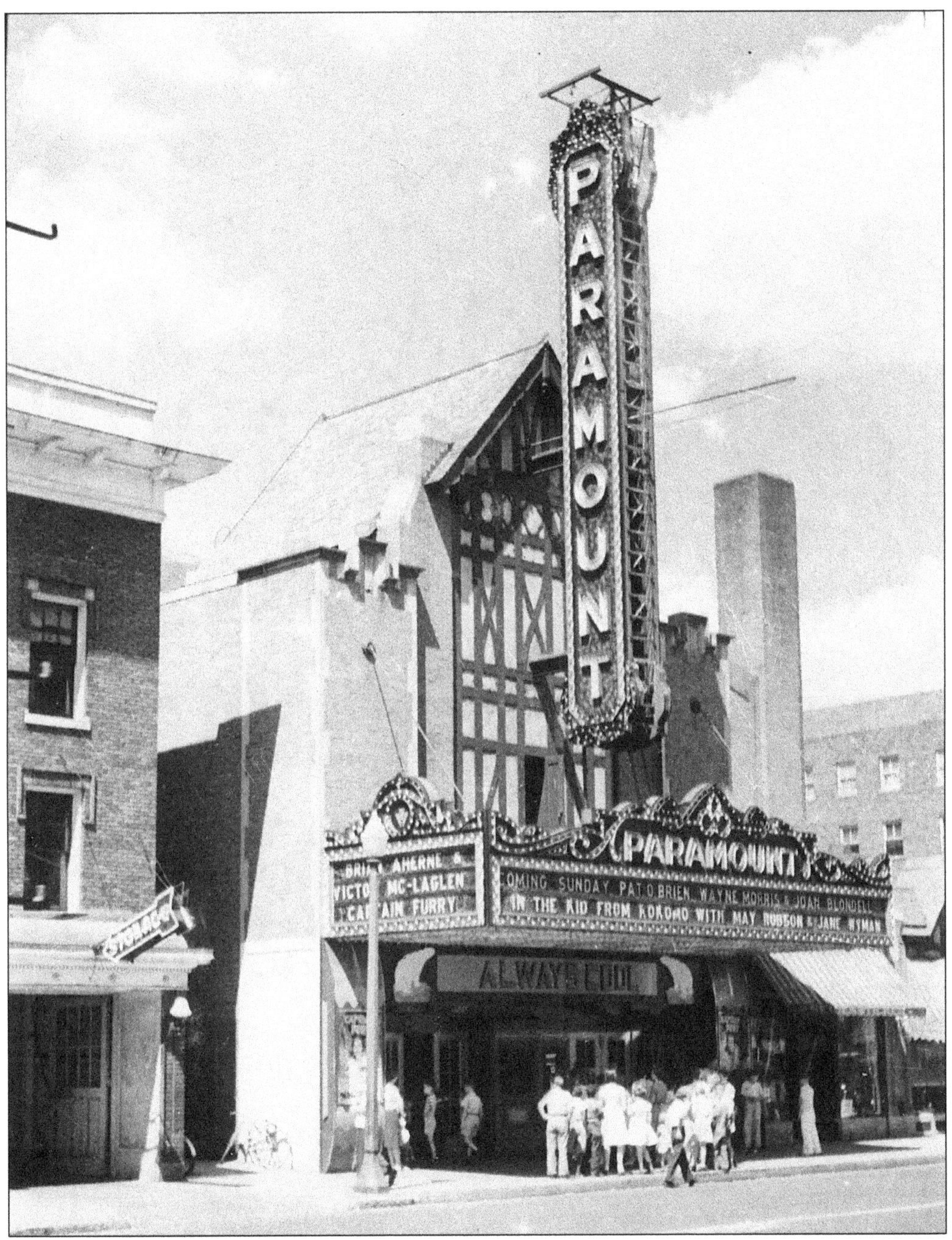

A little farther north on Broad, next to Shetter's Garage, was the new Paramount Theater, which opened April 5, 1931, and had 2,000 seats. It was torn down in 1963. The Gordon and Strand were its major competitors.

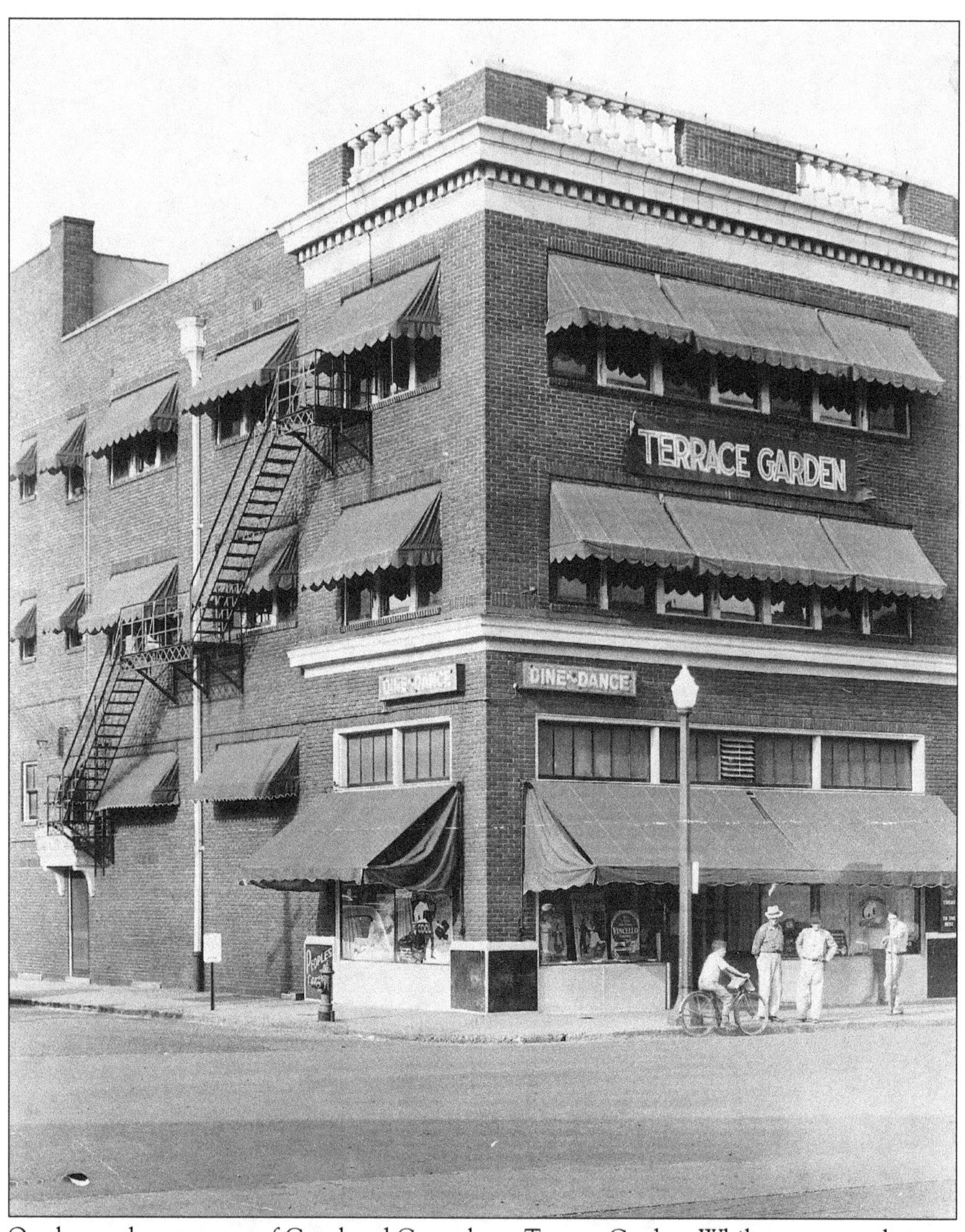

On the northeast corner of Canal and Central was Terrace Garden. While a meat market was on the first floor, the upper two floors served as a night club, with the second floor set aside for line and country dancing, and the third for social dancing. Atop the building was the antennae for Middletown's first commercial radio station—WSRO.

Five

Picture Perfect Postcards

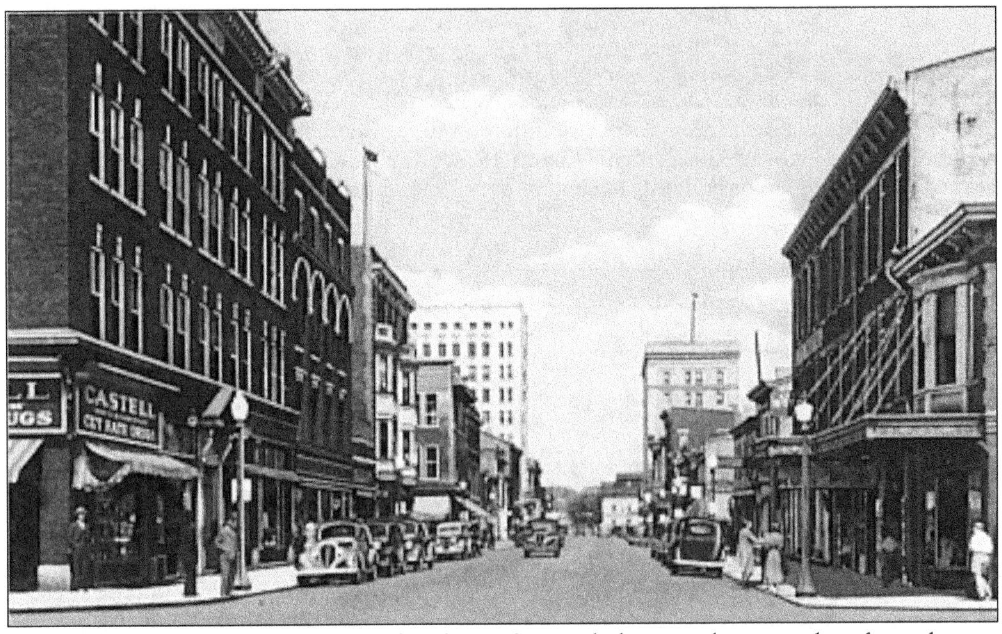

The "picture-perfect" postcard was taken by professional photographers traveling from place to place with the latest equipment, on commission to take views for postcard publishing houses. The printed cards, as well as folders of such cards, were sold at local outlets. It was big business. In 1872, the U.S. Postmaster-General adopted the idea of a penny postcard—a plain card with a stamp. It sold for a penny until 1952. Picture postcards first cost 2¢ to mail, but this was cut in 1898 to 1¢, as free rural delivery was instituted. So millions and millions of the cards, in black and white, sepia and color, were made and are now collected by deltiologists.

In 1905, the Eastman Kodak Company started printing postcards from amateur negatives at a penny a card. In each neighborhood someone bought one of these special Kodak cameras and took pictures, selling them around the community as a friendly service. A few of these are included in this chapter, but most reproduced here are professional cards, such as the one shown here, which is the view from the Castell Building looking west. This is the vibrant Central Avenue of the 1950s and 60s, which would become part of an enclosed mall in the 1970s.

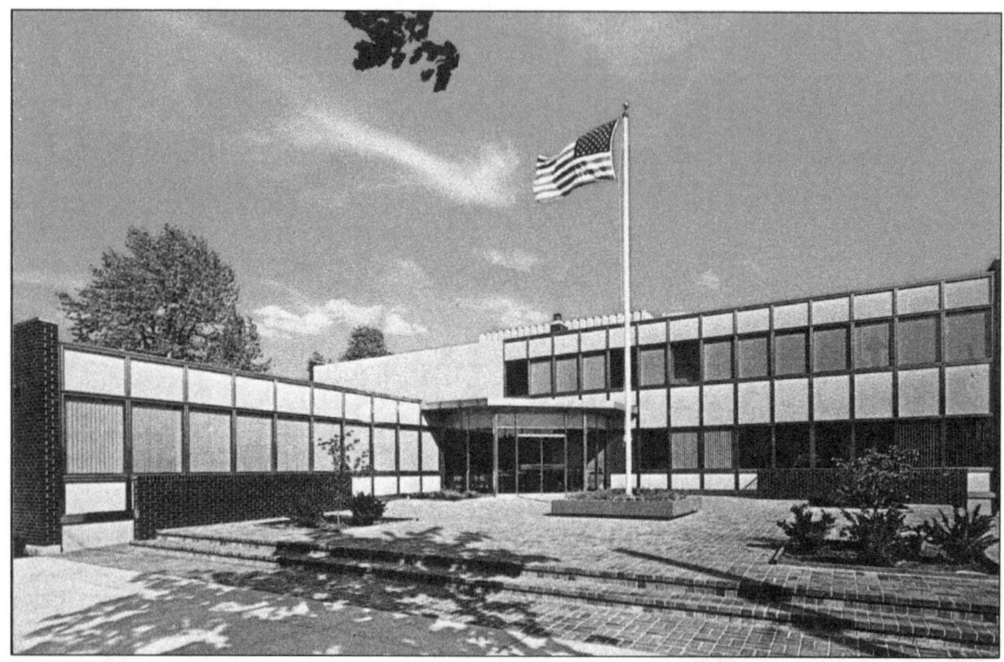

In 1923, the Middletown Civic Association, forerunner of the United Way, was organized. It became the Middletown Area United Way in 1974, which then merged with the Cincinnati United Way. The present building, opened in May 1964, is still in use.

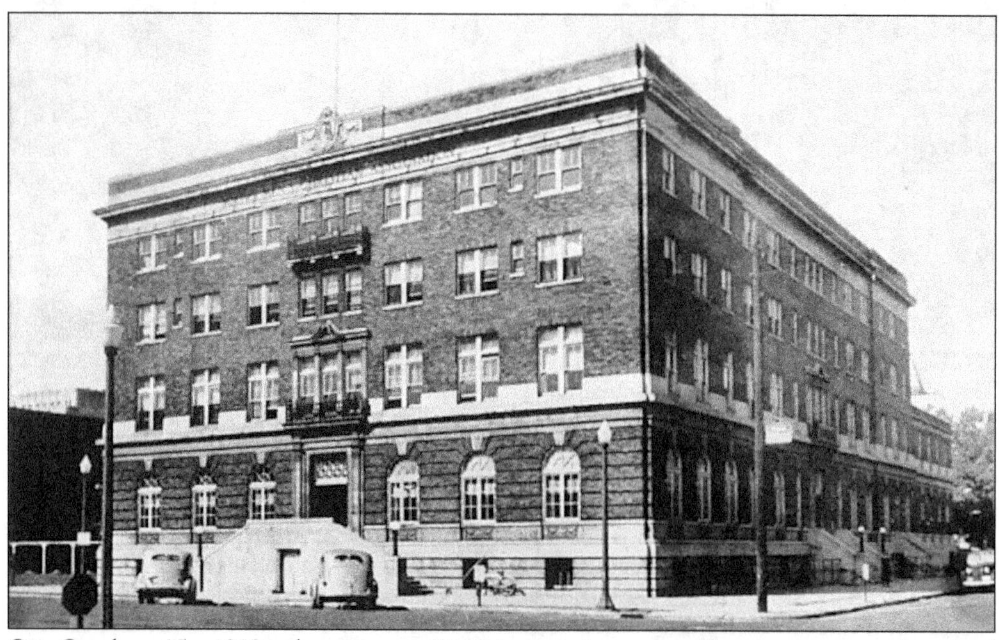

On October 15, 1923, the present YMCA was incorporated—representing the third reorganization of the group. The original structure was erected at Broad and Manchester with an addition, opened September 8, 1985, to the west. The first YMCA was organized here on March 21, 1867.

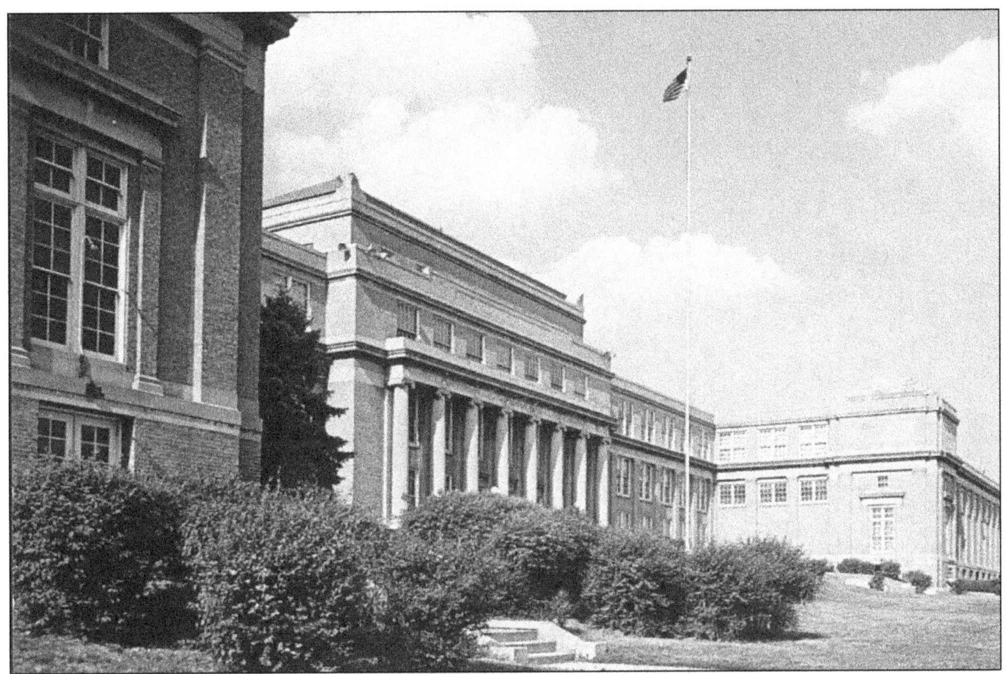

This beautiful high school, now Vail Middle School, along Girard Avenue, opened in 1923, replacing one along Central Avenue which was converted to an eighth-grade building. The Central Avenue building replaced South School, where a high school was organized on the third floor. This school graduated its first class of four in 1871. The present high school along Breiel Boulevard opened in 1969.

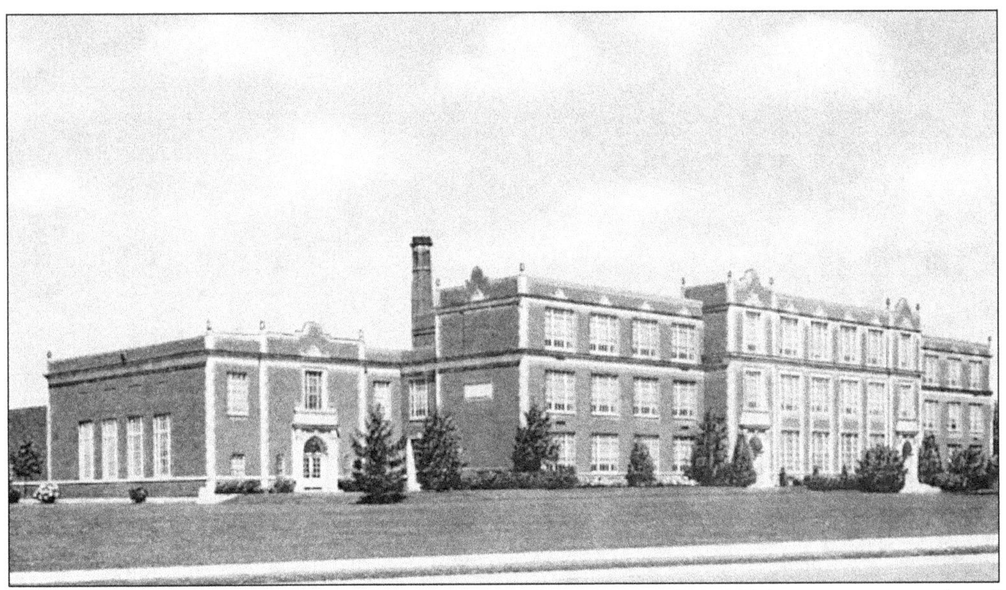

McKinley Junior High School, along Verity Parkway, opened in 1930 to serve central and south Middletown. It has 31 rooms. It became a middle school in 1969, and an elementary school in 1981.

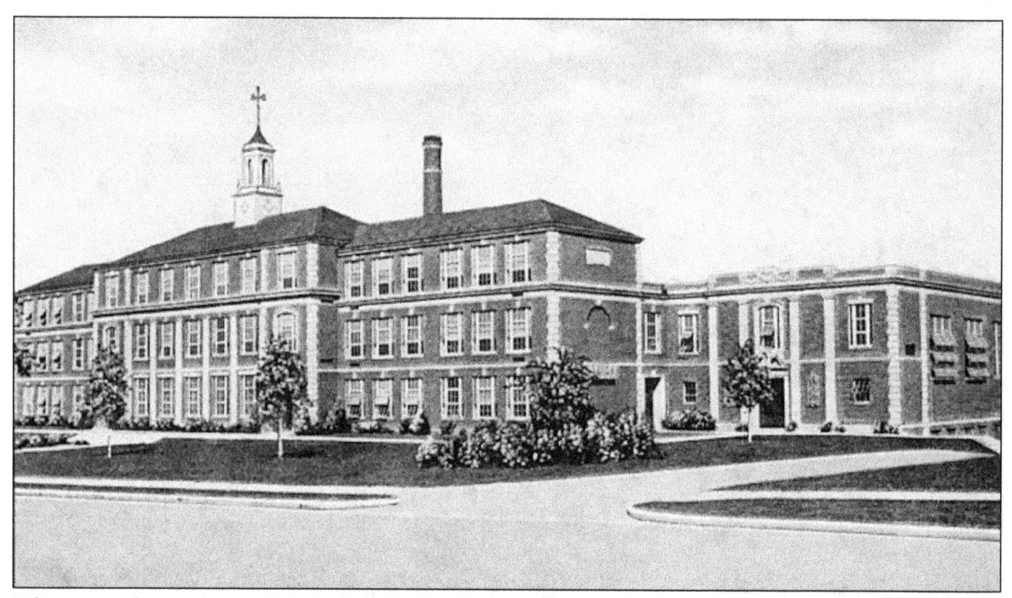

Like McKinley, Roosevelt Junior High School opened in 1930, with 31 rooms along East Central Avenue. In 1981, it too became an elementary school and has been remodeled and refurbished.

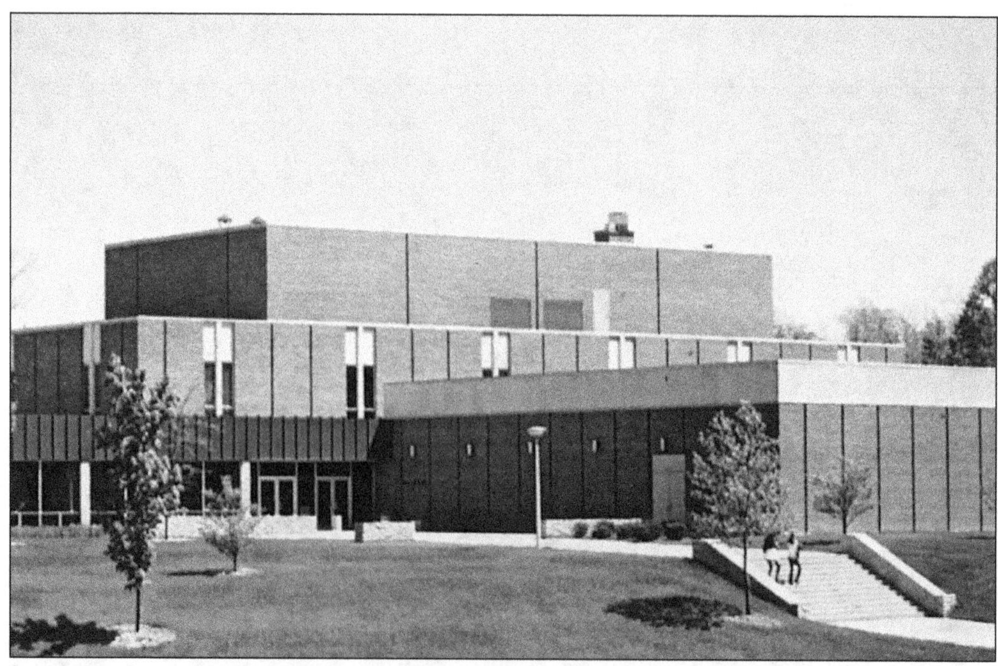

Logan T. Johnston Hall contains the administrative offices of the campus of Miami University-Middletown. The land, deeded at no cost to the university, was a gift from Armco, and was once a part of Armco Park. The campus was opened in 1966.

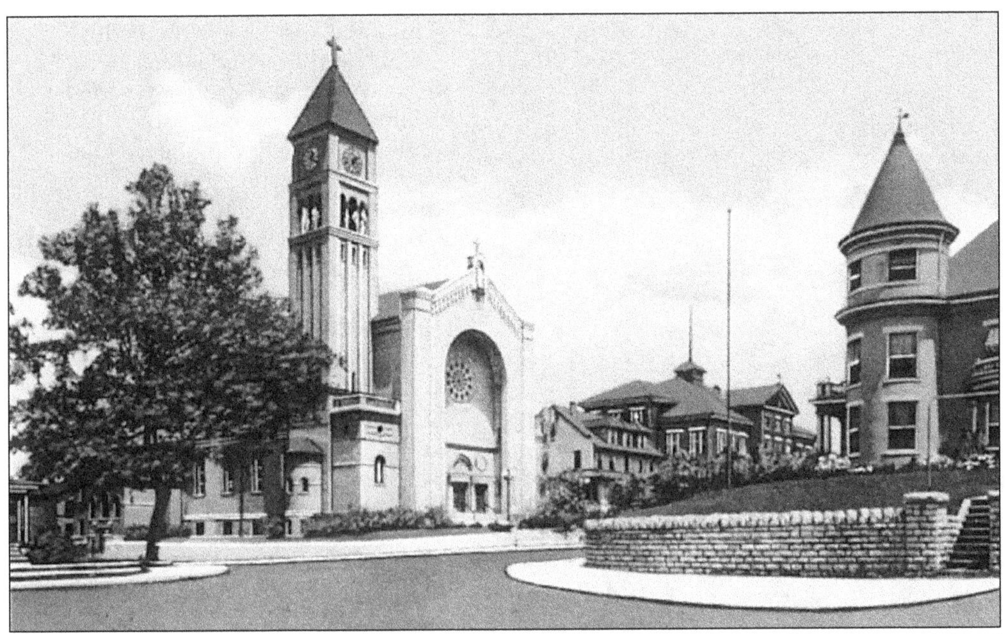

The corner of Curtis and First was the center of the old Saint John's parish, now consolidated with the Holy Family Parish. The card shows the European-design church with its clock tower, the Knights of Columbus quarters, and the red brick school, which was demolished in 1996 to make way for a parking lot.

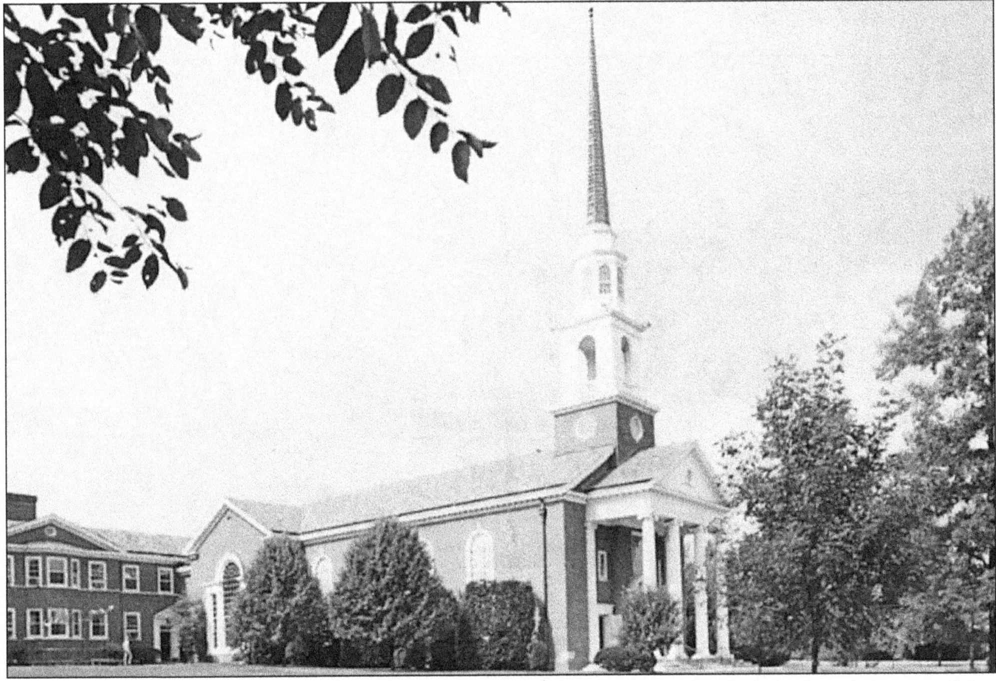

The stately First Presbyterian Church on East Central represents the fourth church home of the congregation. Of Williamsburg design, it was built in 1950. It is a favorite of local architects.

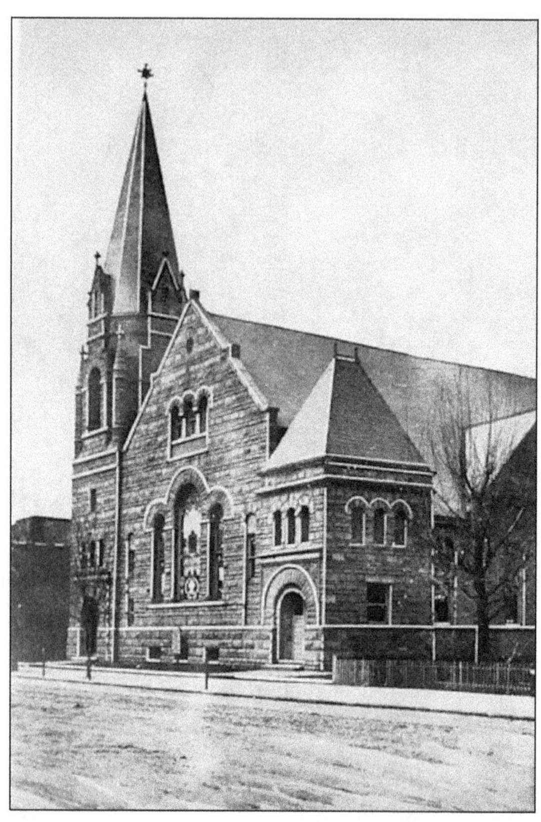

This is the First United Methodist Church at the corner of Broad and Second Avenue. According to the late Wilfred D. Vorhis, who wrote a history of the church, it is old Romanesque Revival architecture planned by Samuel A. Hanneford and Sons of Cincinnati and built of native stone from a nearby Rockdale quarry.

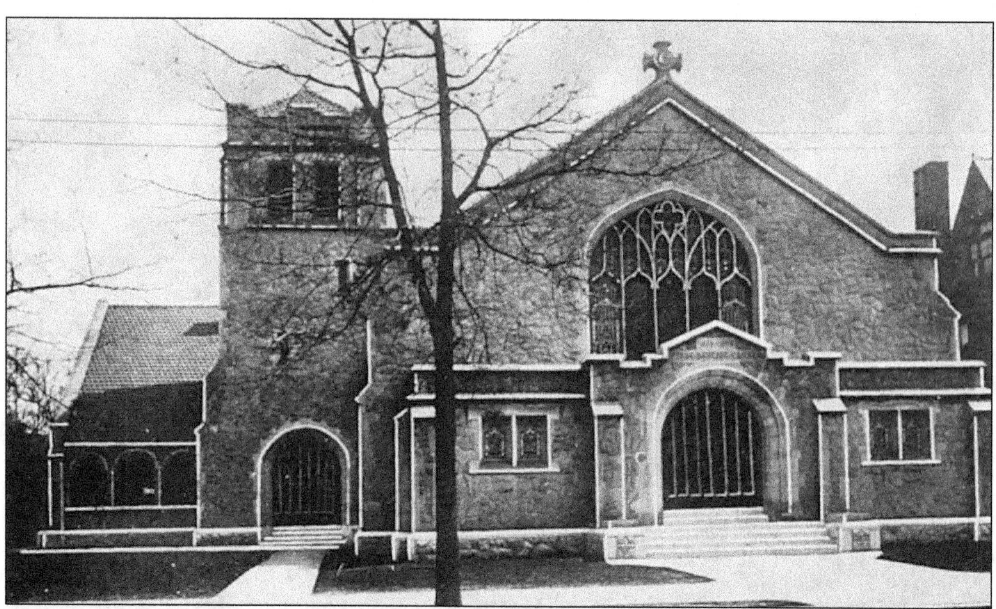

Located at 119 South Main Street, the old First Baptist Church was designed for the congregation in 1904 by one of the world's greatest architects—Frank Mills Andrews. His buildings are found around the nation and the world.

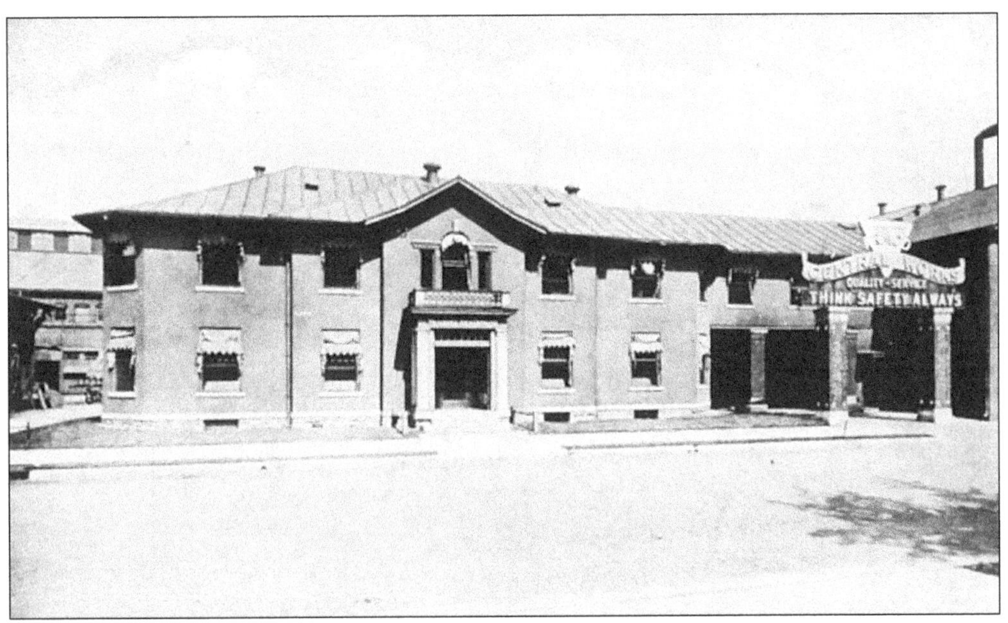

In 1917, Armco established its own school to provide technical training to enhance individual advancement. With the completion of a new general office building in 1917, part of the old office building was set aside for classes.

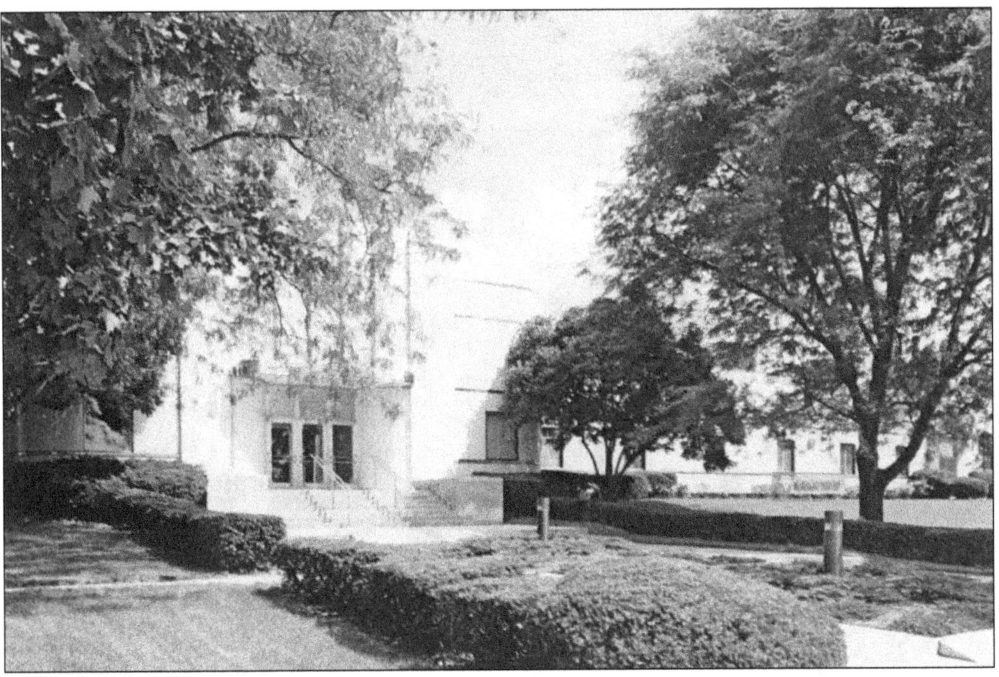

This new research center was dedicated in 1937 by Armco. In 1994, A.K Steel, a company completely separate from Armco, was born. Armco continued to operate from its Pittsburgh headquarters. It retained this property on Curtis Street which became the Armco Technology Center, with 132 technical employees, plus 40 in the Armco insurance group. Outside of Middletown it still employs about six thousand (1998).

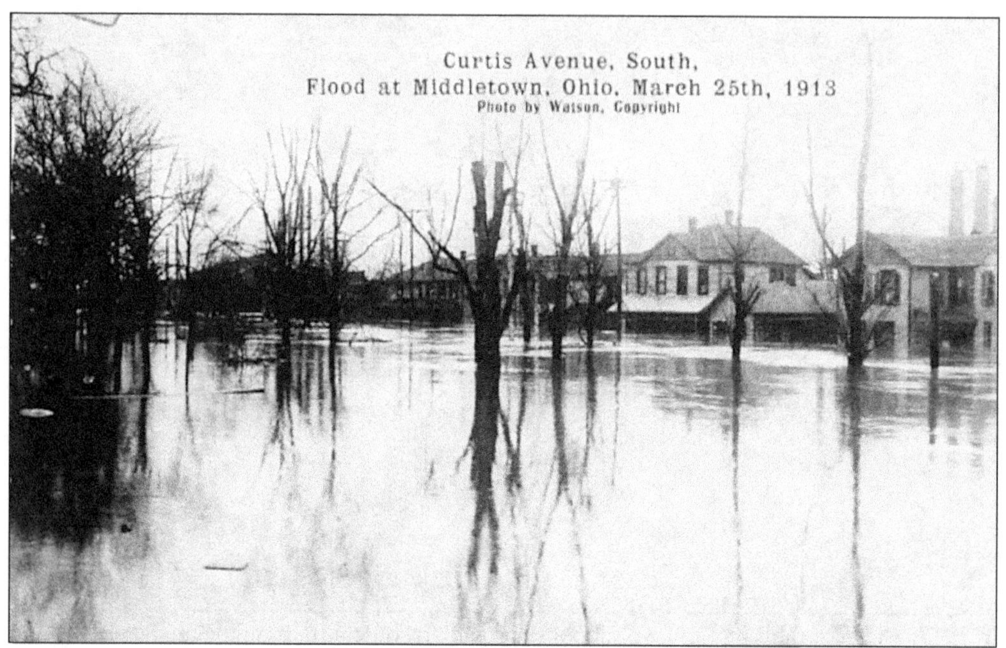

The major physical disaster to hit Middletown was the flood which struck March 25, 1913. It stopped near the foot of the first terrace above the flood plain, which follows the east side of Curtis and Clark Streets.

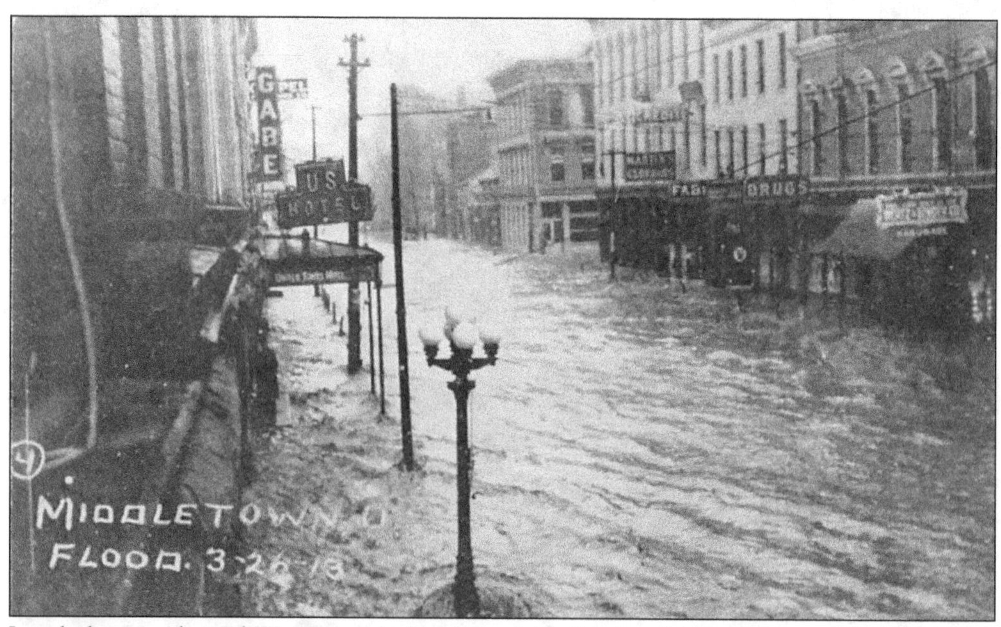

Local photographer Ed Watson took this shot of the flood on Main Street on March 26. The Great Miami River had crested that morning at 5 a.m. Watson took many shots of the flood which can be viewed at the Canal Museum or the public library.

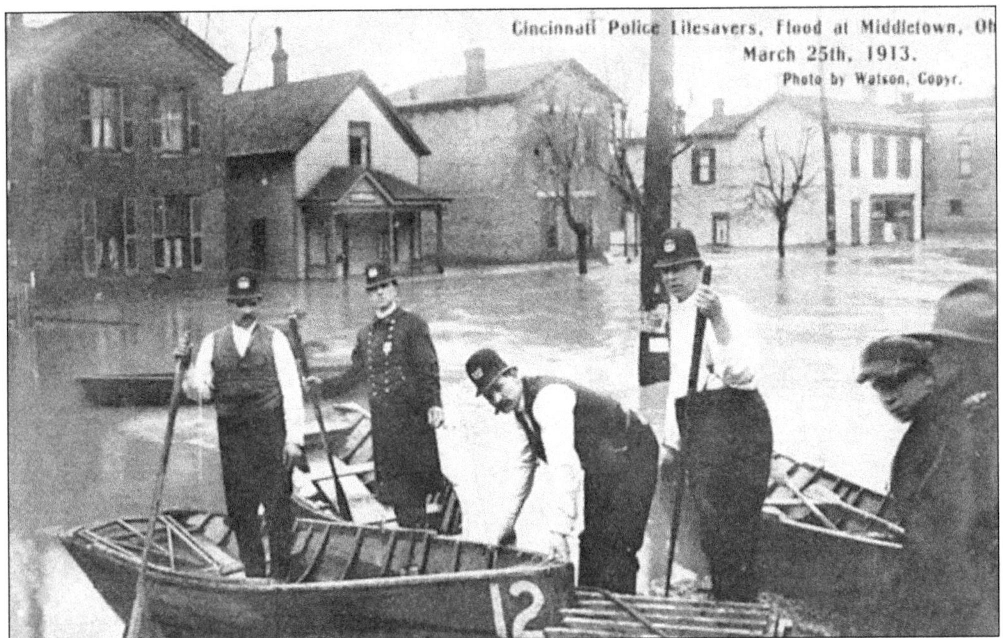

Cincinnati sent up 18 boats, and 10 policemen had volunteered to come to rescue those stranded by the rising waters. The boats came by way of the Big Four Railroad. This photo shows a group of policemen on Curtis Street near Central.

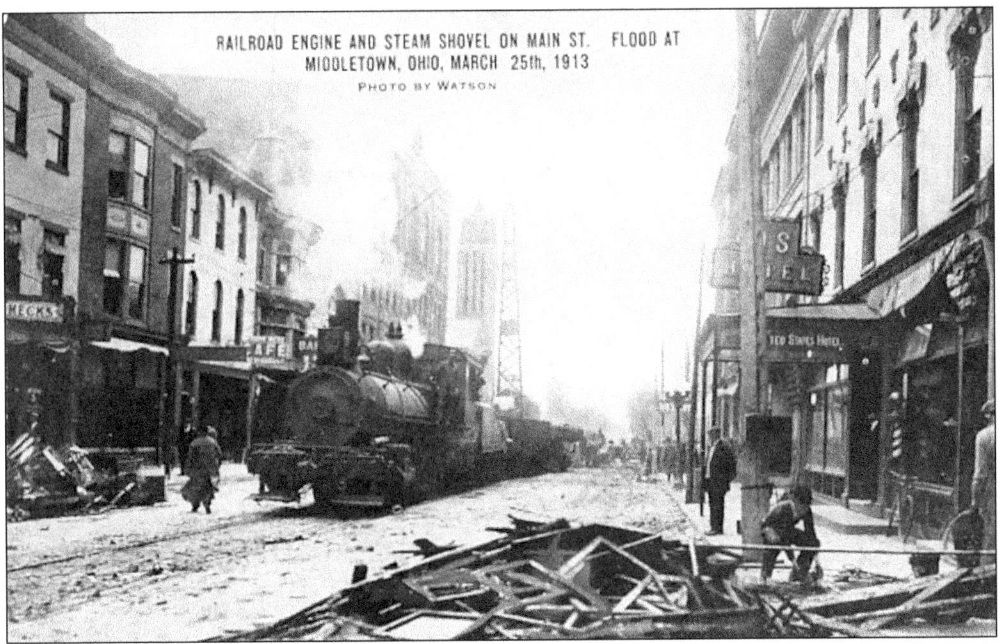

Armco loaned out their locomotives, which were able to travel on the trolley line's rails. With such help, the city was the first in the valley to be cleaned up. The engine seen here is on Main Street in front of the U.S. Hotel. Valley citizens banded together, and through the Miami Conservancy District built five dams which have prevented serious floods.

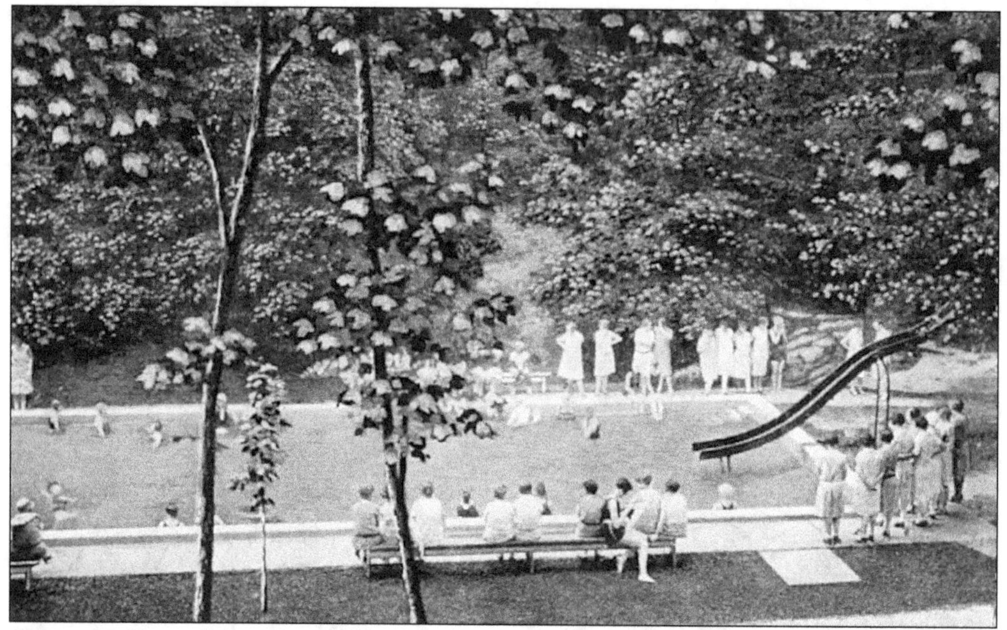

George M. Verity believed in the importance of recreation. In 1914 he was introduced to golf and decided to buy up abandoned land behind his Main-Street home, where a nine-hole golf course was laid out. Then he built a pool at the site of an east-end home near Armco Park. It was opened to members of his new golf club, which became known as Forest Hills.

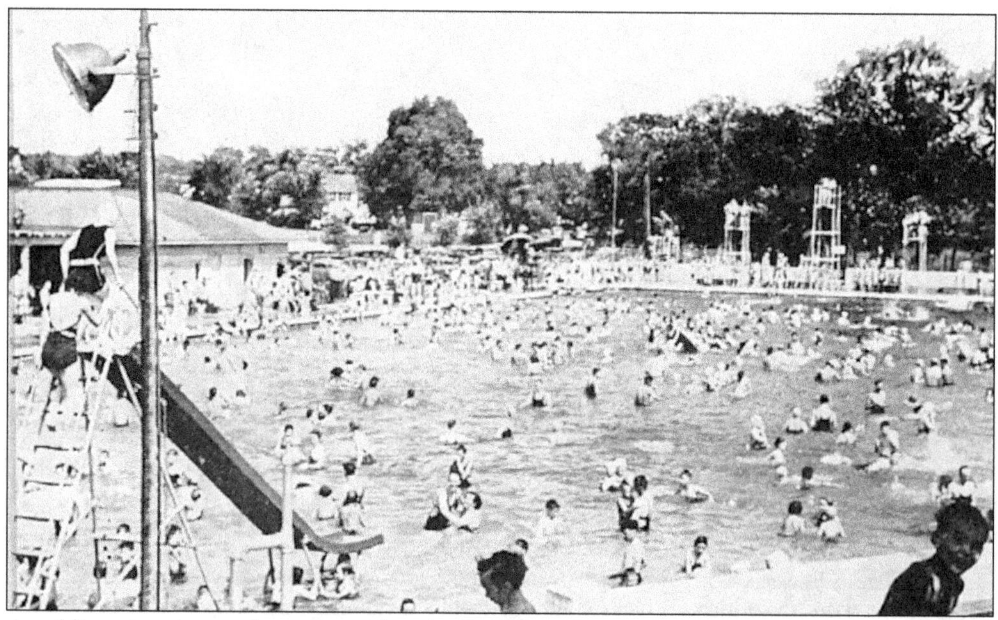

A public swimming pool was created in the Bulls Run Ravine, which ran through Sunset Park. The first pool was finished in 1922. After being remodeled many times, this pool was completely replaced in 1979.

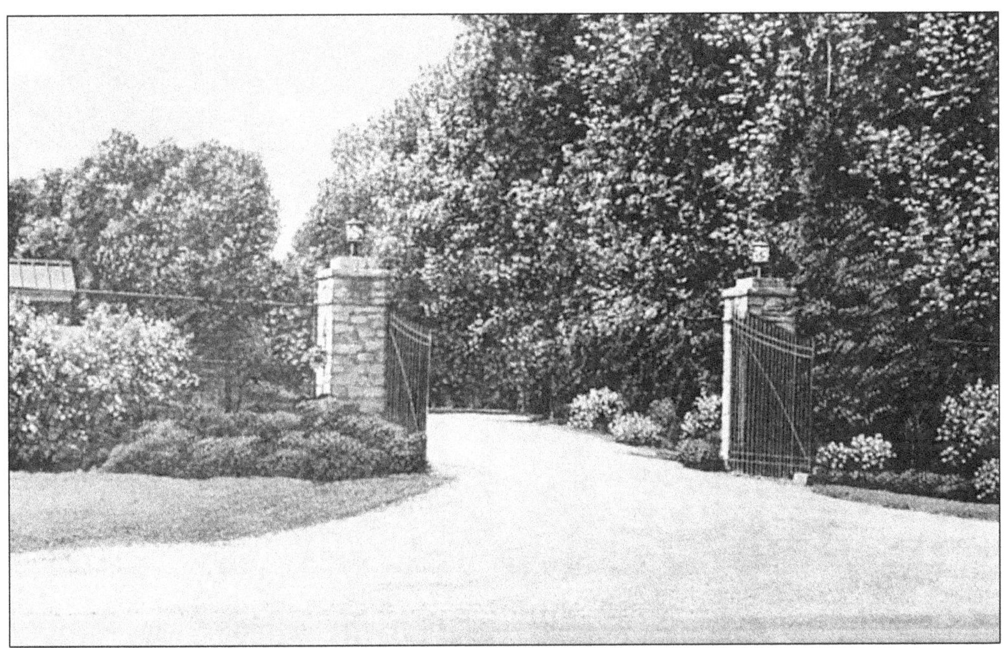

These landmark masonry gates once guarded old Armco Park, which closed in 1968. A crane from Mecco Construction Company saved them and moved them 60 feet to the south, placing them farther apart at the new entrance to the Sunset Branch of a local bank. They are still there.

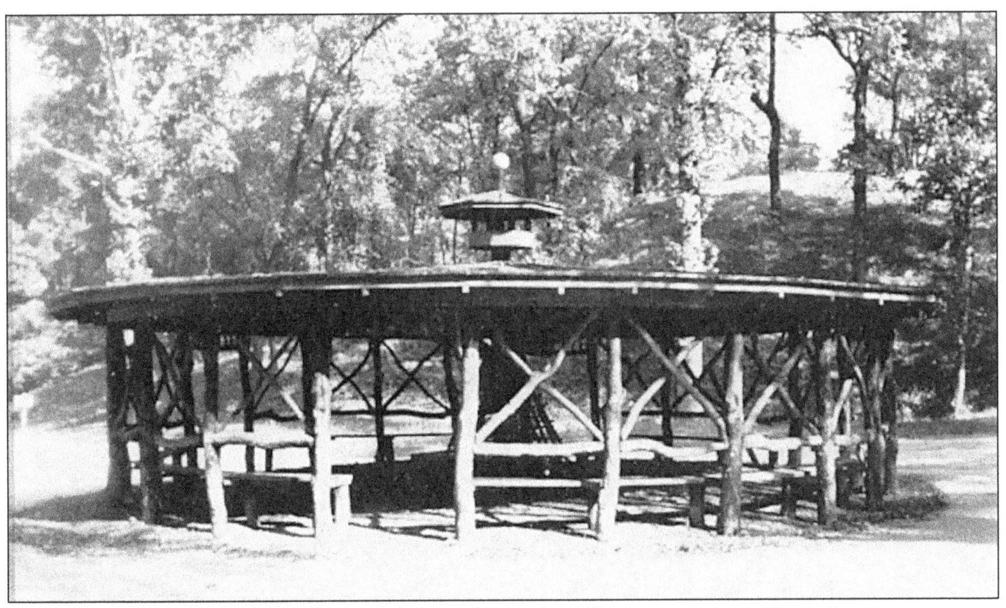

Opening in 1922 in the hills and dales of east Middletown, Armco Park became an area recreational center due to the generosity of Armco. This shelter house was at a park crossroads, one leading to the popular children's play area, "Bunny Hollow."

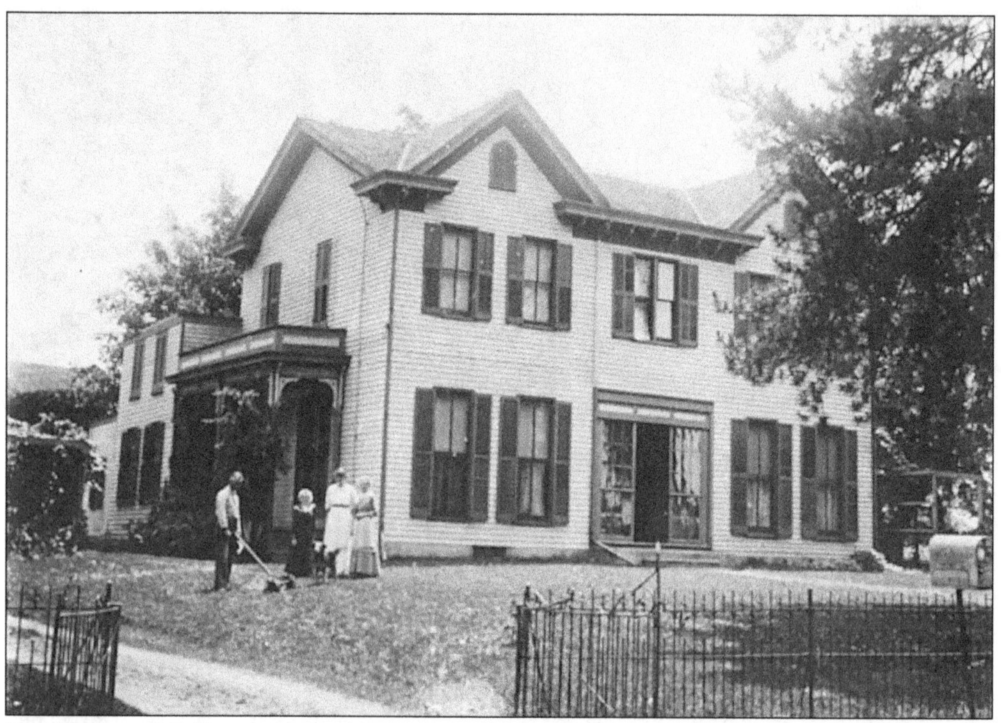

Dr. Abraham H. Iler, the legendary doctor of Blue Ball, now part of east Middletown, who practiced medicine for 51 years, lived in this lovely home with his family. The home was razed to make room for a road leading into Towne Mall.

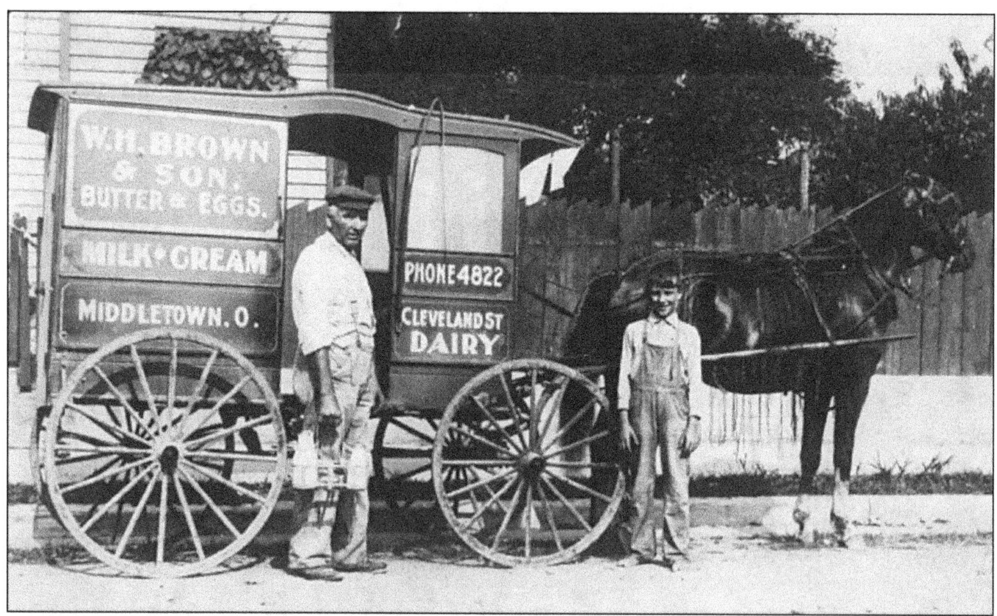

William H. Brown and his son, Harry, ran a dairy on Cleveland Street from 1909 to 1918. Its delivery wagon was typical of those that traveled local streets at the time delivering milk, bread, and ice to patrons.

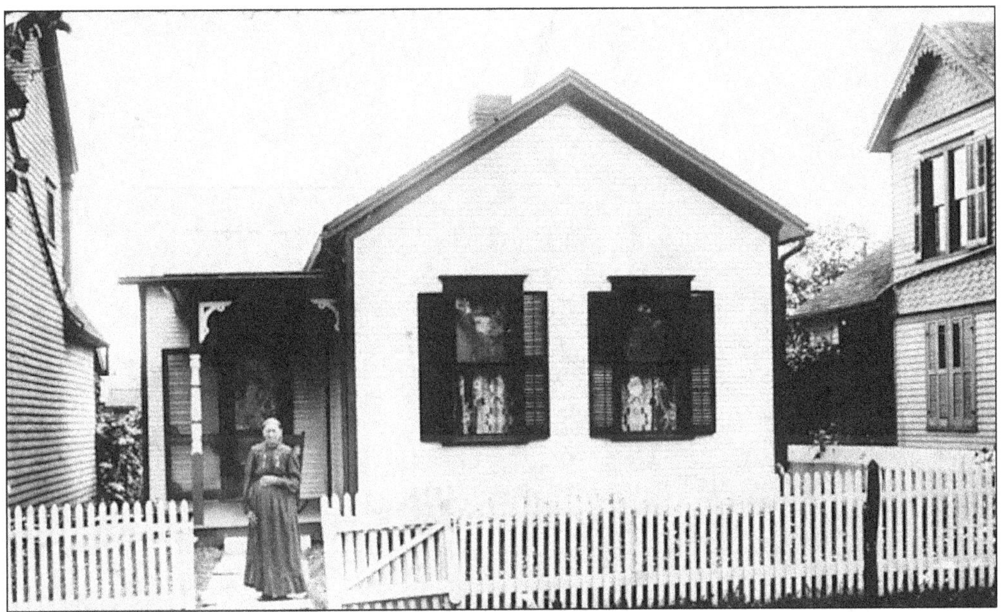

This little old woman lived in a retiree's cottage on Beech street. A neighbor, Virginia Keister Peters, as a girl, recalled that her name was Elizabeth DeGroat. This photo was taken in the 1920s.

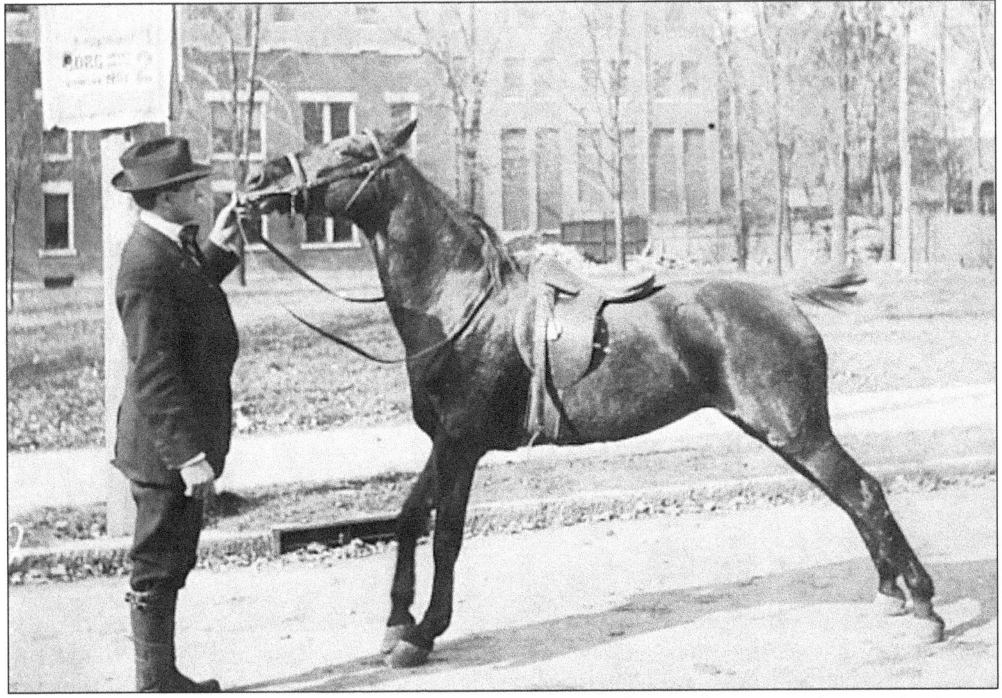

This last personal postcard in this group of four shows an unknown horseman showing his horse. This was on North Main in front of the Sorg Paper Company. On the pole is a showbill for the Sorg Opera House.

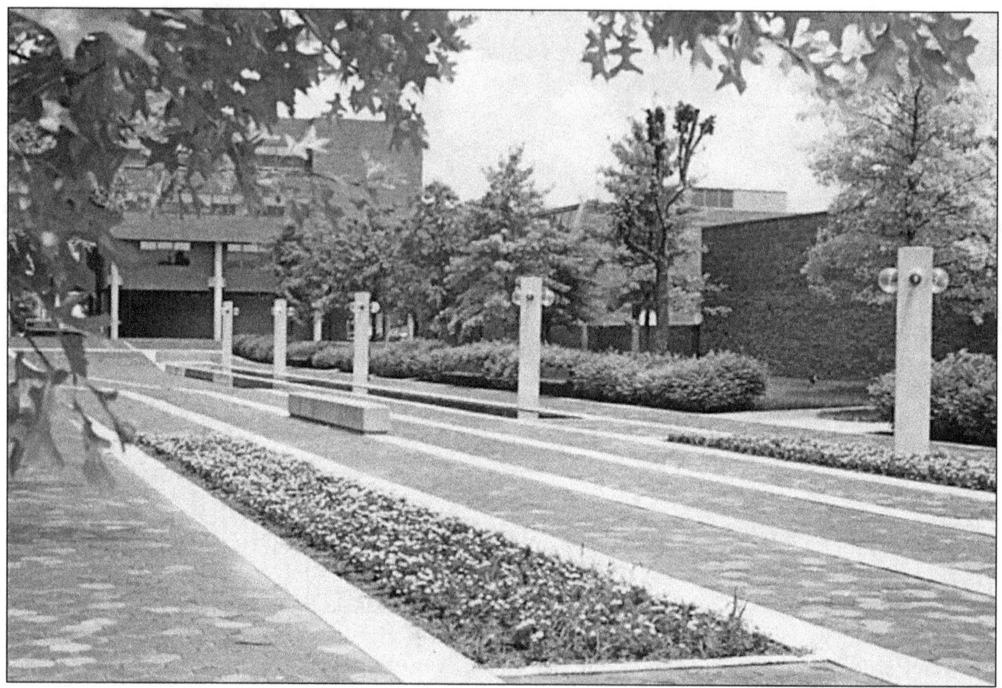

The City Building, in the left of this postcard, was designed by world-famous architect Harry Weese. It anchors the City Centre Plaza, the Ed Rusk Center (Middletown Area Senior Citizens), and Arts in Middletown. Not shown, to the south, is the Women's Center.

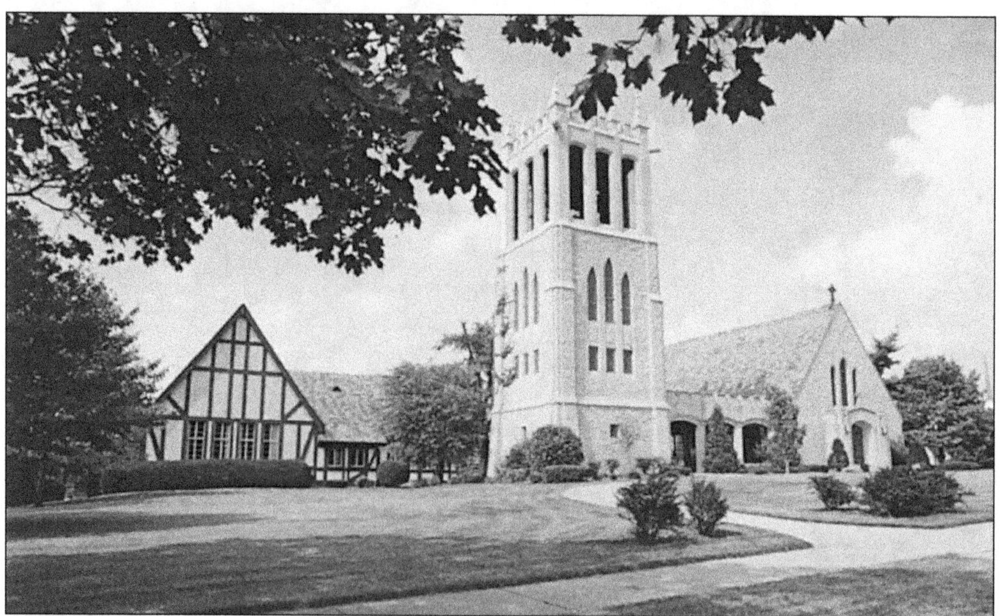

The Church of the Ascension, an English-type structure, was dedicated in 1929, and the beautiful Gothic bell tower was added in 1964. It has a 35-bell carillon, with bells ranging in size from 34 to 3,750 pounds. It is a local landmark. In 1998 Middletown saw its second carillon tower, which was built on the City Centre Plaza by the Casper family, memorializing Jack A.Casper.

Six

The Lens Captures Special Events

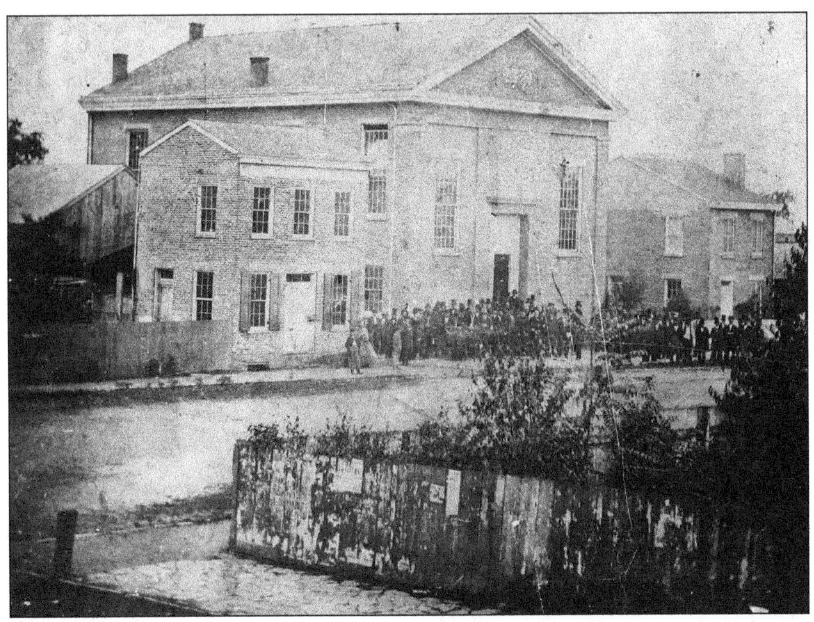

A photographer who had a "nose for news" often sought newspapers and magazines for assignments. Some of the memorable shots by local *Journal* photographers are among those found on the following pages. This photo is thought to be the oldest outdoor photo of an important event. It was taken by Dr. Jonathon W. Leight, described by a grandson as a "part-time" photographer. Thomas Leight remembered being told that it was a picture of an early convention at the old Methodist Protestant Church on Broad Street, of which Dr. Leight was one of the founding members. Long since torn down, its congregation is now known as Christ Methodist and worships in a new church edifice. The original church in the picture is described as being "a substantial brick building," erected in 1865, with a church parsonage to the south. The house on the north belonged to the Sebalds, and their brewery was behind the church.

Surrounding a home standing on the southwest corner of Broad and Central (then Third Street) was the old board fence, which served as a bulletin board for the community. Note the cobblestone sidewalk and the cut limestone gutter stones. The picture was taken sometime in the 1870s, and reveals many secrets of old Middletown.

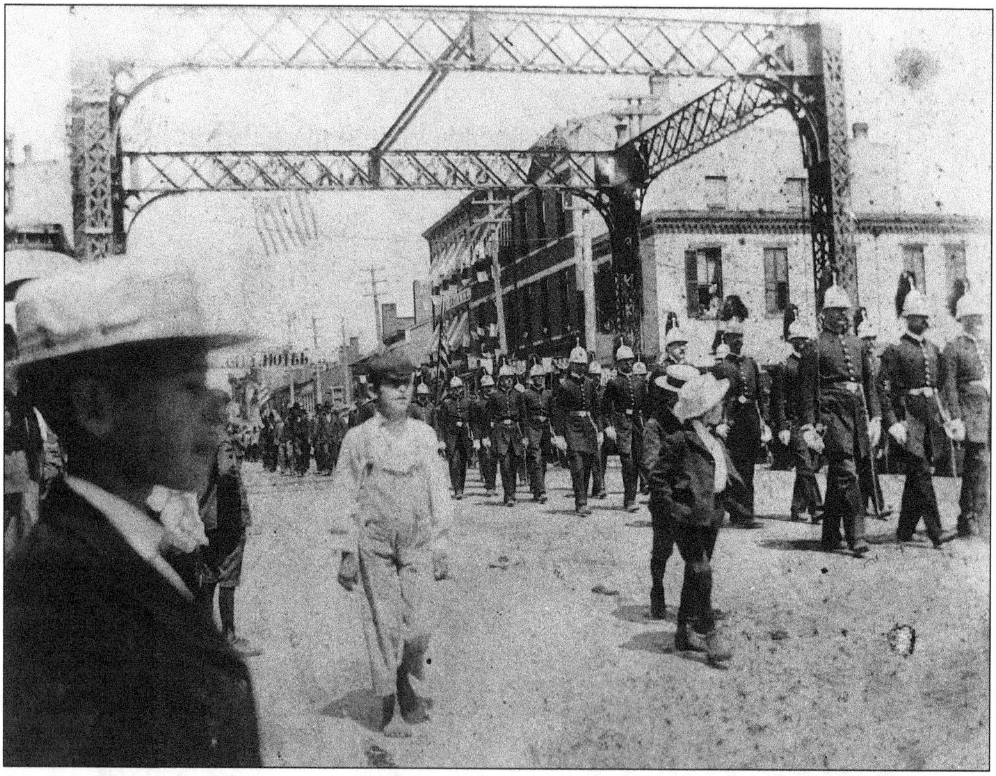

On September 16, 1898, Captain W.M. Sullivan, with his Company L, First Regiment Ohio Volunteer Infantry, returned home from the Spanish-American War and paraded up Central Avenue. Some five thousand people, including students released from school, turned out to greet them. Here they march under the superstructure of the canal bridge.

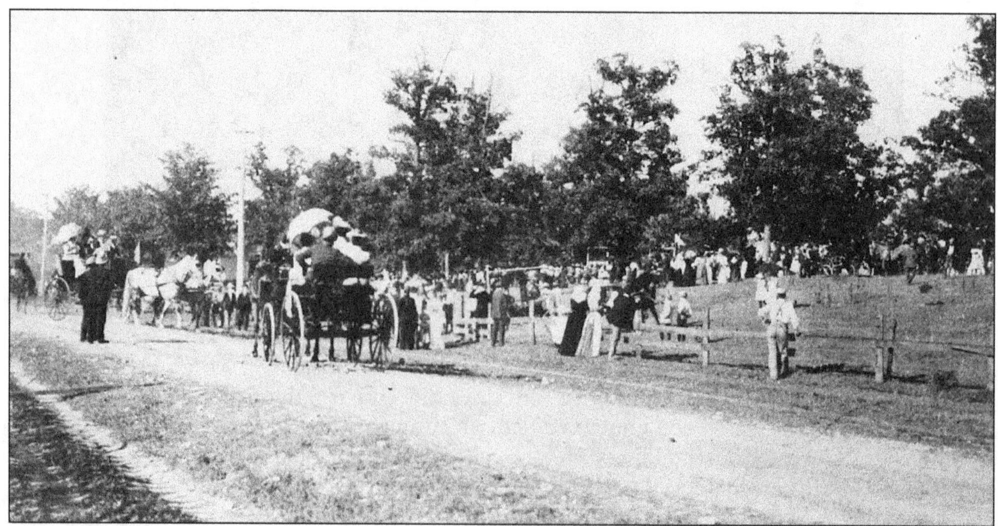

July 12, 1900, was a gala day for the people of Middletown. They gathered at Doty's Grove along the canal to watch the laying of the cornerstone of the American Rolling Mill Company, which had announced plans to build a steel plant here.

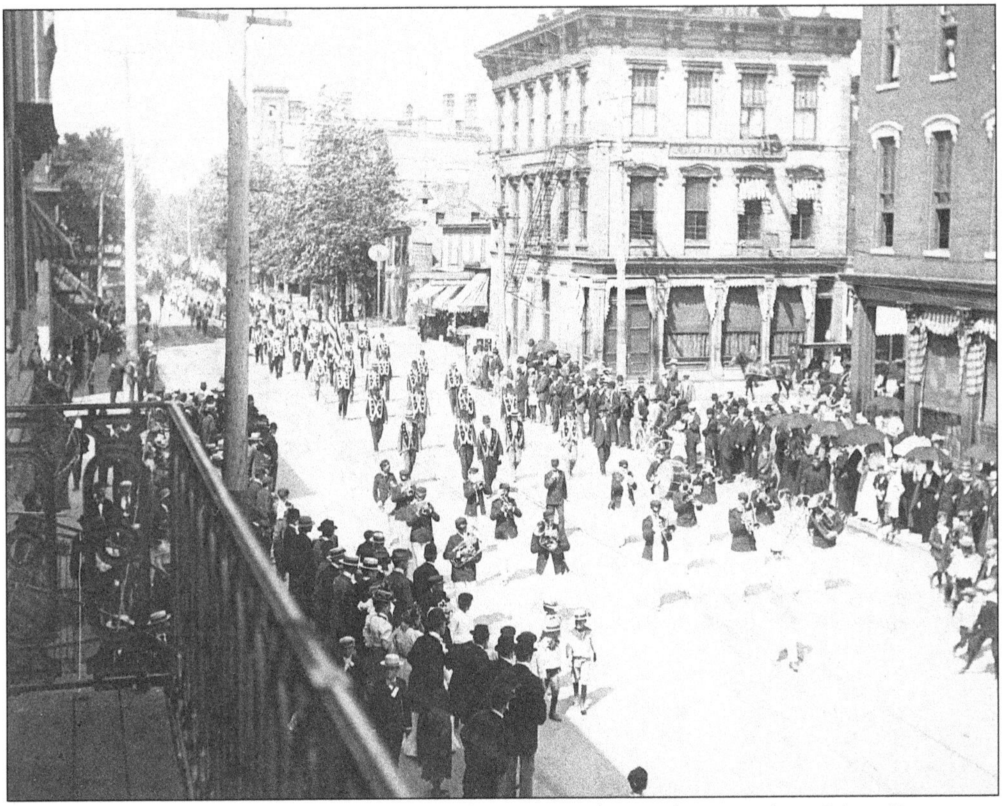

This unmarked photo, taken around 1900, shows a parade marching south on Main Street as it passes the intersection with Central. The Merchant's National Bank is on the corner.

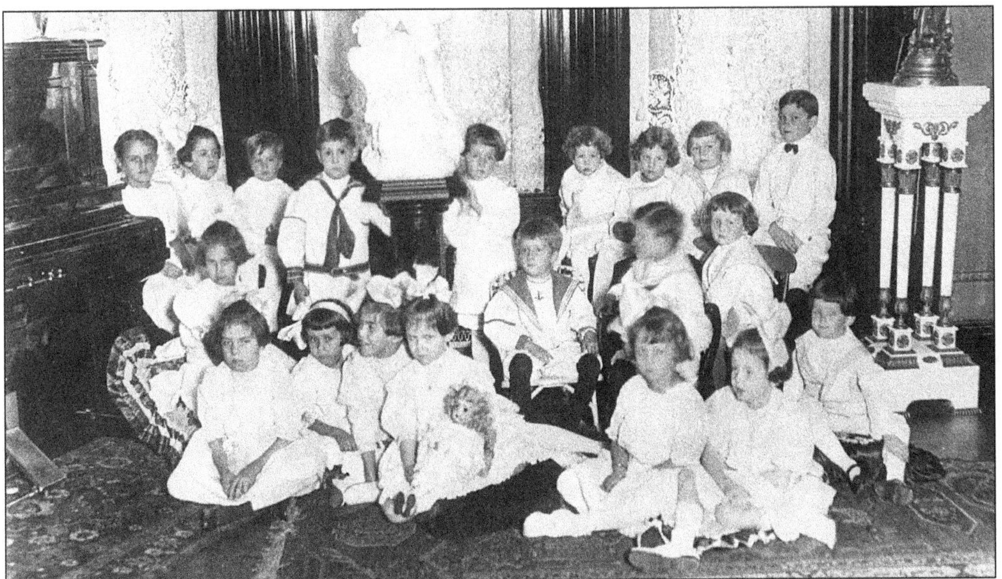

Each summer, Mrs. Paul S. Sorg held a neighborhood party for her visiting granddaughter, Jane Drouillard. This photo is from 1902. Seated in the center rocker is Master Robert D. Oglesby, of a prominent Main Street family.

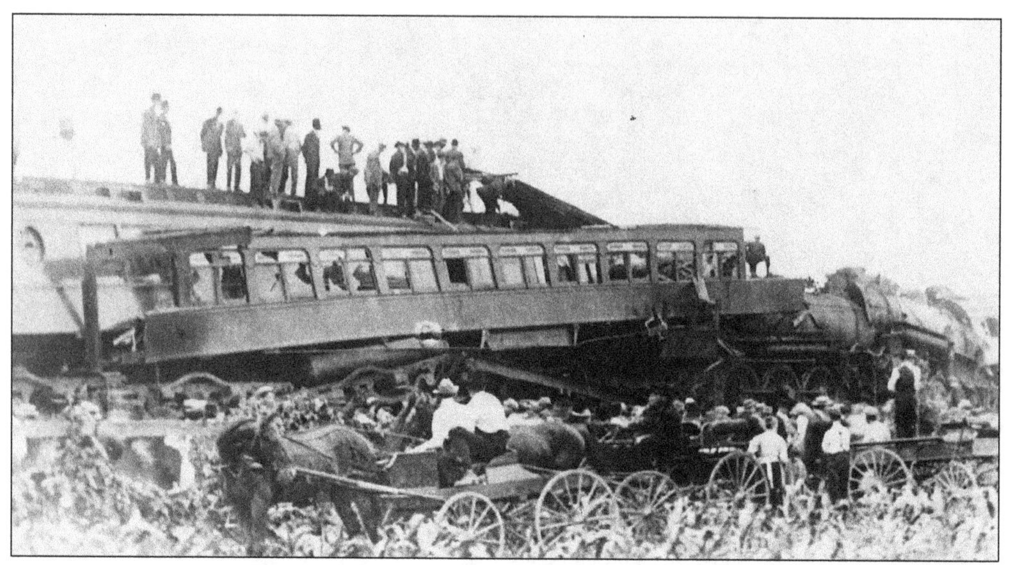

On July 4, 1910, a passenger train on the Cincinnati, Hamilton, and Dayton line drove head-on into a freight that was backing into a siding. The crash could be heard miles away, and Middletonians rushed across the bridge with rescue units.

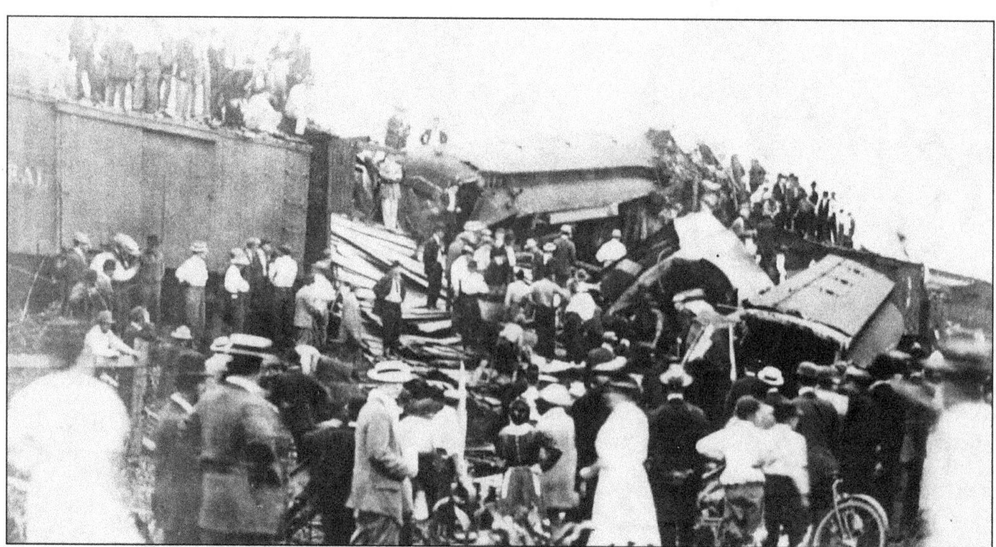

The wreck claimed 36 lives and 50 injuries. Since there was no local hospital, the injured had to be rushed to a Hamilton Hospital. The wreck caused local residents to realize the need for a hospital, and this resulted in a drive for such a facility.

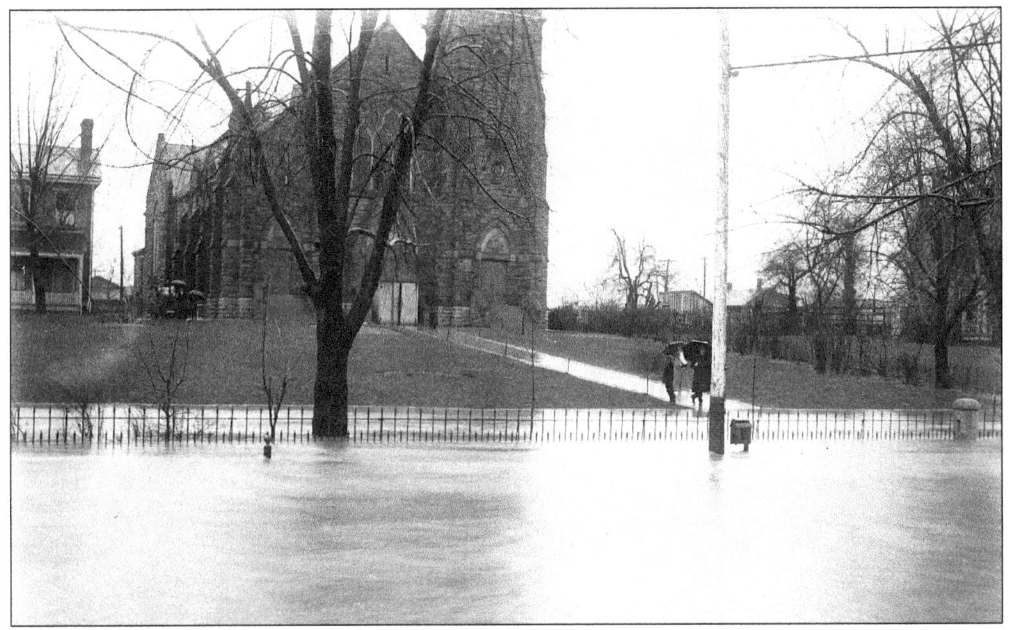

The flood, which struck March 25, 1913, was photographed by others besides Watson. Here, James Buchanan snaps a picture of his father with his umbrella in front of Holy Trinity Church on Clark Street. This beautiful Catholic church is still standing.

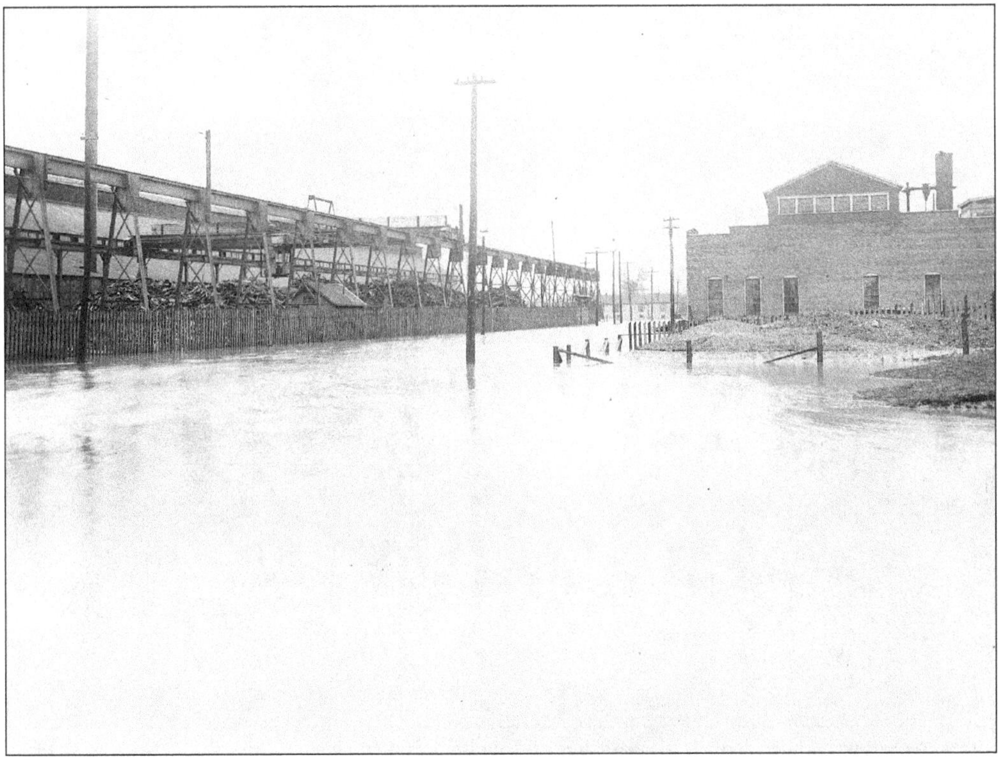

This is the mill yard of the old Central Works of Armco along Curtis Street during the 1913 Flood. The photo was taken by Armco photographer Tom Portsmouth.

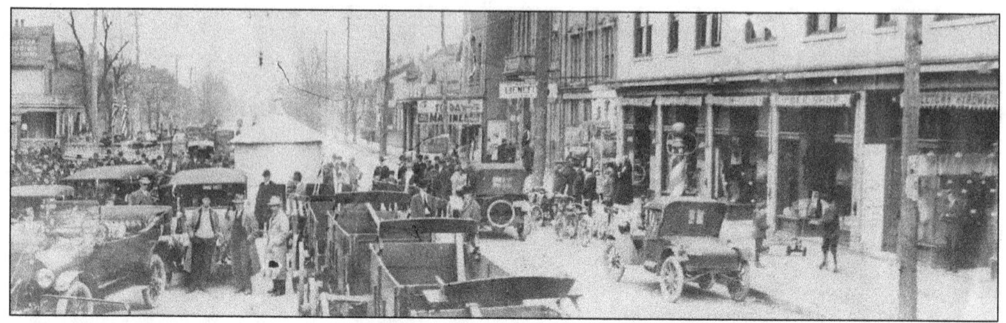

This is the 1914 Street Fair on North Broad Street. The tall building on the left is A.B. Shetter's store, where farm vehicles and automobiles were sold. Broad Street was once the site of the farmer's market. Shetter's store was sold and became Dohn's Hardware.

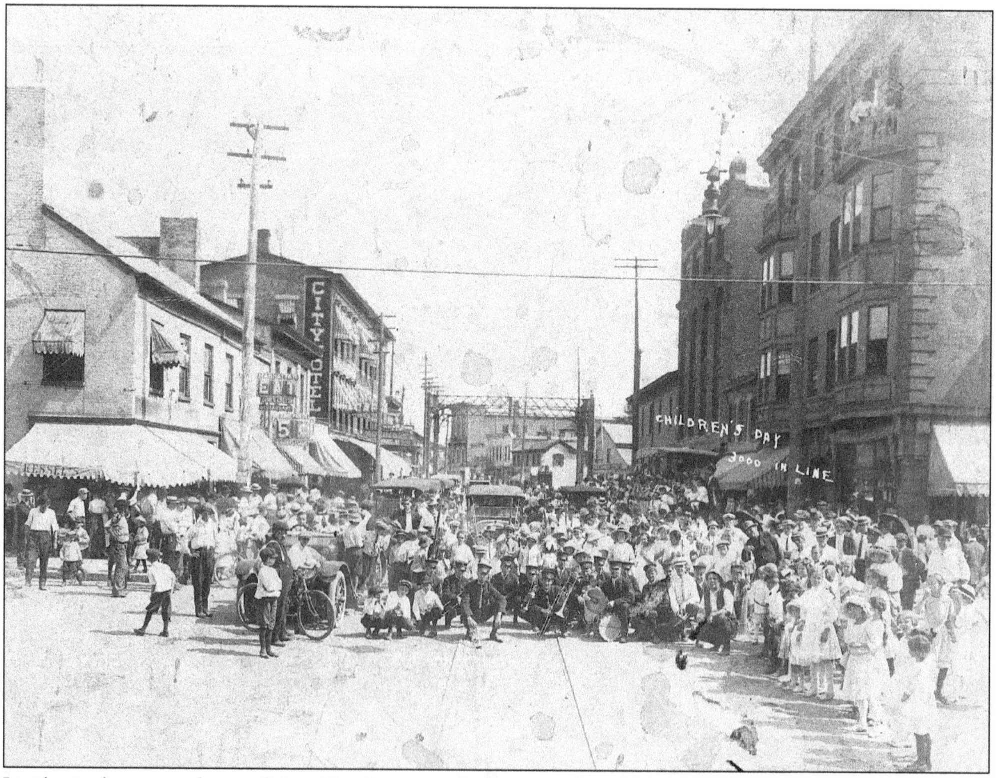

Little is known about this old photograph except that it was taken on Children's Day, August 18, 1913. The superstructure of the canal lift bridge is seen, along with the Central Avenue buildings. It states that three thousand people were in the parade.

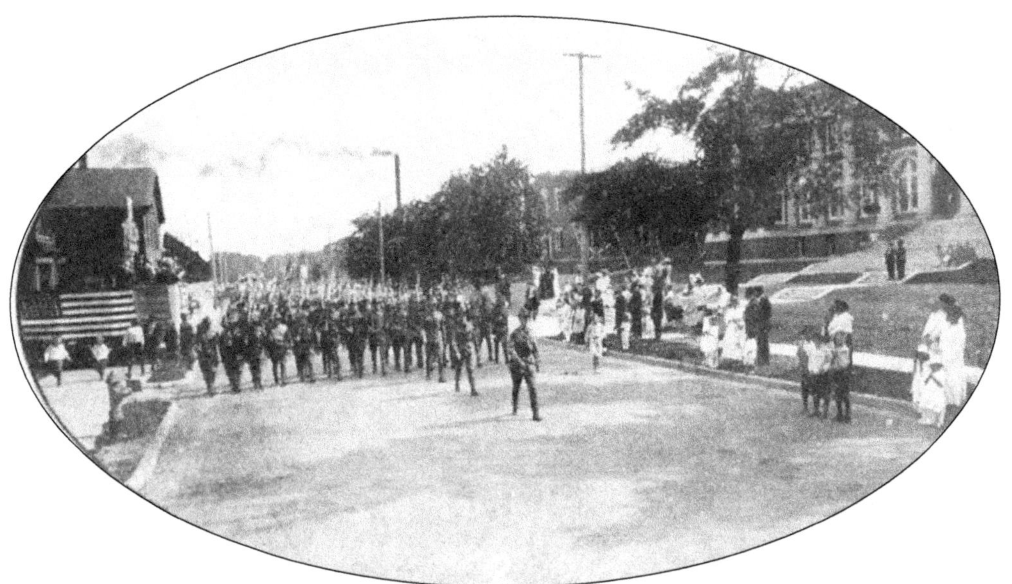

The Home Guards of WW I days are shown passing the reviewing stand in front of the Armco General Office in 1918. They were organized after the Ohio National Guard had been pressed into service on December 21, 1917. The city provided them with an official Home Guard uniform and a rifle.

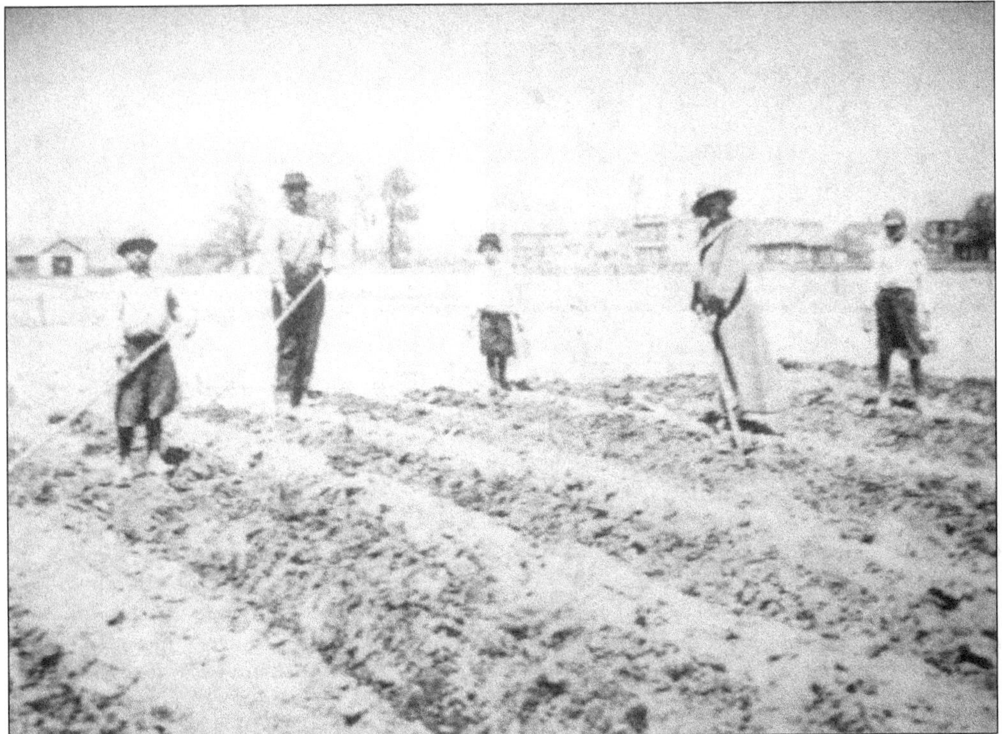

The Alexander Child's family is shown at work in June 1918 in their Armco "Victory" garden, on land provided by Armco for their employees. The George Child's family had a garden adjacent to it.

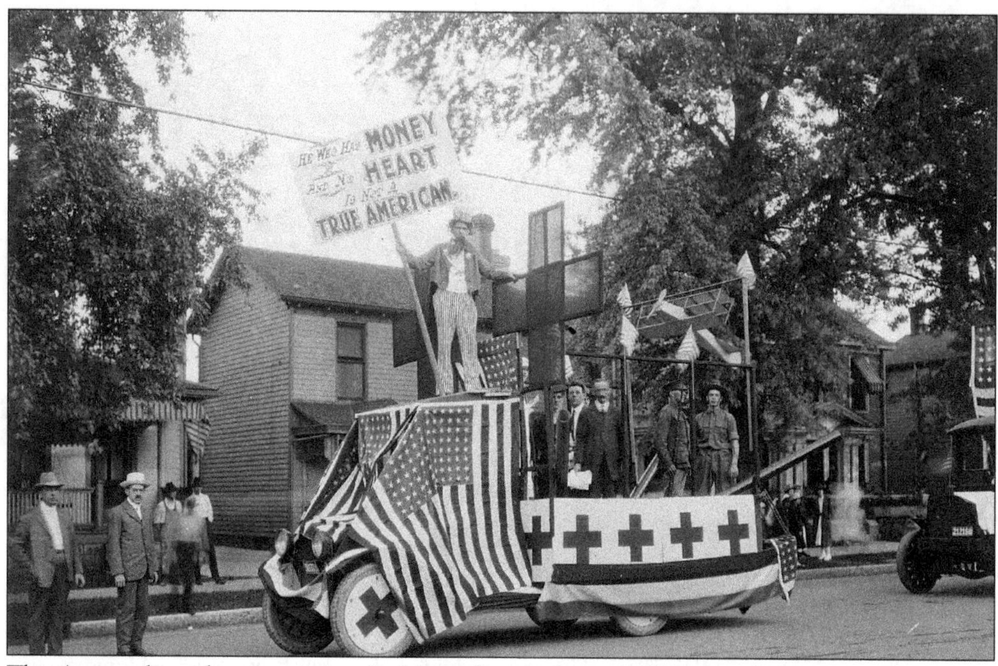

This Armco photo shows a unit in a Red Cross Parade during WW I. Armco was a strong supporter of the war effort, even sponsoring an Armco Ambulance Corps on the European front.

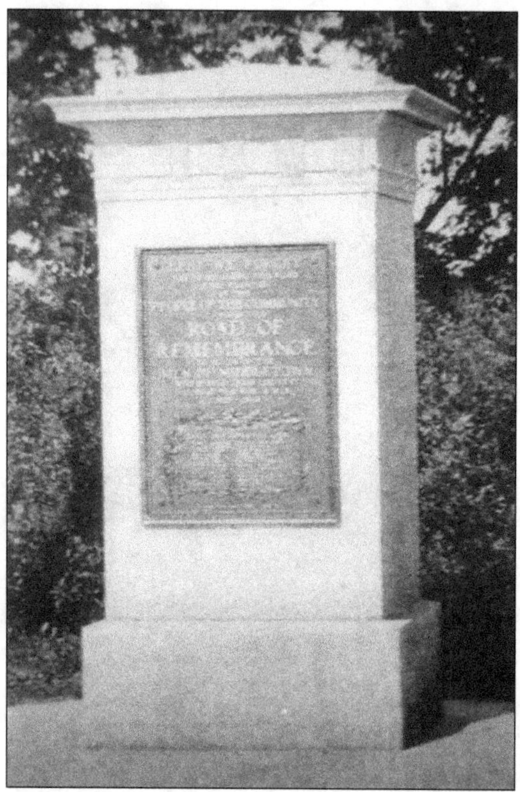

On Labor Day, September 6, 1920, the people of Middletown dedicated the "Road of Remembrance" at Main and 14th. Along the 2 miles of highway south to Elliott's farm (now near Garden Manor), trees were planted honoring the local dead of WW I. A monument was placed at each end, and the one at 14th Avenue is now at the American Legion Home on Main Street.

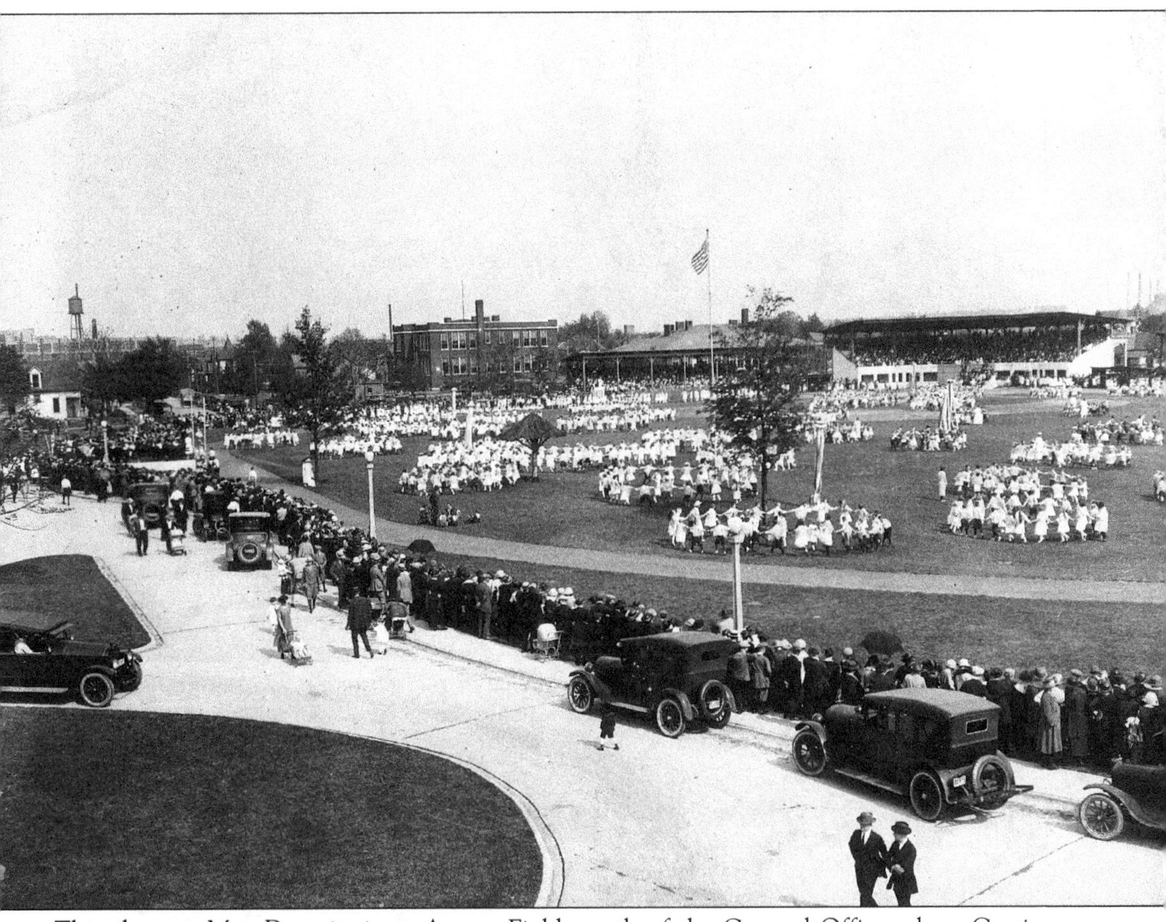

This shows a May-Day picnic at Armco Field, south of the General Office, along Curtis, May 7, 1921. About ten thousand people showed up. Schoolchildren with the colors of their respective schools are shown around the May poles. The new Bureau of Recreation was in charge.

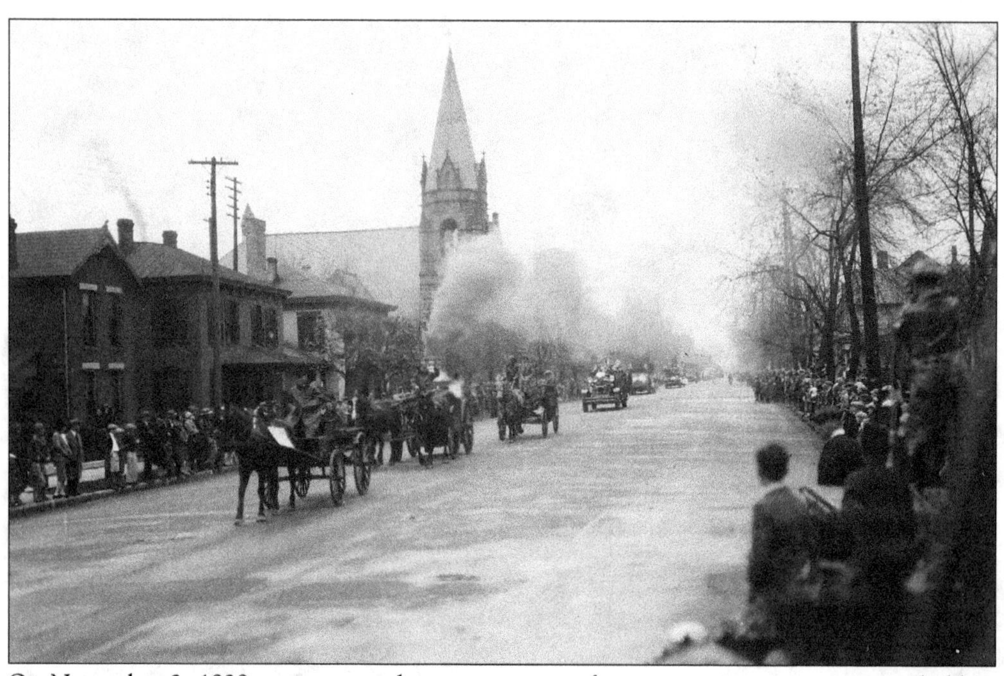

On November 2, 1929, a great parade—a panorama of transportation progress—was held to commemorate the ending of the Miami-Erie Canal. Here, the parade moves past the First Methodist Church on Broad Street.

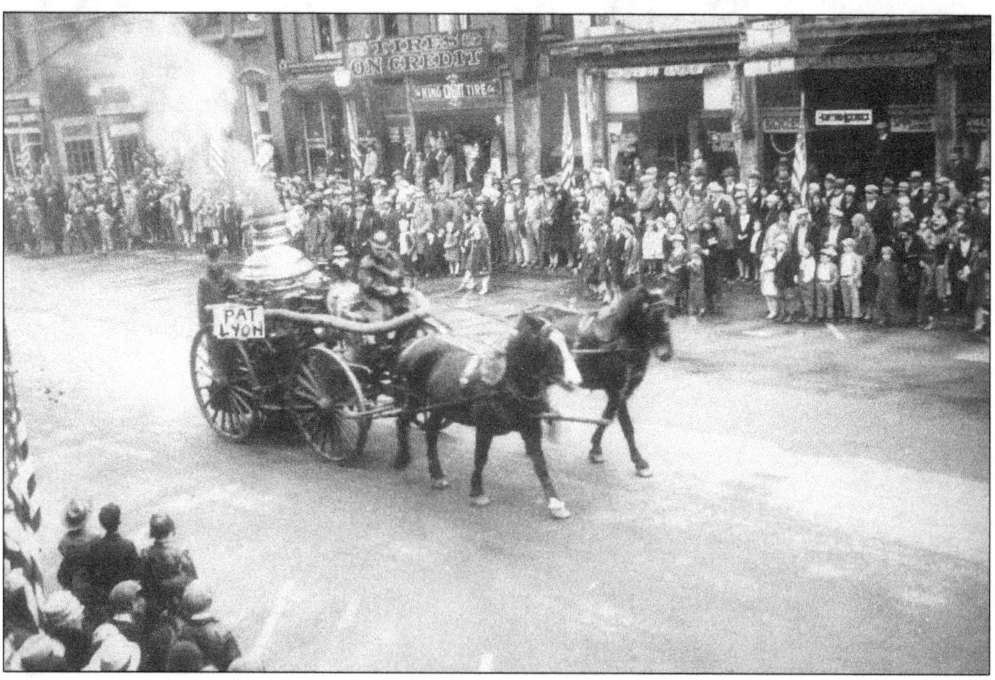

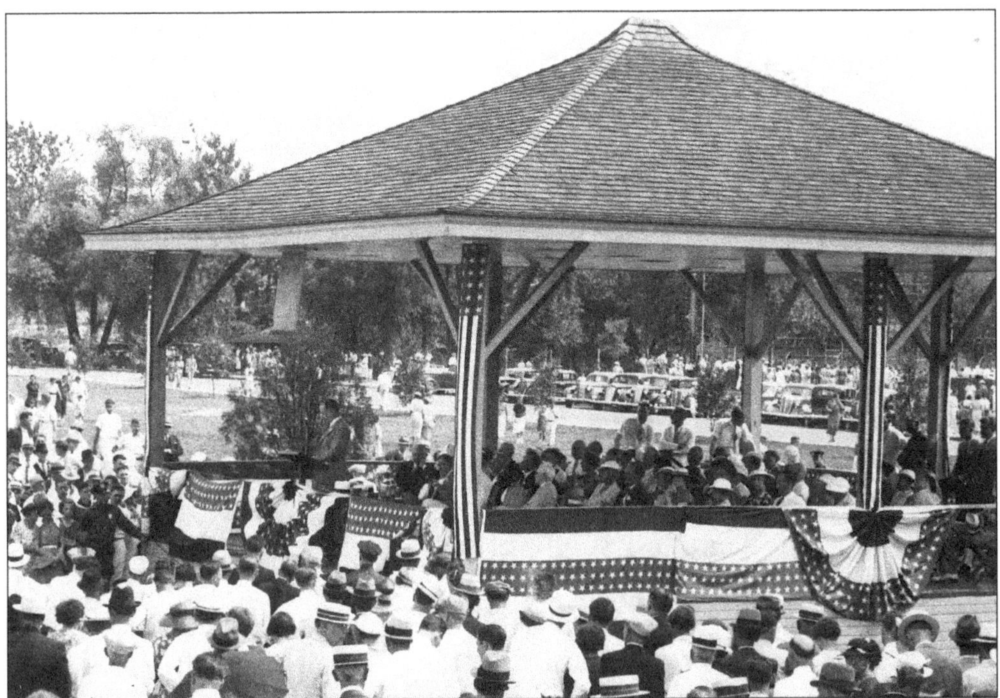

June 6, 1936, was set aside by the City Commission to show appreciation for "A Man and His Work—George M. Verity—1900–1936." Over three thousand marched in the parade, while an estimated ten thousand took part in some way.

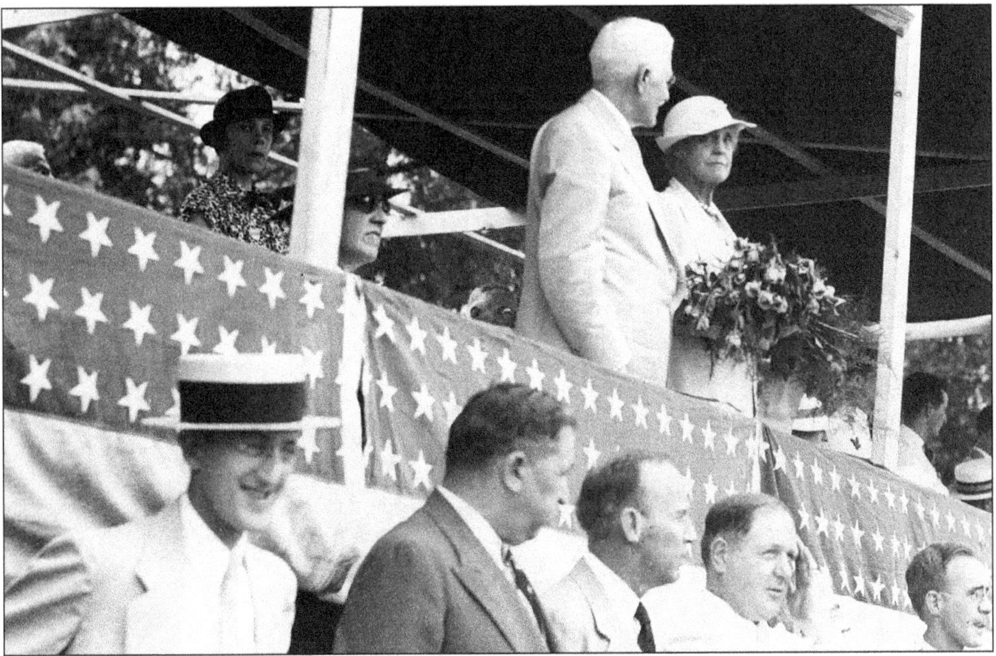

Here George M. Verity and his wife appear on the bandstand at Sunset Park. The program began at 3 p.m. Verity spoke briefly, with the major address being made by former Governor James M. Cox, an old Verity friend.

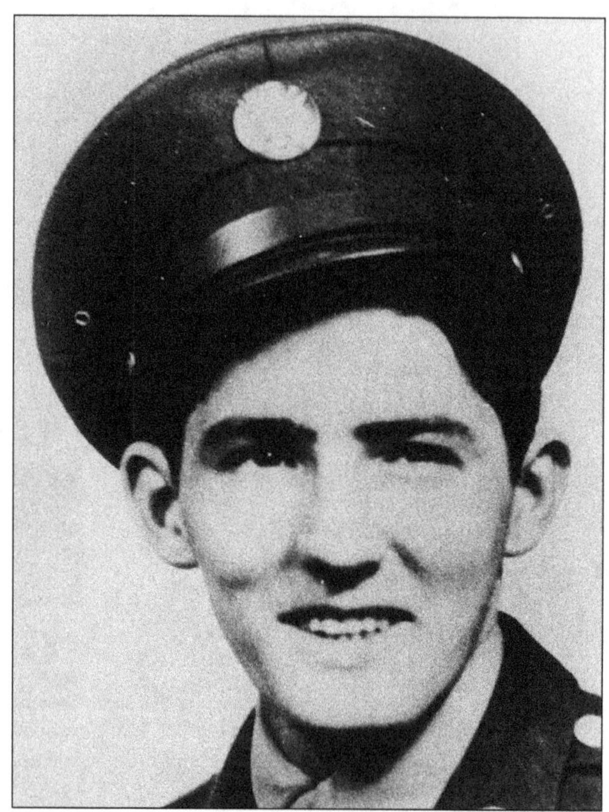

On May 23, 1944, near Ponte Rotto, Italy, Private First Class Patrick L. Kessler, shown in the photograph, so distinguished himself as to be awarded posthumously the Congressional Medal of Honor. On October 15, 1967, the local Ohio National Guard Armory was dedicated to his honor. In 1966, Kessler Auditorium at Post 218 of the American Legion was named in his honor.

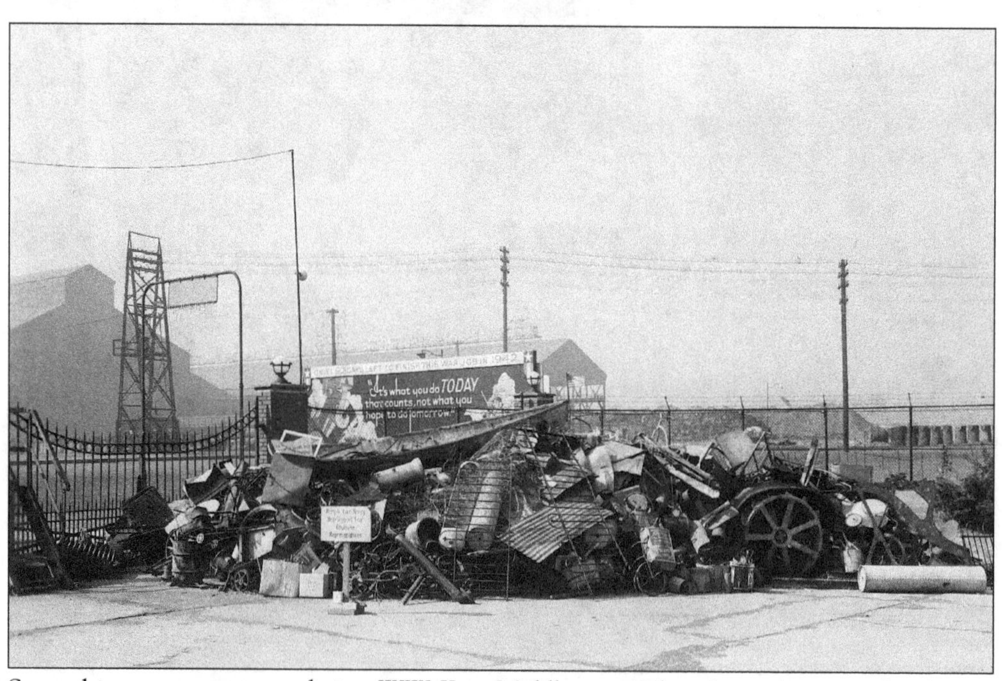

Scrap drives were common during WW II in Middletown. This photo shows a pile of scrap collected near an Armco gate.

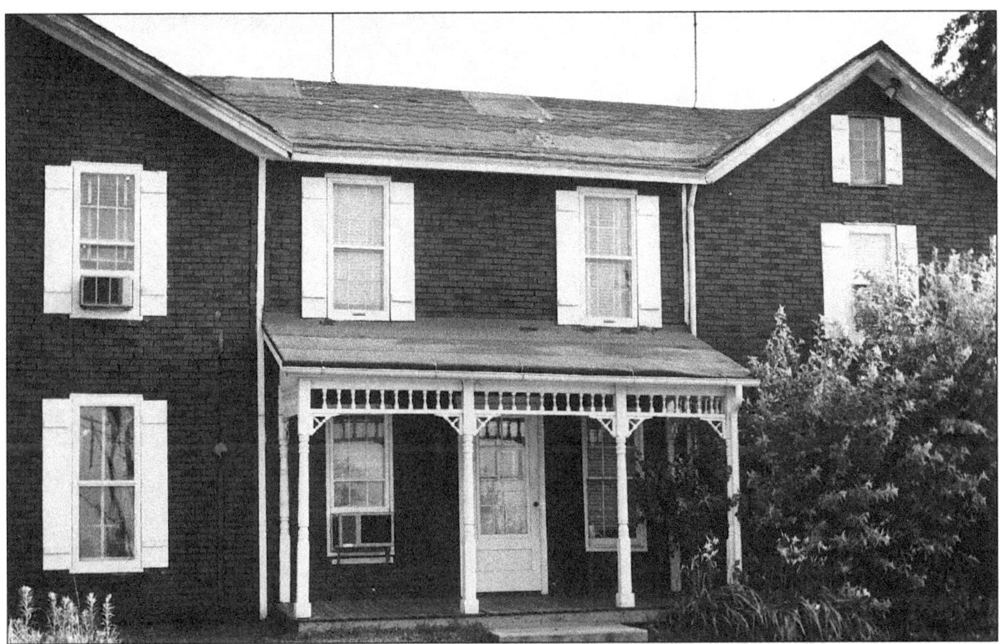

On September 1, 1947, Chief Engineer Larry H. Beckwith put Middletown radio station WPFB on the air. It was owned and operated by Paul F. Braden, whose initials gave the station its identity. Its home was the former farmhouse shown in the photo.

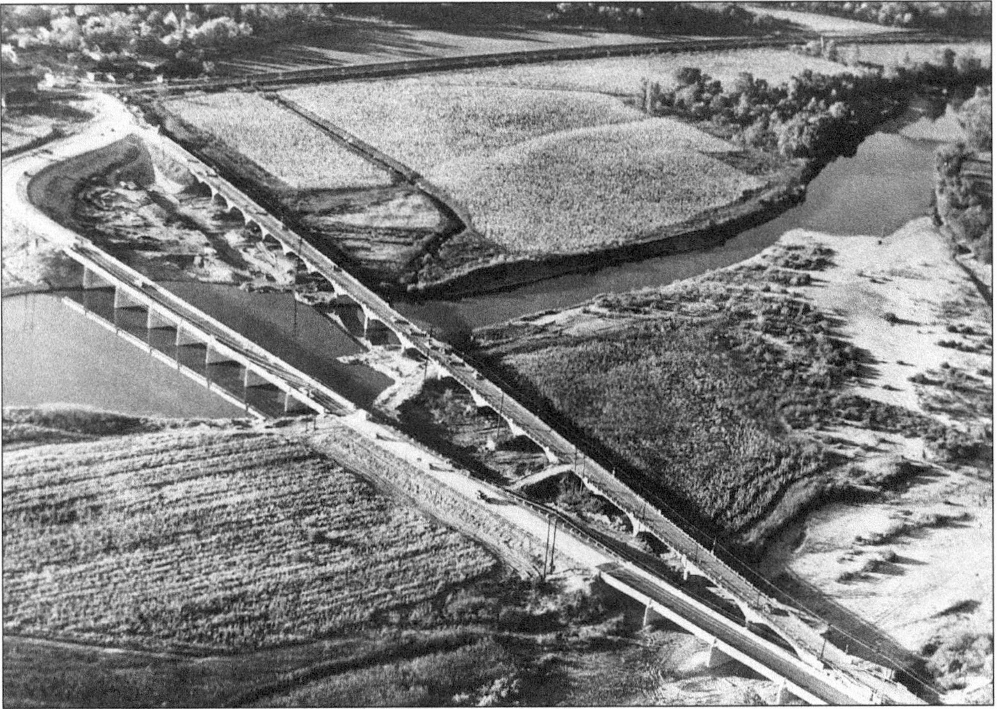

The new West Middletown Bridge (Route 122) was dedicated on October 19, 1948, by Ohio Governor Thomas J. Herbert. It replaced a crumbling viaduct. This picture of the old and new was taken by Bob Barnett, a *Middletown Journal* photographer.

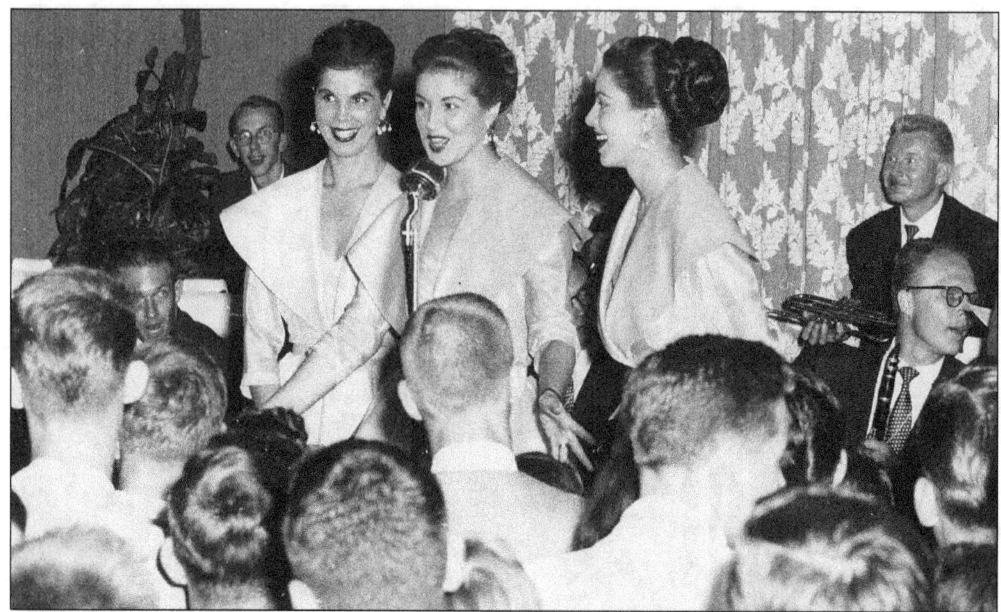

The Middletown High School Prom Jubilee was held May 30, 1953, at LeSourdsville Lake. It is remembered because of its entertainment, which featured the McGuire Sisters, longtime national celebrities who listed Middletown as their hometown. They returned for a concert at the Sorg Opera House on March 11, 1991.

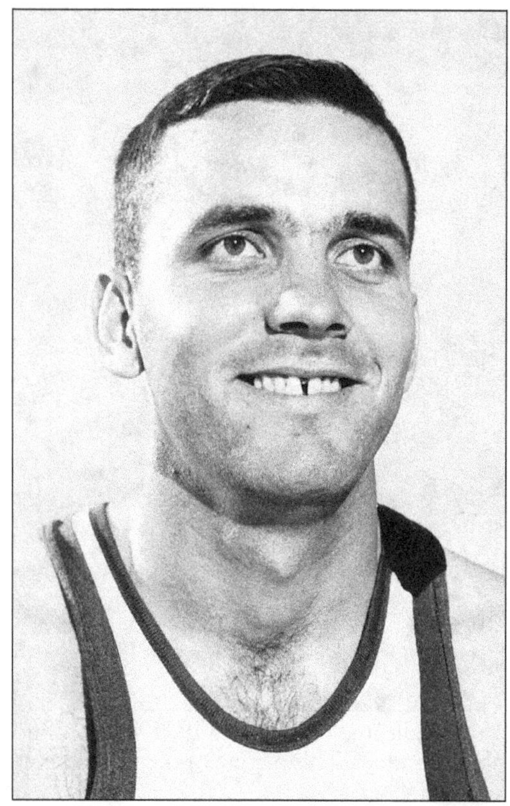

In more recent years, the two Carter Brothers—Chris and Clarence, prominent on the national sports scene, have brought fame to the city. Another celebrity from the city is Jerry Lucas, a phenomenon in local school sports in the 1950s. He went on to be a star athlete at Ohio State University and in the National Basketball Association. Lucas is also an author, with one title selling over 2 million copies. Jerry Nardiello, longtime *Middletown Journal* sports editor, provided this photo.

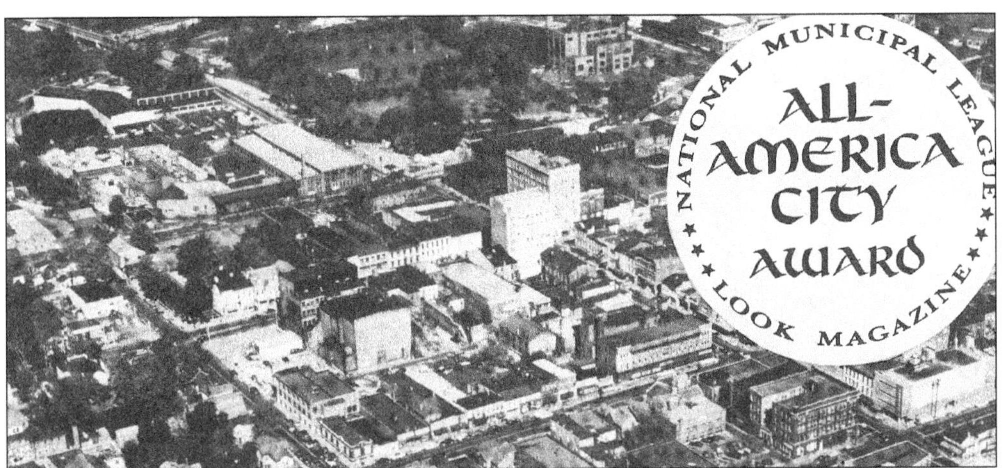

On January 8, 1958, Middletown was saluted as one of the All-American Cities of the Year. The citation was awarded for its handling of the problems of post-war growth. Knight Goodman made the official presentation before the awards panel.

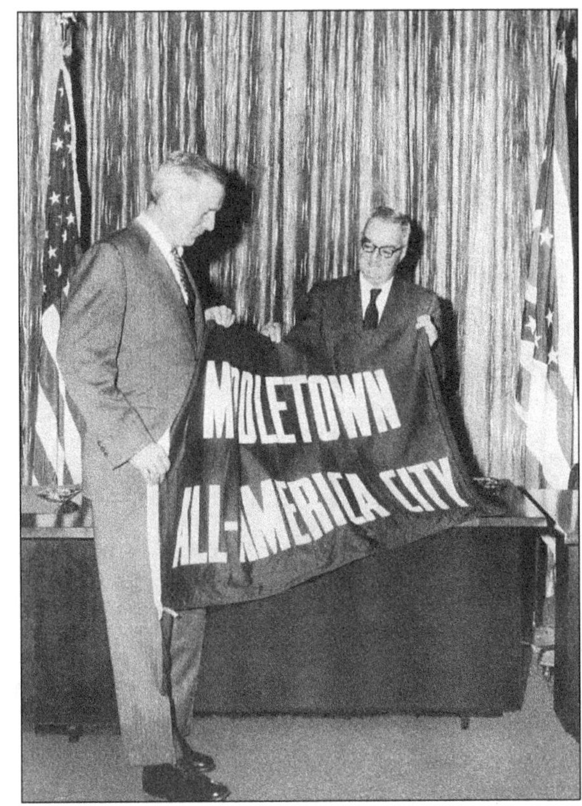

Francis Carmody, chairman of the city commission, and David Driscoll, civic leader and industrialist, accepted the official flag, now hanging in the Canal Museum. A parade was held to celebrate the honor.

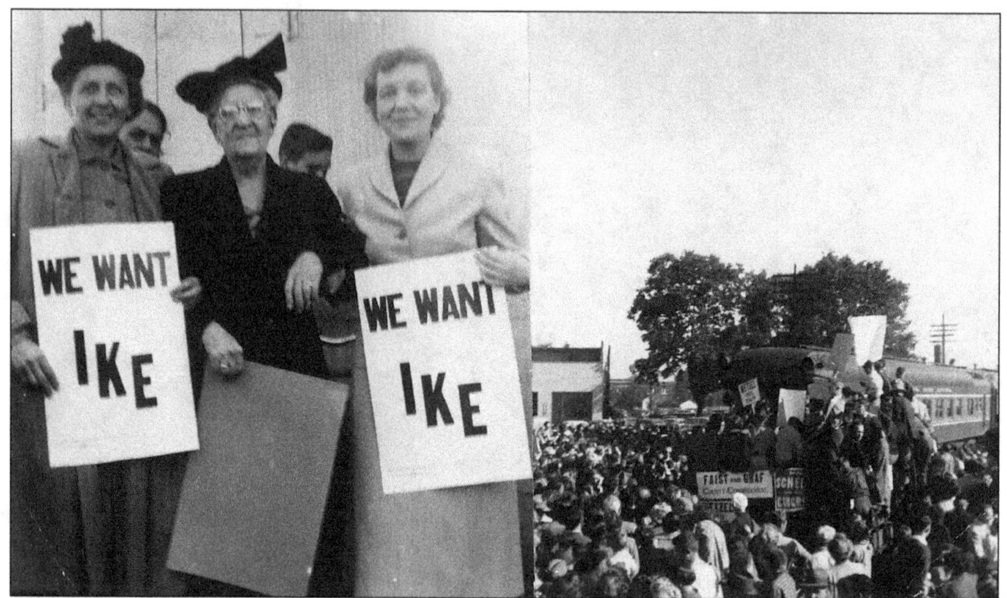

Fourteen men, on the way to the White House, have stopped at Middletown—Harrison, Lincoln, Johnson, McKinley, T.R. Roosevelt, Harding, F.D. Roosevelt, Truman, Eisenhower, Nixon, Kennedy, Ford, Carter, and Reagan. Eisenhower was here on September 23, 1952.

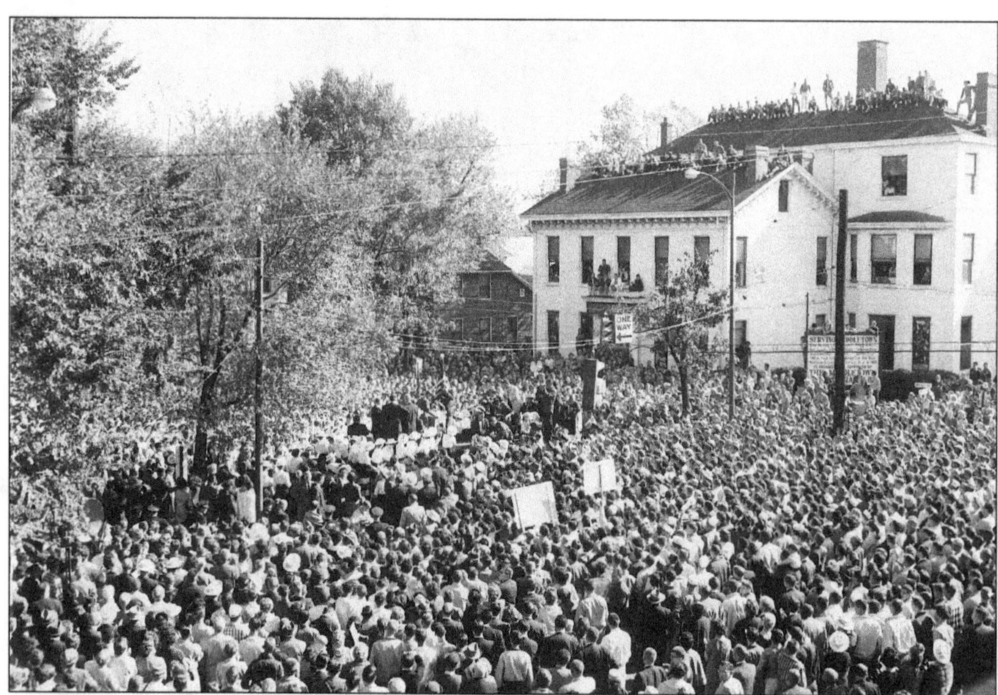

Candidate John F. Kennedy arrived in the city on the chilly night of October 16, 1960, according to Paul Galeese, then-manager of the Manchester Hotel, where he stayed. The next morning he spoke to a large rally (shown here) arranged by Frank Dobrozzi, Democratic leader.

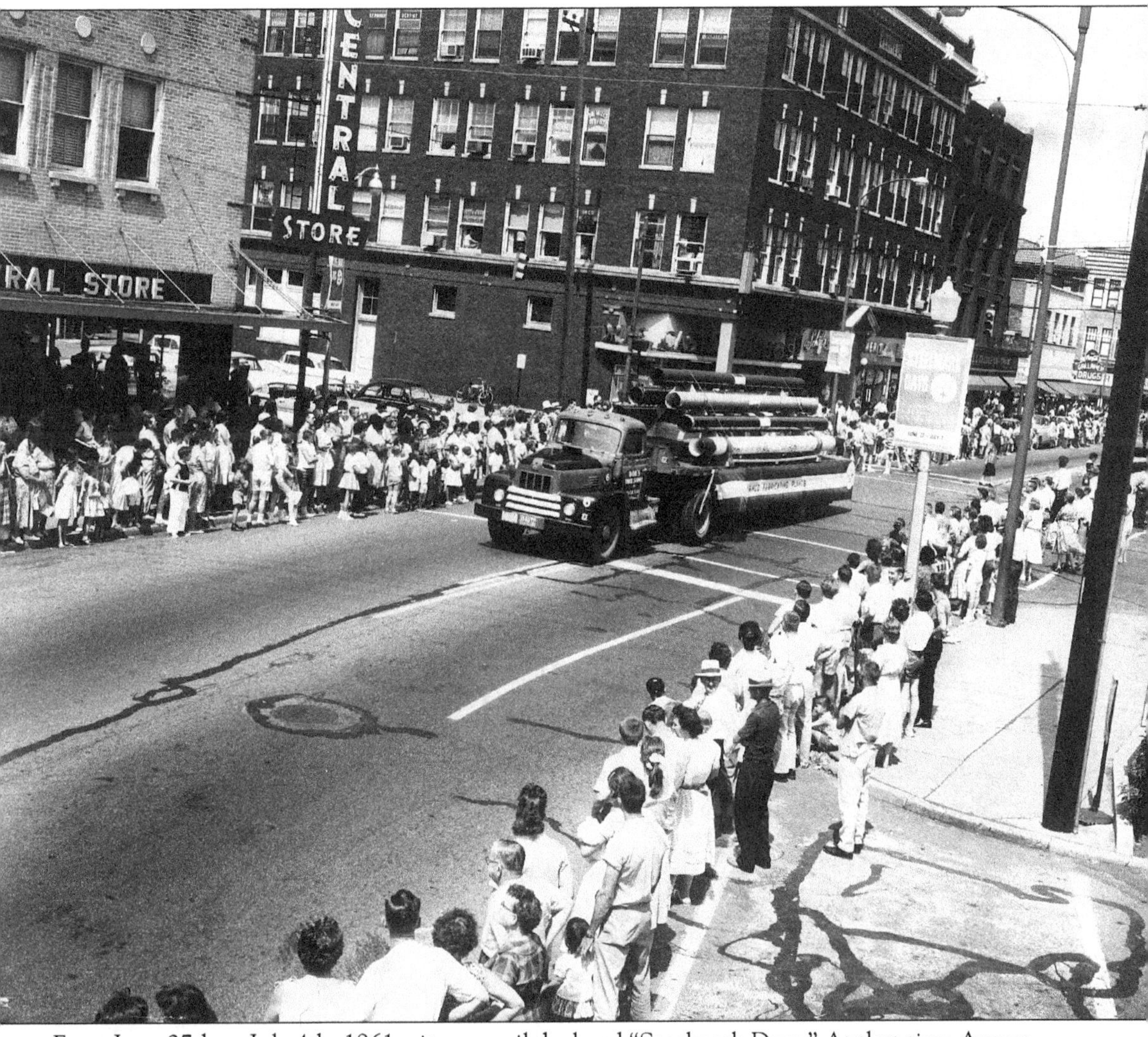

From June 27th to July 4th, 1961, city council declared "Steelmark Days." At that time Armco was in its hey-day, operating steel plants in ten cities, fabricating plants in 25 states, and Armco International, a subsidiary, had manufacturing warehouses and offices in 52 foreign locations. The Armco corporate banner flew over offices in 139 different countries on six continents. It employed more than 50,000 people with 1,000 at the home office along Curtis Street. On the drawing boards were plans for a new, state-of-the-art plant along Lefferson Road. It employed around seven thousand workers in local plants. Middletown, as some said, was Armco. Before the end of the century it would be split up. In May 1989, it formed a partnership with Kawasaki Steel of Japan, but another change on April 7, 1994, would create A.K. Steel.

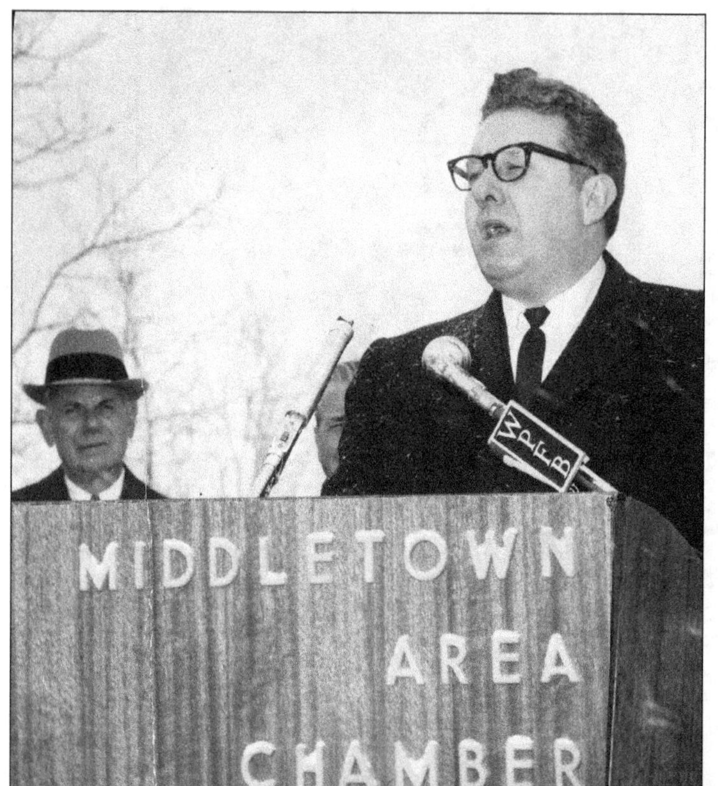

On January 28, 1965, a ground-breaking ceremony was held for the Middletown campus of Miami University. William Donham, chairman of the city commission, gave the official welcome at the podium, with Logan T. Johnston, chairman of the campus committee, waiting to deliver his speech, "The Middletown Dream."

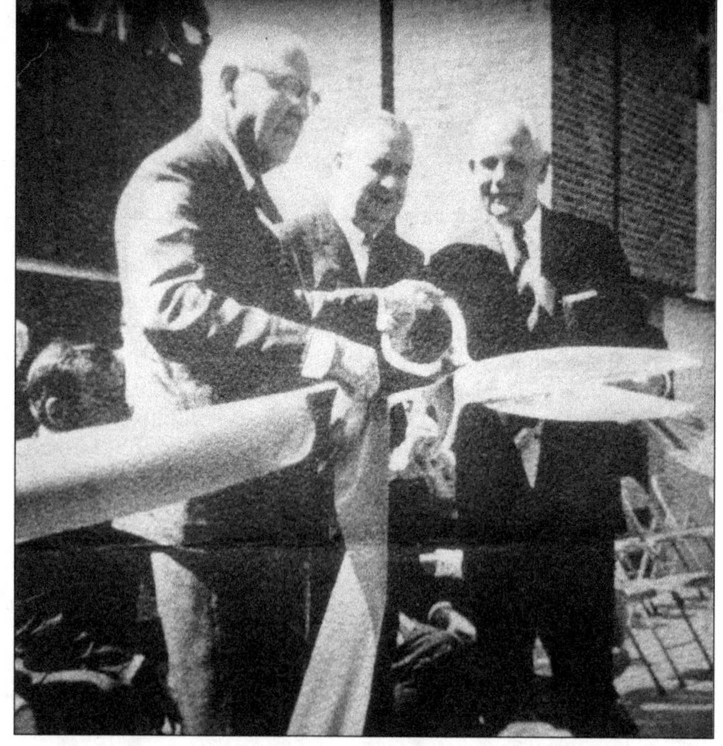

At the campus dedication, September 5, 1966, over two thousand students and spectators looked on as Colin Gardner (left), Governor James A. Rhodes, and Logan T. Johnston share the chore of ribbon cutting. By the time the university celebrated its 30th anniversary in 1996, the Middletown campus had become one of the city's major educational and cultural resources.

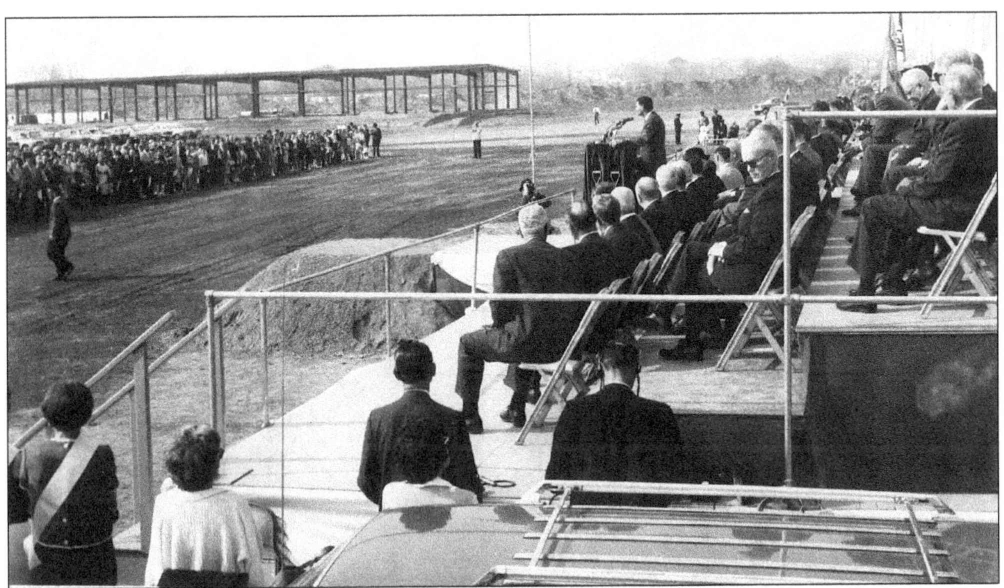

Armco's Project Six Hundred, so-named as the original project was to cost $600 million (but rose to about $1 billion), was launched on the old Lefferson farm in April 1965. Governor Rhodes and Logan Johnston spoke at the groundbreaking shown here.

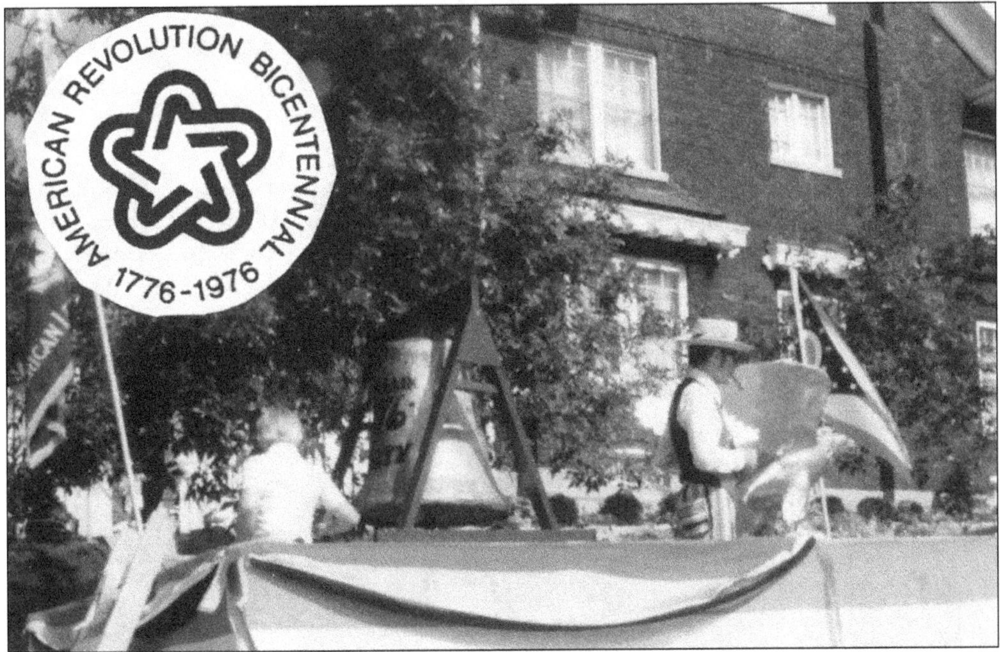

On July 4, 1976, Middletown joined the nation in celebrating its Bicentennial with a full day of special activities highlighted at 5:30 p.m. with a parade made up of 60 units, beginning at Sunset Park. However, the American Revolution Bicentennial had been a well-organized, two-year observance, beginning February 3, 1974, with a "Salute to 1776," a motion picture presentation. A long list of activities for Hometown Heritage Days covered a six-month period prior to July 4th, ending with a cornerstone ceremony for the new city building that was under construction. J.W. Keiser was chairman.

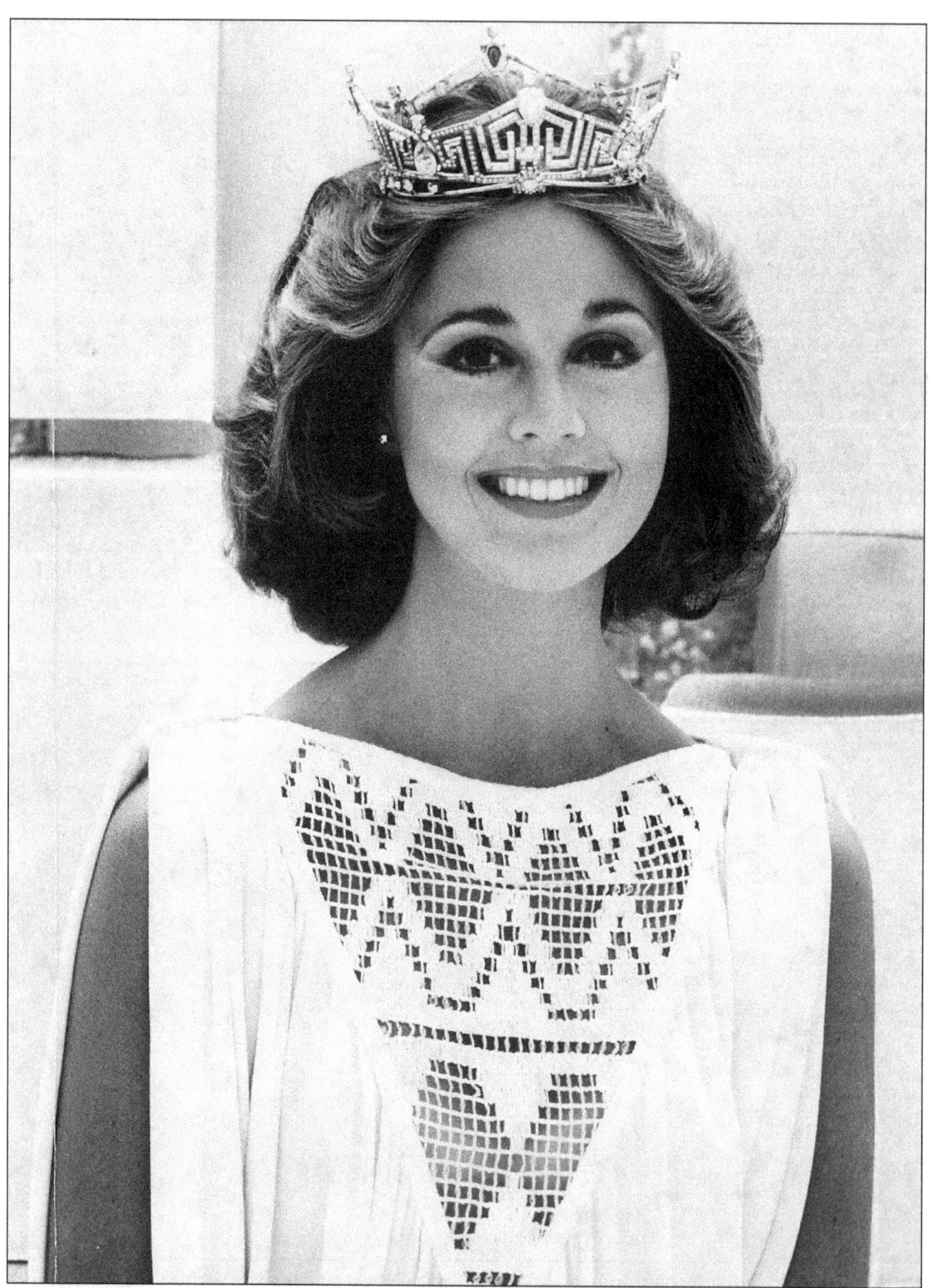

On September 10, 1977, Susan Yvonne Perkins of Middletown was crowned "Miss America" at Atlantic City. Her parents were Mr. and Mrs. Paul Perkins of Shawnray Drive. She returned here on October 28, and the city made elaborate preparations for her homecoming, including a big parade. She had climbed the ladder from "Miss Miami University" to "Miss Ohio" before taking the national crown. She was a graduate of Monroe High School. Now, as Susan Perkins Botsford, she lives in a Boston suburb with her husband, Allen, and her two sons.

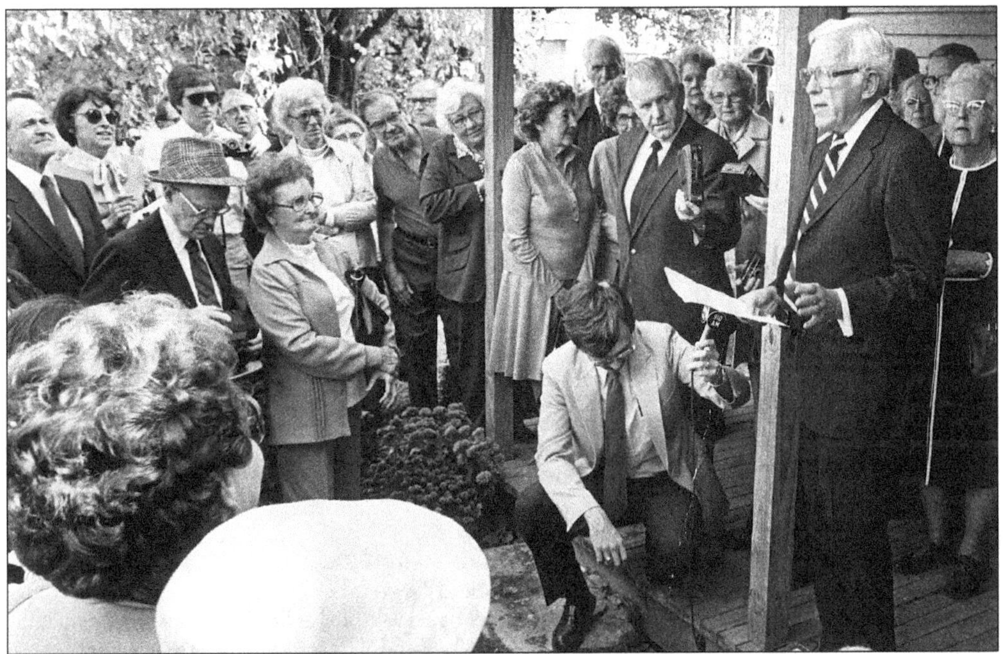

A historical replica of a Locktender's House that once stood at Amanda, and was rebuilt at Verity and Tytus, was dedicated on November 1, 1982, as Middletown's Canal Museum. C. William Verity, an Armco official, gave the keynote speech. His grandfather chose the city as its site due to the canal being here. Before this, the Middletown Historical Society's collection had been housed at the city building. The Society was organized in 1966.

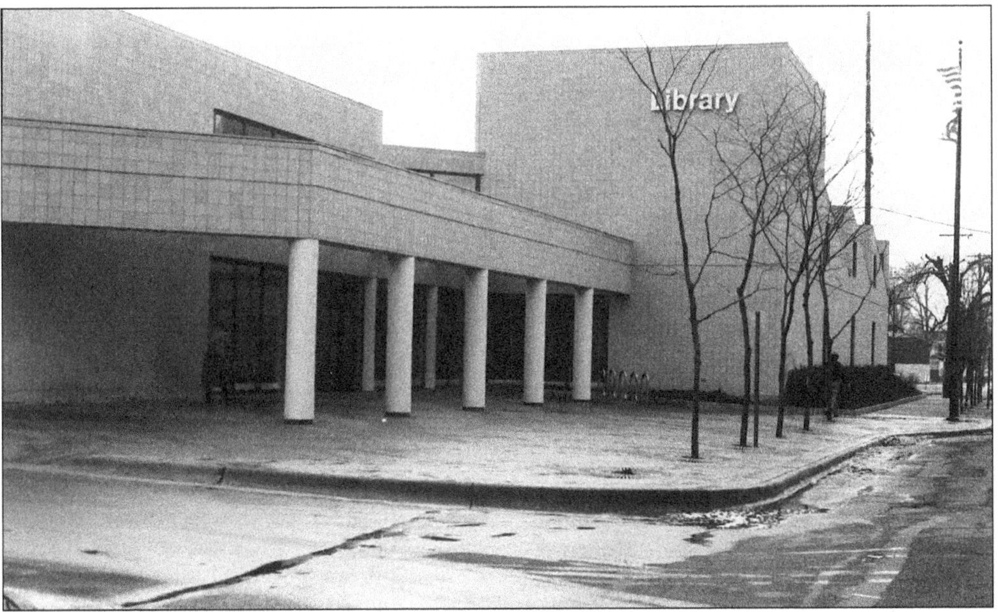

The new public library on Broad Street was dedicated on January 23, 1983, 70 years after the original library at First and Curtis opened. Douglas J. Bean was head librarian. The modern facility, designed by Lorenz and Williams, cost $4 million, financed by the city with a bond levy.

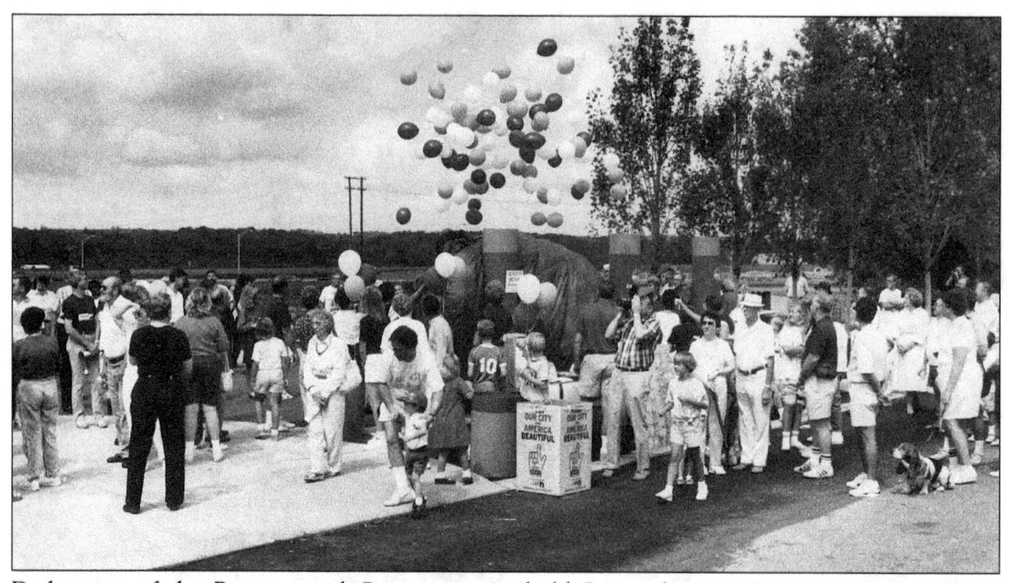

Dedication of the Bicentennial Commons was held September 9, 1990, at 1 p.m. With it came the first viewing of the honor bricks and the overlook of the lake and river. The official groundbreaking for the lake had been June 11, 1989. The Bicentennial Parade was September 21, 1991. Various legal complications would delay the lake completion. Much of the work on Bicentennial Commons was financed by private and local funds. An appropriate memorial was set in place by the Middletown Historical Society. Finally in 1998, the Miami Conservancy Building, at the southwest corner of Carmody and Central, was moved to open up the river view, after the west end of Central had been rebuilt in 1997.

The Middletown Mail.
WESTERN JOURNAL.
MIDDLETOWN EMBLEM.
MIDDLETOWN HERALD
The Middletown Journal.
MIDDLETOWN LEADER.
Middletown Daily Argus.
MIDDLETOWN SIGNAL
MIDDLETOWN NEWS.
THE DAILY SIGNAL.
THE DAILY JOURNAL.
THE MIDDLETOWN DAILY NEWS--SIGNAL
THE MIDDLETOWN JOURNAL

Of the many newspapers published in Middletown—their mastheads appear in this photo—only the *Journal* has survived. It was founded January 12, 1857, as the *Western Journal*. It soon became the *Middletown Journal*, making it one of the oldest newspapers in Ohio. Two brothers, A.C. and C.H. Brock, were printer and publisher. A subscription for the weekly publication was $1.50 a year. From weekly to bi-weekly, it became a daily on April 1, 1891. Its major competition was the *News Signal*, which it purchased in 1928. In 1932, the *News Signal* was disbanded, while the *Journal* continued to publish a morning edition using the *News Signal* masthead until 1940. In 1977, local ownership passed to the Thomson Newspaper Publishing Company, and its publisher Frank Myers retired in 1980. The events recorded in this chapter have all been reported by the *Middletown Journal*.

Seven

On Camera: 1950 to the Millennium

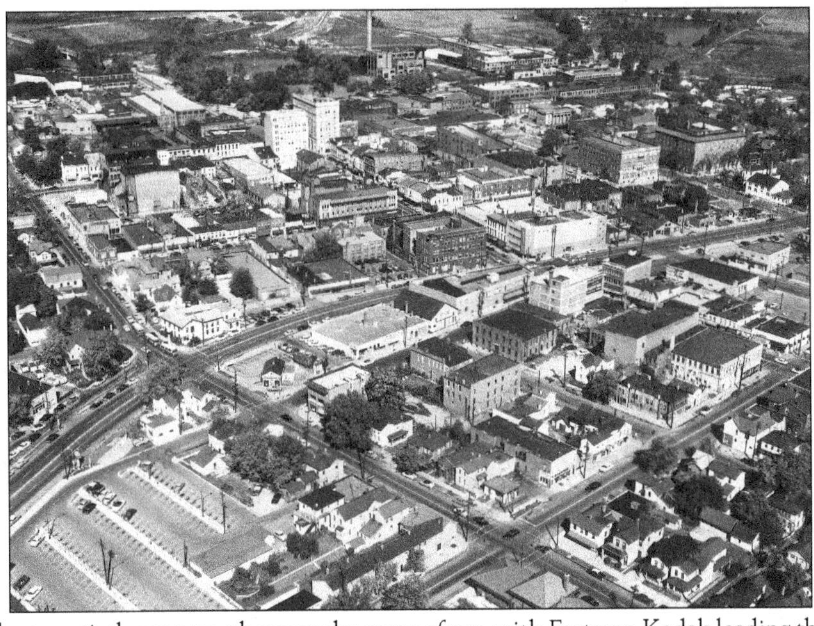

During the twentieth century, photography came of age, with Eastman Kodak leading the world. But later in the century, Japanese film companies entered the competition. Early in the century, Kodak introduced the cheap and reliable "Brownie," which found its way into most homes. Then came the simple, reliable "Instamatic," with its drop-in cartridge. But eventually, the 35-mm became the standard, as did color film. As the Millennium approached, many camera shops closed as the new video tape replaced the camera. The surviving 35 mm camera became a sophisticated mechanism, making amateurs into professionals.

During this century, photographers took to the air and with special lenses were able to take clear, detailed pictures from the sky. One such nearby firm was Dayton's Mayfield Photos, which recorded the city's growth and its industrial complexes from the 1930s on. Here a Mayfield camera views the city on a clear day in 1955. Many such negatives are on file locally. Aerial views proved valuable to the city and its industries in planning and expansion. Modern enlargement and computer enhancement techniques make such pictures even more useful. A careful study of the above photograph will show how much the city changed in the past half century as it enters the Millennium.

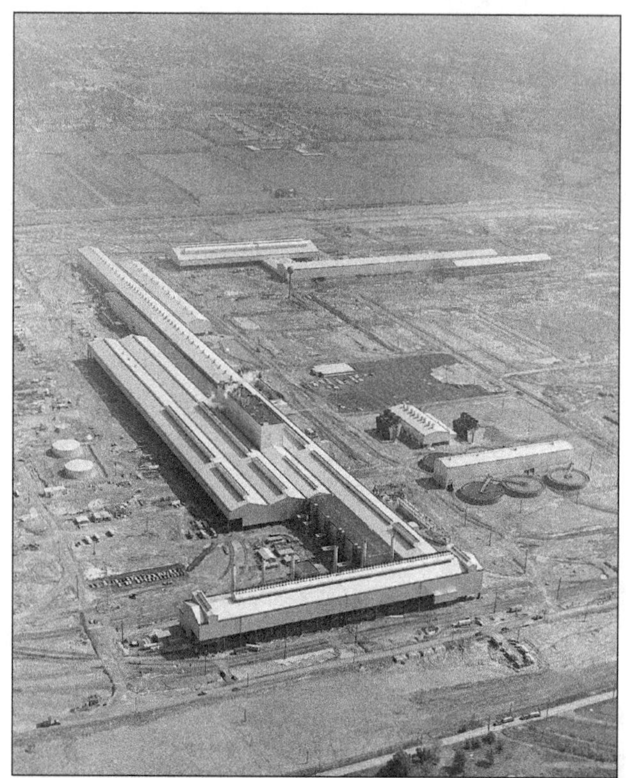

As Middletown entered the 1950s, the Armco Steel Corporation dominated the local industrial scene, with three large plants here. In 1958 it acquired National Supply, and in 1959 it completed a $50 million expansion. Then came Project Six Hundred and a new plant in 1968, shown here.

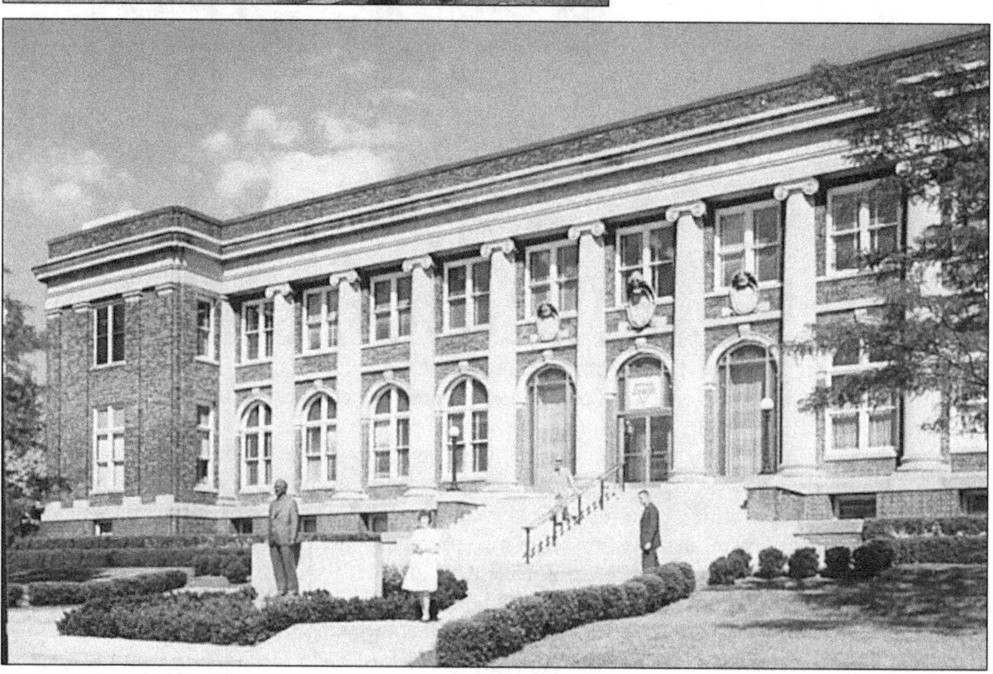

Until 1985, this building served as corporate offices of Armco, but then headquarters were moved to New Jersey and then to Pittsburgh. In 1994, with A.K. Steel formed, it moved into the former Armco complex. The 1990s proved to be a period of downsizing both for A.K. Steel and for the old Armco.

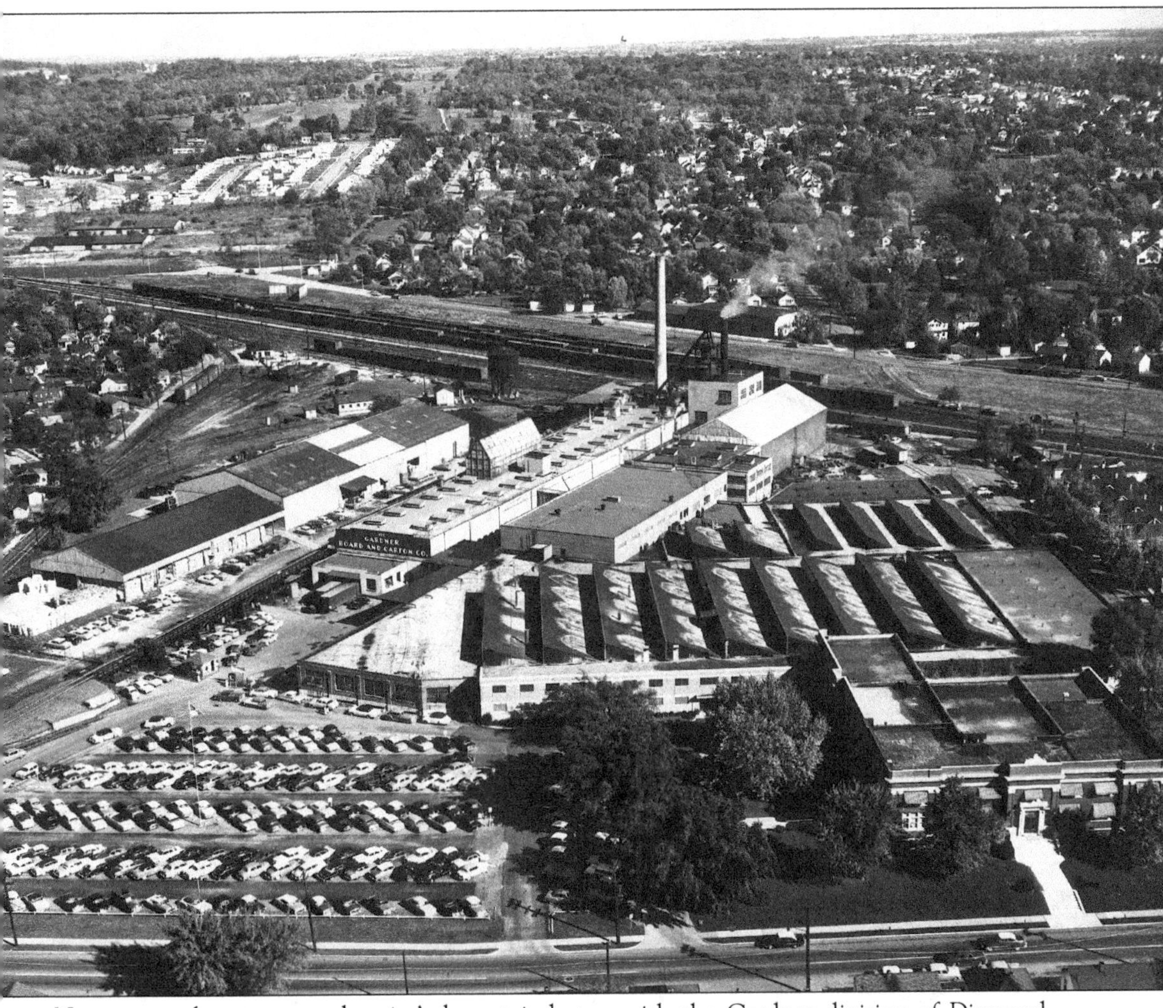

Next to steel, paper was the city's largest industry, with the Gardner division of Diamond National being the major producer with a thousand employees. Sorg Paper was an important part of the paper group, as was Crystal Tissue and Inland Container. Several firms here, as the 1950s began, would be absorbed by other companies or just disappear. Venerable Harding-Jones paper machines were moved out. Wrenn Paper closed. Continental Can became Middletown Paper Board. Interstate Folding Box became Corson Packaging. Fairbanks Container became a unit of Packaging Corporation of America, now Tenneco Packaging. And Pollock Paper became St. Regis, then Miami Packaging.

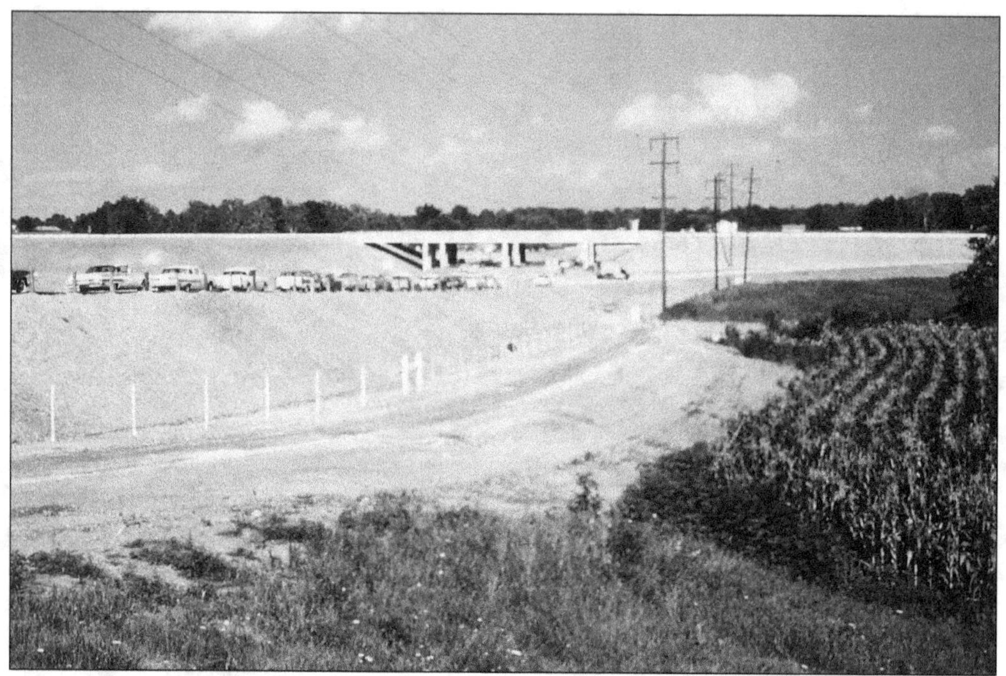

The project which had the greatest impact on Middletown during the past 50 years was the building of Interstate 75. It replaced Route 25 as the major link between the Midwest and the South. The Middletown interchange opened Sunday, July 31, 1960, at 5 p.m. This photo was taken by William Culbertson, through whose farm the new road ran.

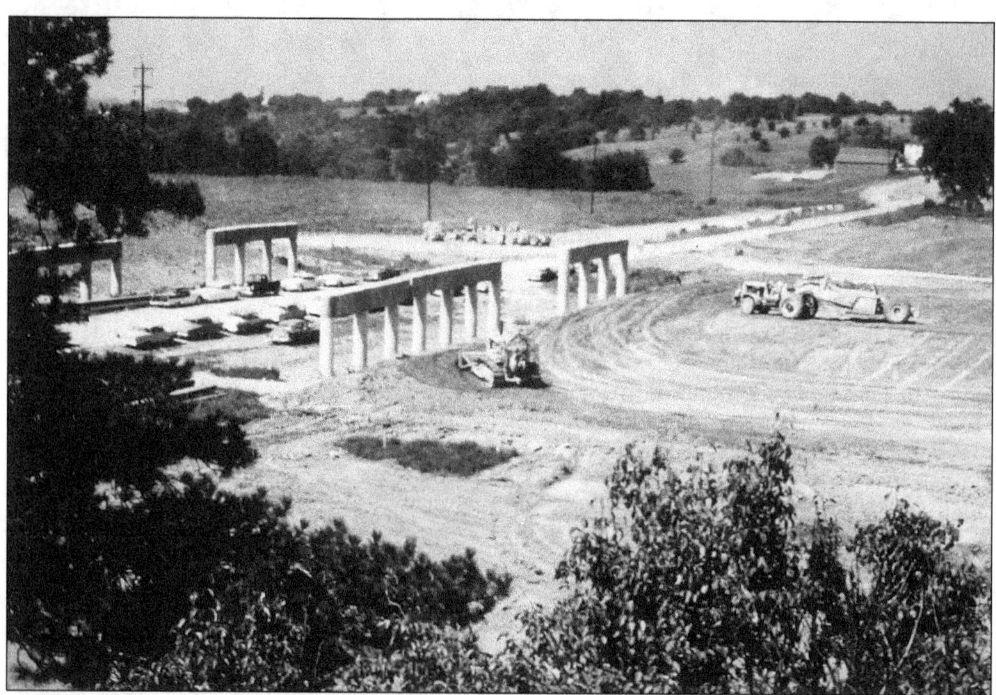

Culbertson took this photo showing the construction underway. It would link Sault Saint Marie, Michigan, with Tampa, Florida, at an original cost of about $4 billion.

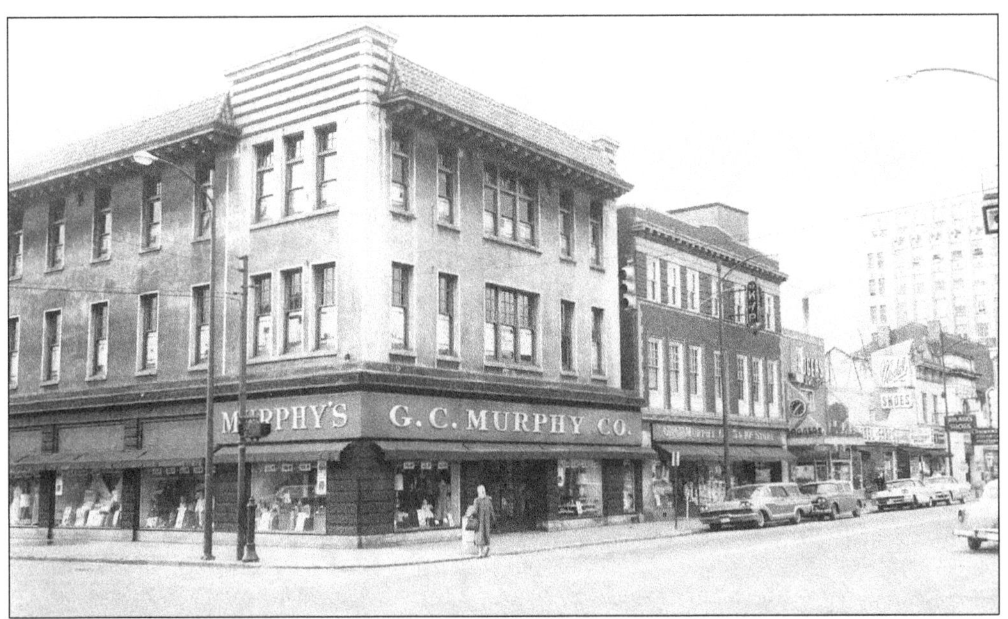

Artist and illustrator Peter Rudokas, using a Ziss-Ikor camera, took the following set of pictures of downtown Middletown in 1962, as it appeared before the mall. The southwest corner of Central and Broad was the city's focal point.

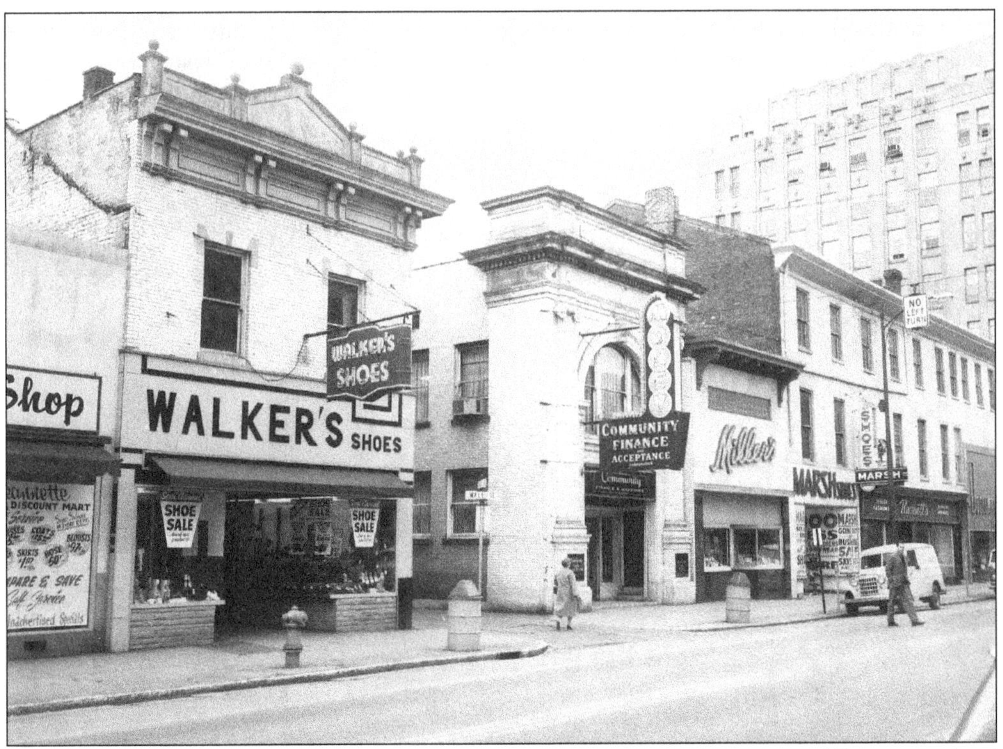

This photo continues the view along the south side of Central, showing Middletown Federal Savings and Loan building (now Fifth-Third Bank). With the building of the mall, Miller's Jewelry would move across the street. It is the city's oldest jewelry store.

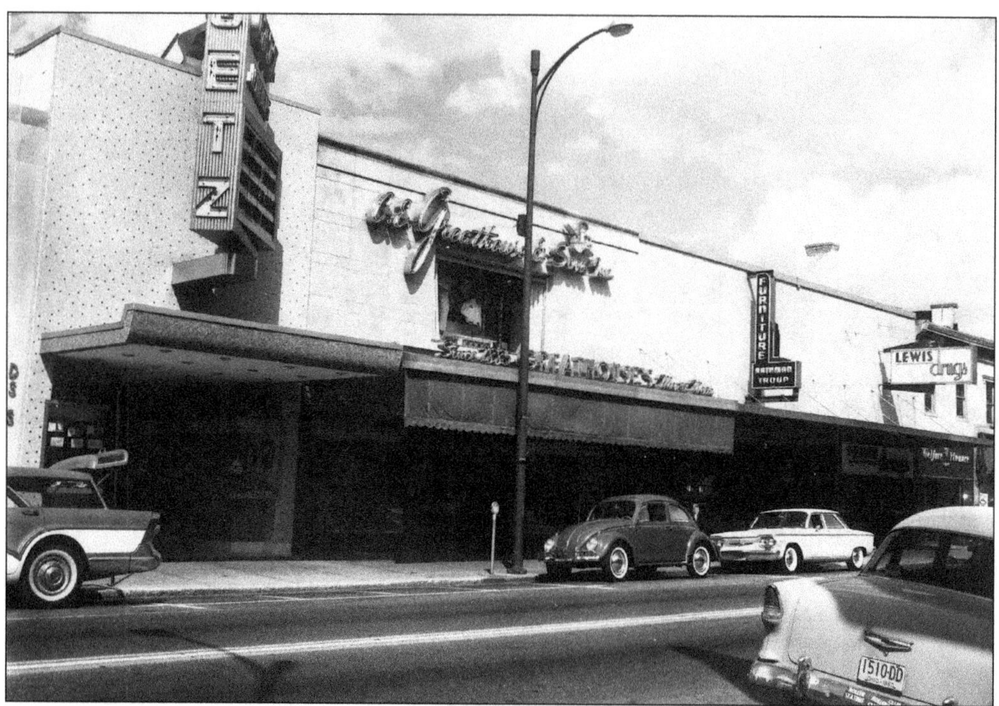

Across Central, on the north side, the photo shows Lewis Drugs, Rathman-Troup Furniture, C.E. Greathouse and Son Men's Store, and Getz Jewelry. Both the furniture and men's store would continue to operate in the mall for several years, while Greathouse would close in 1981 and Troup-Joffe in 1995.

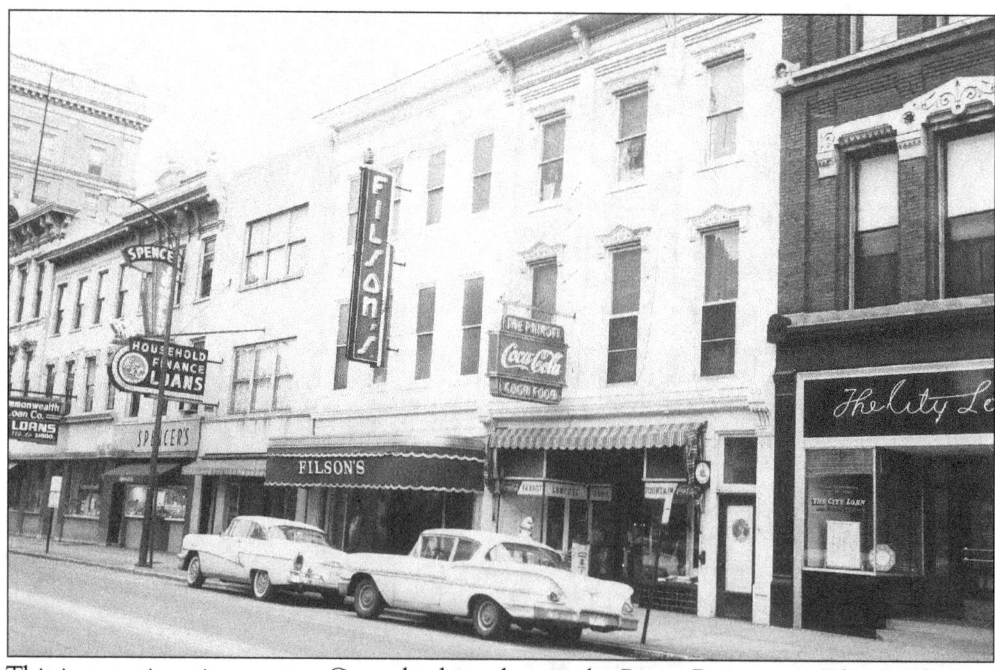

This is a continuation west on Central, where the popular Parrot Restaurant, Filson's Clothes, and Household Finance were located. The tall building is the First National Bank.

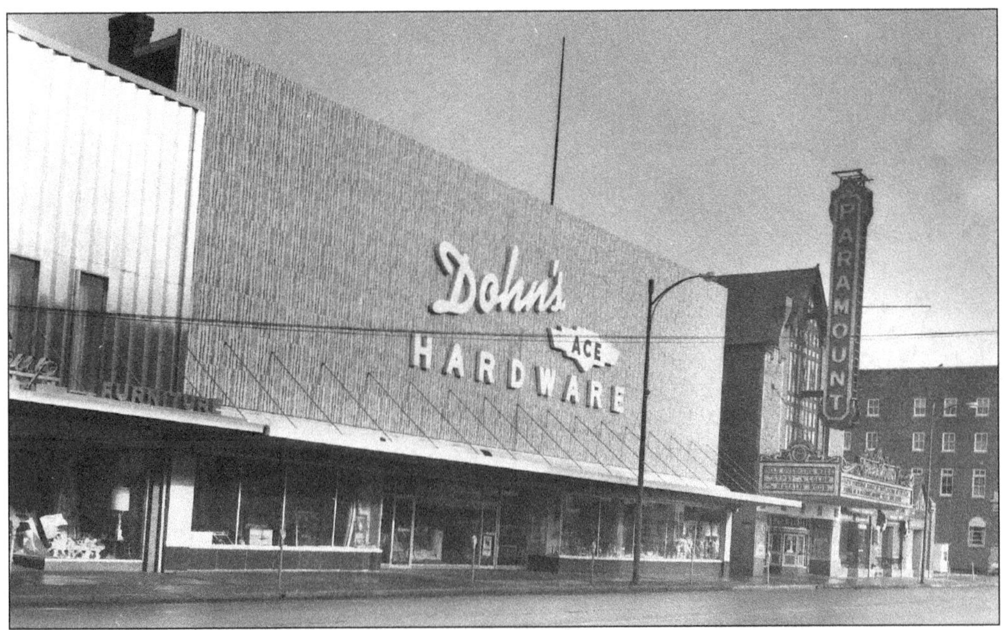

Up north on the west side of Broad was the large Dohn Hardware Store, still in operation, and the beautiful Paramount Theater, torn down in 1963 for a city parking lot.

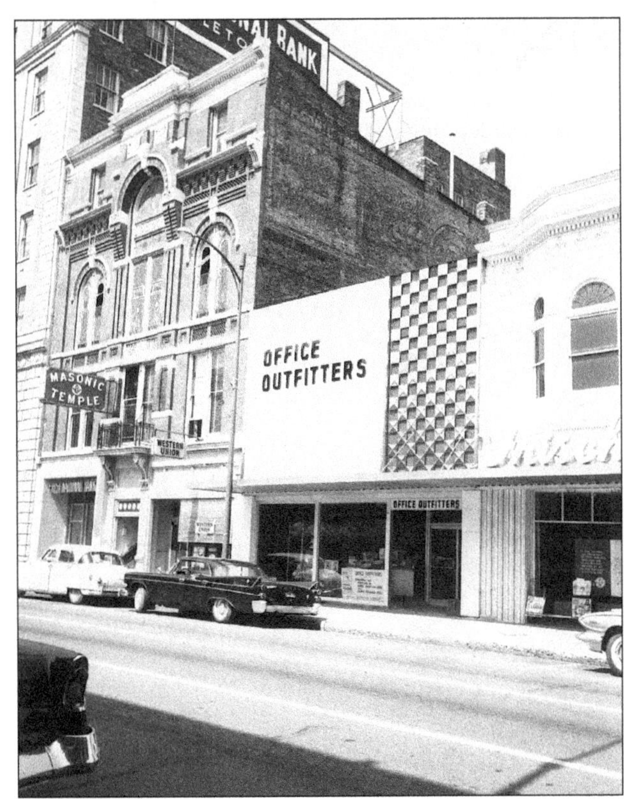

Here we see past the First National Bank, up North Main where Inwood's Office Outfitters and Frisch's Restaurant had a good trade. The Masonic Temple has moved, and its building was purchased by the bank.

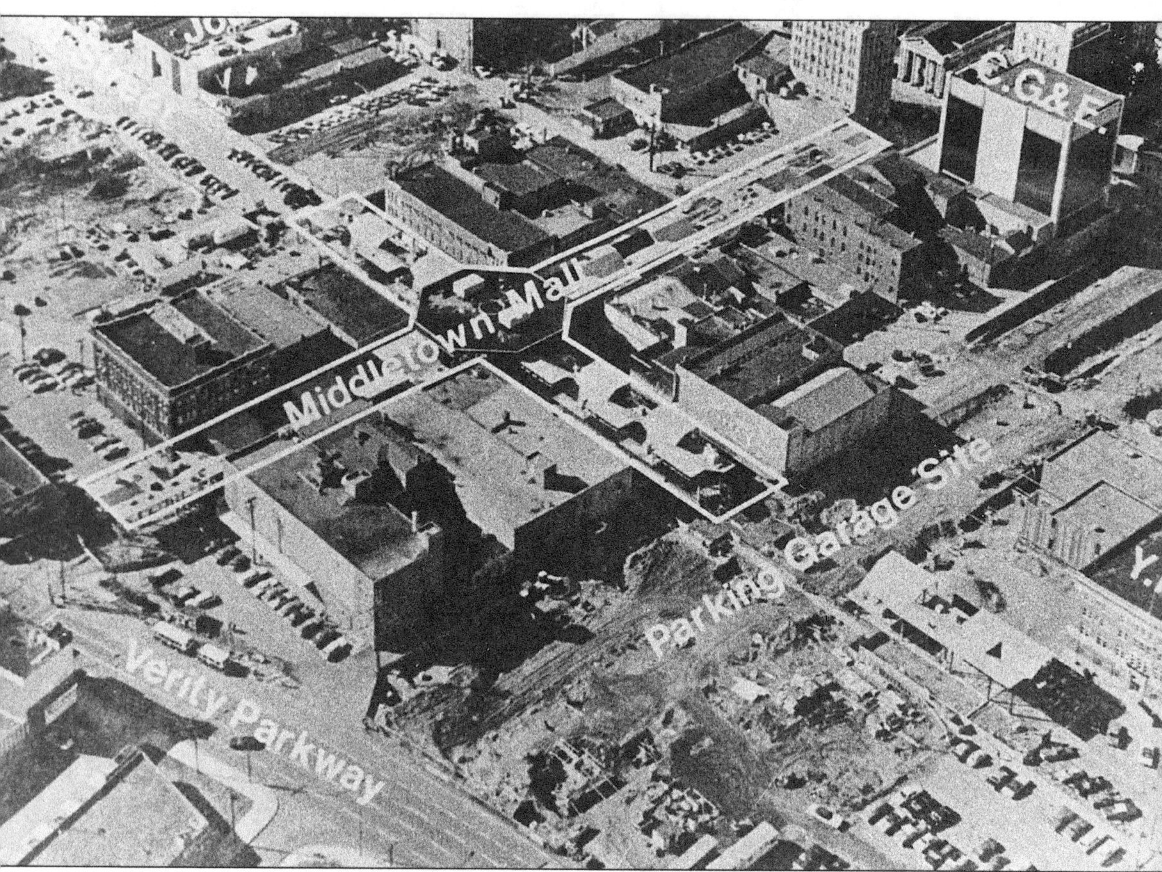

With the Middletown Shopping Center, which opened in 1958, and the neighborhood shopping centers, downtown businessmen were seeking a way to bring back trade to the center city. An experimental downtown "Center Plaza" in the summer of 1959 led to a decade of planning for a fully-enclosed downtown heated mall and a parking garage. In 1968, a federal grant made this feasible. On April 12, 1973, at Central and Broad, a ground-breaking ceremony was held for the new mall, with C. Dudley Inwood, commission chairman, and Dale Helsel, city manager, making remarks. Paul Christiansen, director of community development, was successful in getting federal and state grants, which largely built the project. The garage opened later on February 3, 1975. This photo, taken in late 1972, shows the mall area.

The year 1973 began with utilities being relocated, as caught by this *Journal* photographer. Utilities, as well as storm and sanitary sewer lines, were all relocated to the rear of existing structures in four service courts. The main concourses of the mall were 49 feet in width, compared to Central's 66 feet and Broad's 82 feet.

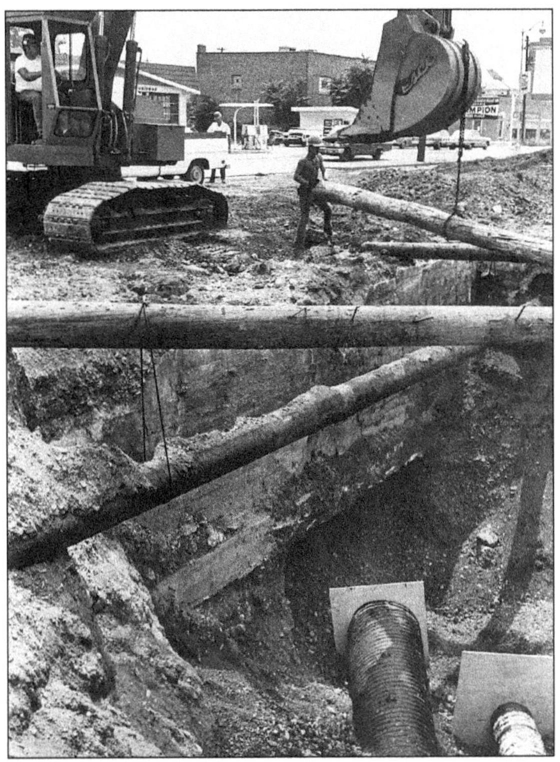

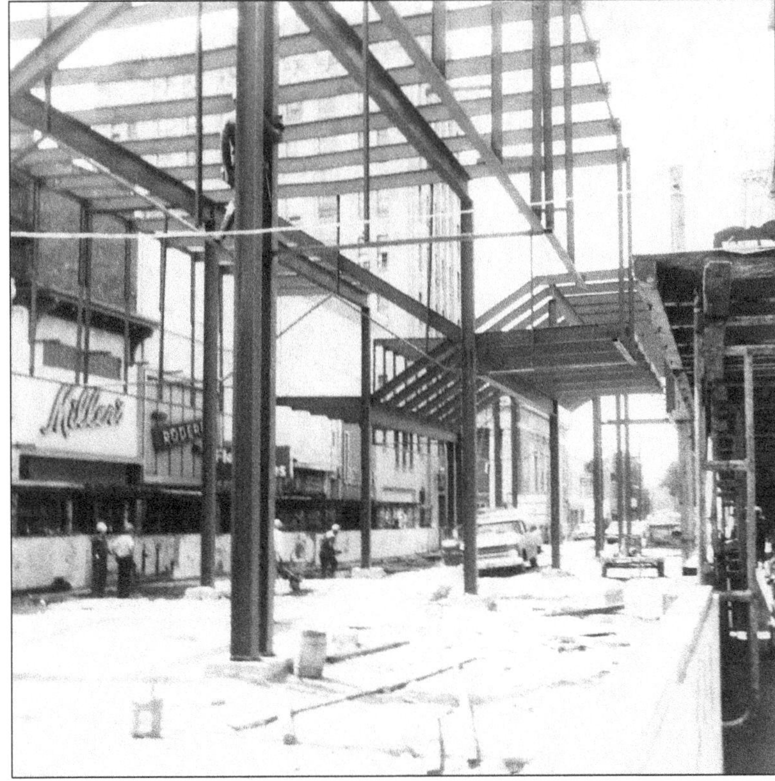

By August 1973, this mall canopy framework was being put in place. Some 16 loads of steel went into the framework.

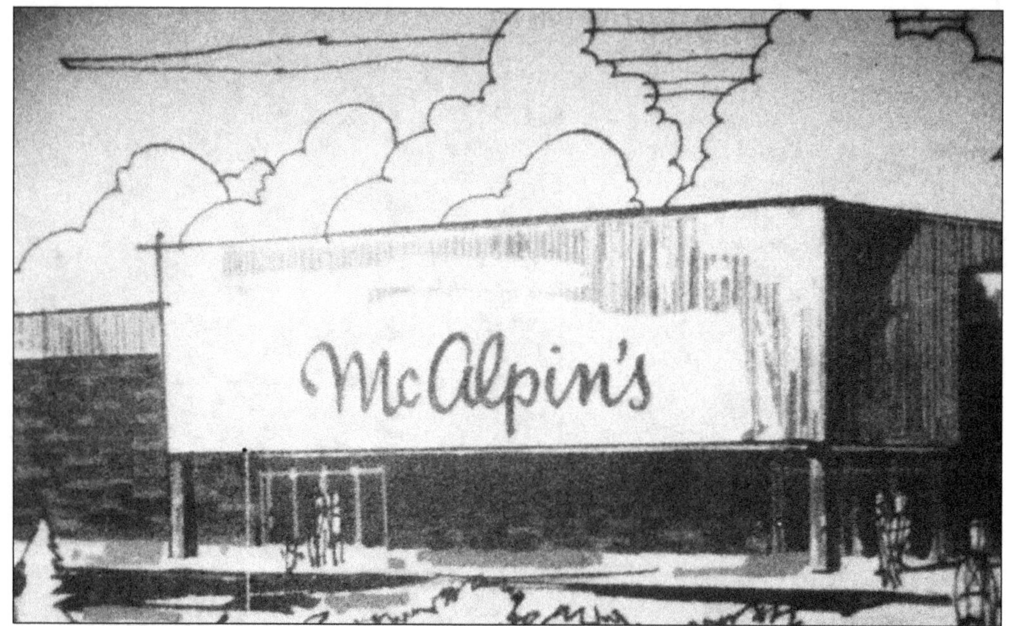

Although the City Centre Mall was a fine structure, it was in the wrong location, and it would be Towne Mall, adjacent to Interstate 75, that would generate most of the business. It began with the opening, February 16, 1975, of McAlpins, the first anchor store, followed by the full mall on February 9, 1977.

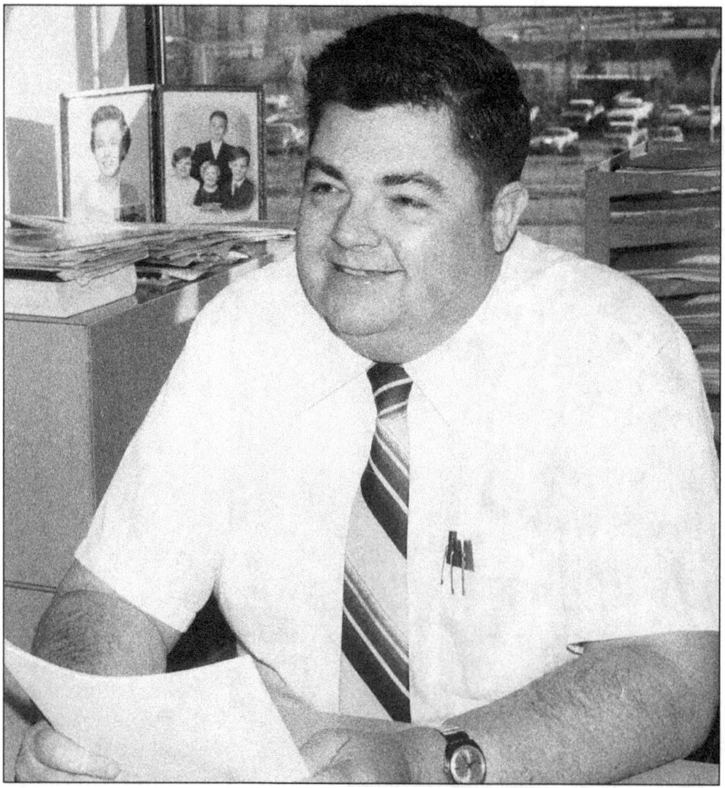

As 1964 City Engineer William Klosterman had foreseen, Middletown would grow to the east by planning sewer and water extensions for the area. Beginning in 1988 as city manager, he devised annexation strategies that would finally extend Middletown corporate boundaries to Interstate 75—a plan finally realized in 1994. Also, he was responsible for designing the Inner-Belt Thoroughfare System.

The last half century before the Millennium saw the rise of African-America leadership in the city. James Saunders served 16 years on the city commission, becoming the first African American to serve as its chairman. Also, he led the OKI Regional Planning Board, Middfest International, and the United Way. Ebie Banks was first on the school board, Allen H. Morgan Sr. was a city official, and Dr. William D. Patton was a member of the health board. Besides individuals, African-American churches and the local chapter of the NAACP, along with other groups, also provided leadership. The Martin Luther King Jr. Memorial Way is a tribute to their dedication.

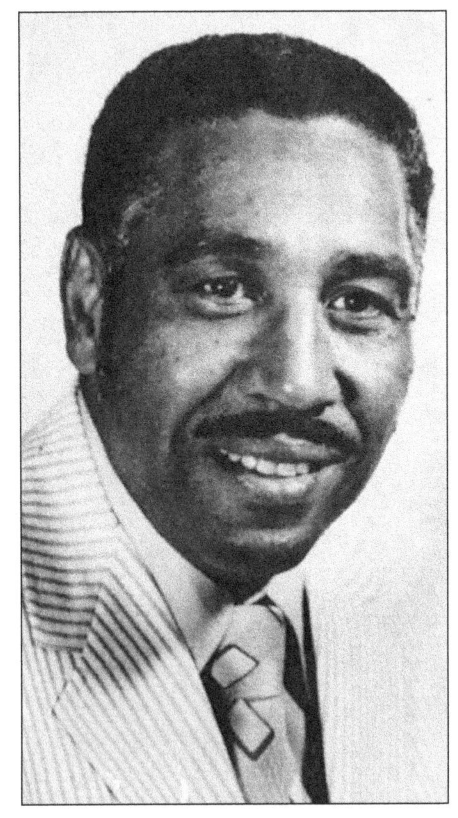

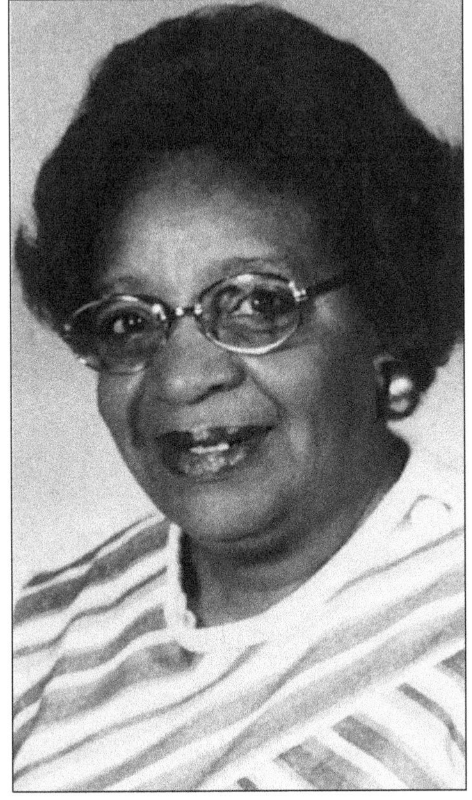

Rossella Harper was appointed, in 1972, the first African American to serve as coordinator for the Middletown city schools. Also, she became director of the "Right to Read Program," a member of the Civil Service Board, and director of Community Playhouse. Louise McBain, after serving as an elementary principal, took over the high school math department. Jean W. Gear was a principal and published poet.

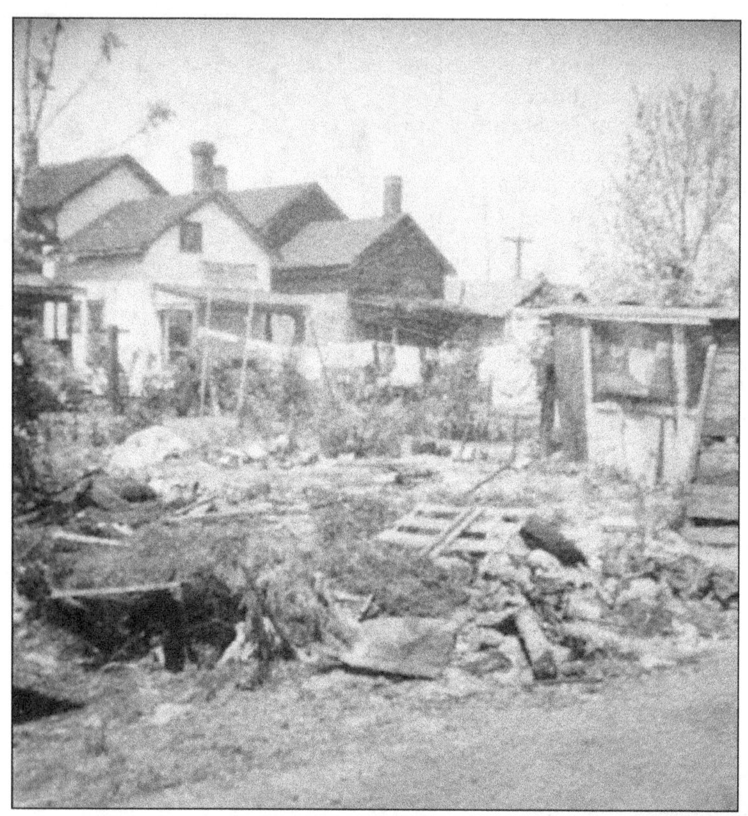

During the 50 years, the city changed physically through slum clearance, with its Garfield Renewal plan approved by federal officials in 1959. Some 350 sub-standard dwelling units were torn down. In 1973, another grant aided in the clearance of the deteriorating downtown. The South Prospect project was aimed at rehabilitation.

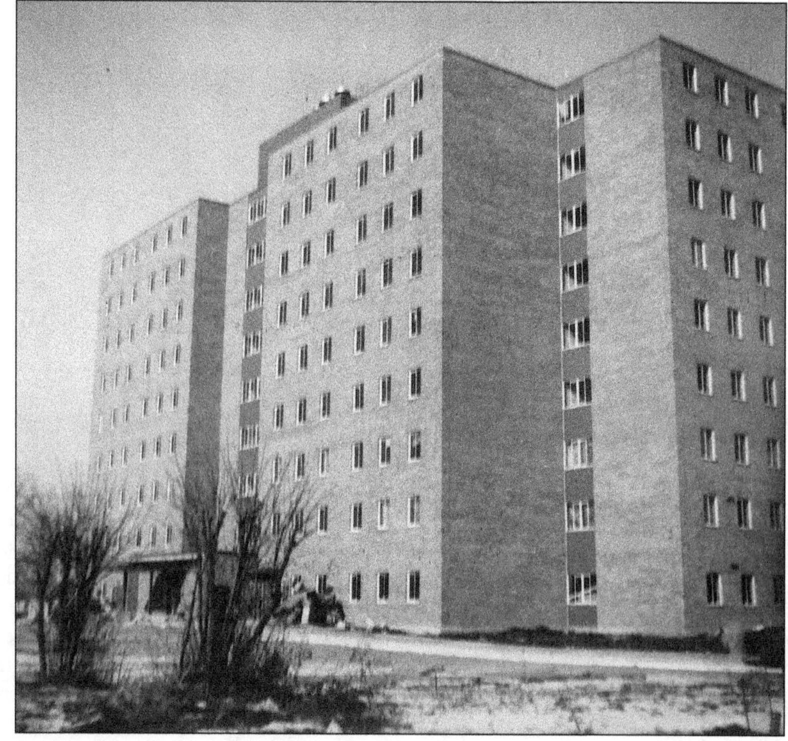

In 1961, an application was submitted to the Metropolitan Housing Authority. In 1965, a new town house facility stood at 600 Verity Parkway in part of what was Lakeside Park. J. Ross Hunt Towers was completed in 1972. There were other smaller complexes with a total of 650 public housing units by 1993.

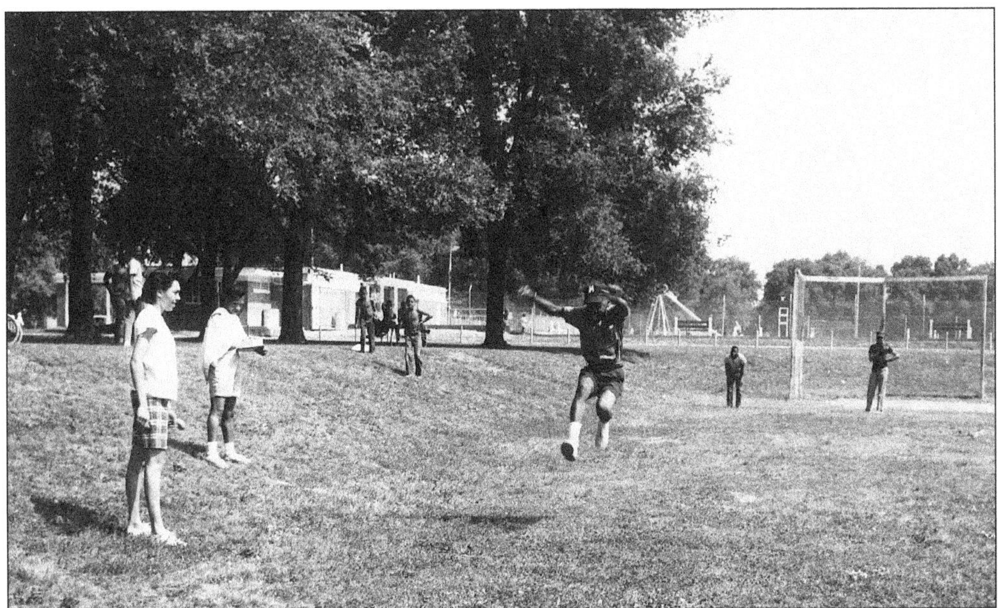

The 1950s opened with Walter "Steve" Geckeler as Middletown Parks Director He promoted a levy for park expansion. Improvements were made at Frederick A. Douglass Park (shown here) and others—each of which had a planned, supervised program with trained recreation leaders each summer.

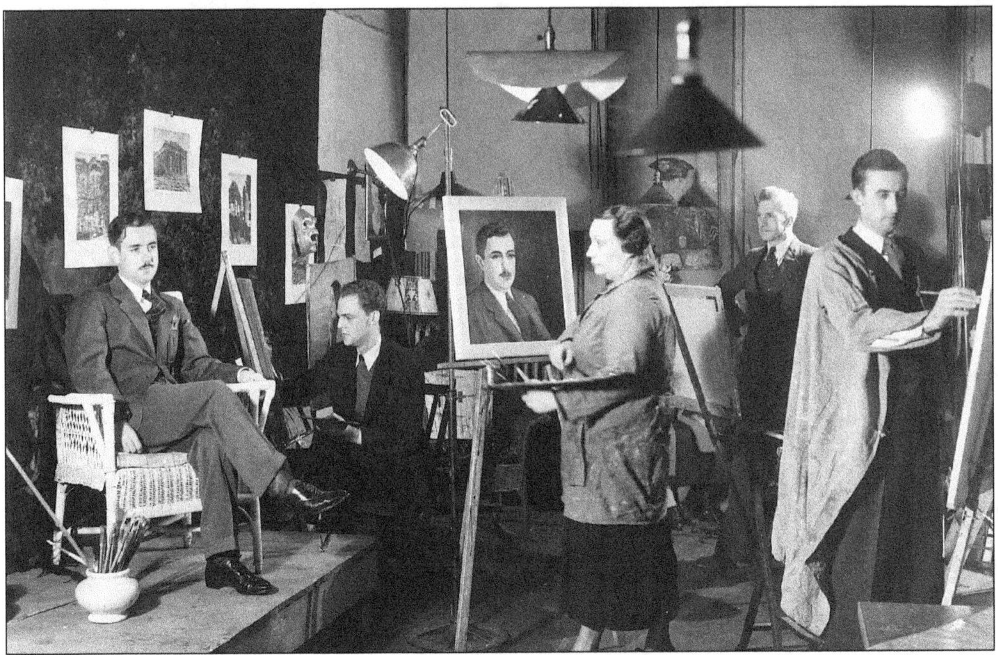

Not only did the city have programs for the physical wellbeing, but there were also cultural facilities. The art committee of the local Federation of Women's Clubs held the first Art Week in 1927. In 1957, a Fine Arts Center was organized. The first group of artists worked in a studio at the American Legion Building, shown here. When the AIM building was completed in 1975, the center was moved there.

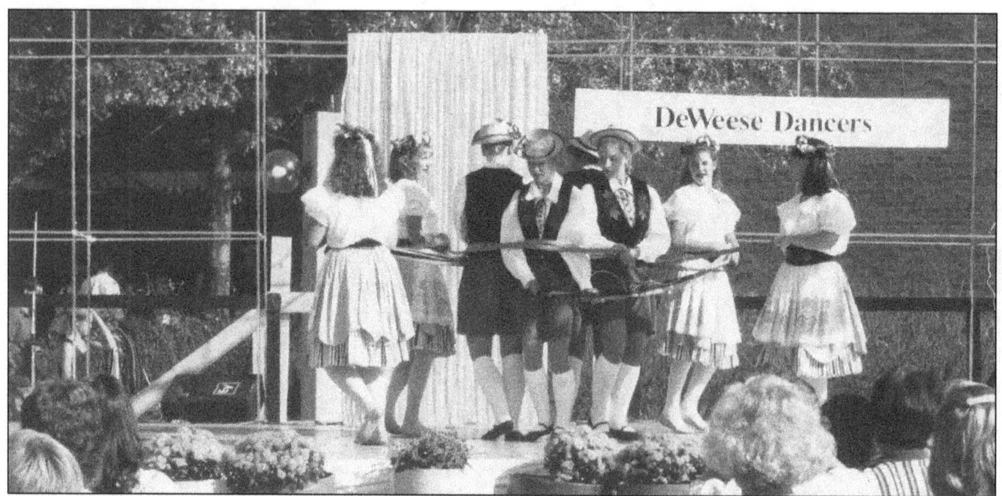

An early fall community activity is Middfest. It originated in 1978, suggested by civic booster, John Renick, and the name by M.G. McCall. In 1981, the Middfest International Foundation was established when it was decided to feature the culture of some foreign nation each year.

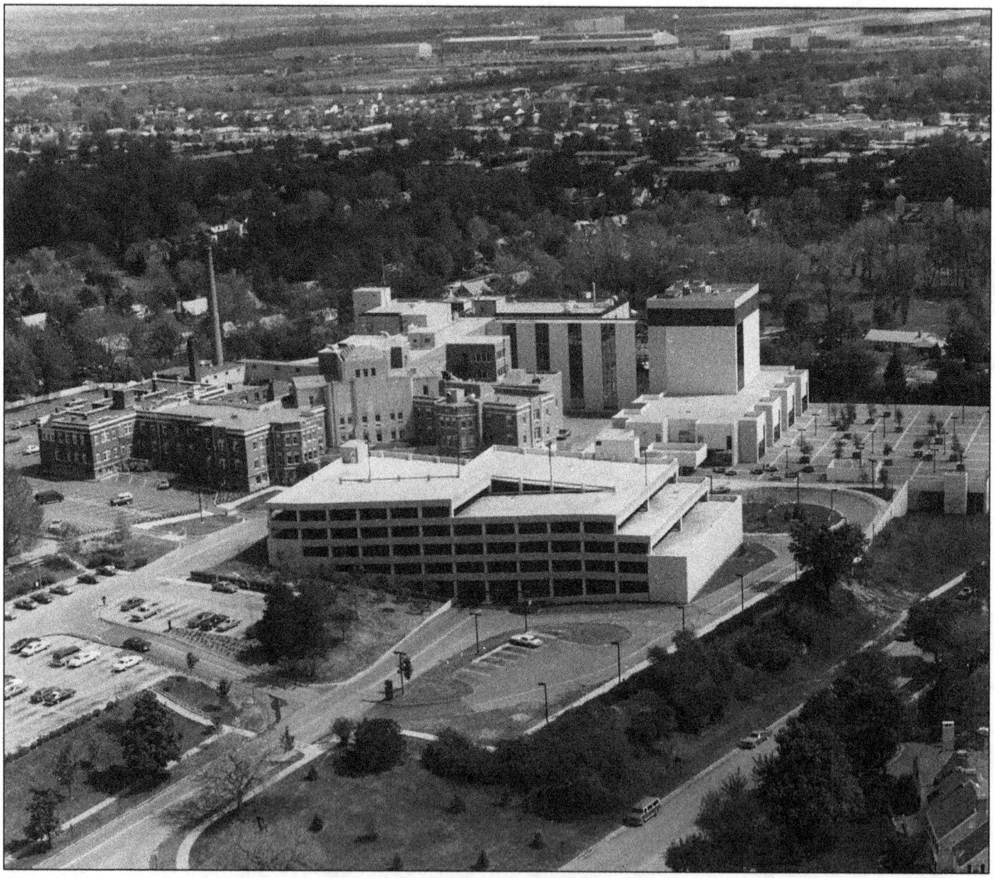

The favorite social event of the winter is the annual Charity Ball, held since 1921, to finance a project for the hospital (shown here). It is sponsored by the Federation of Women's Clubs.

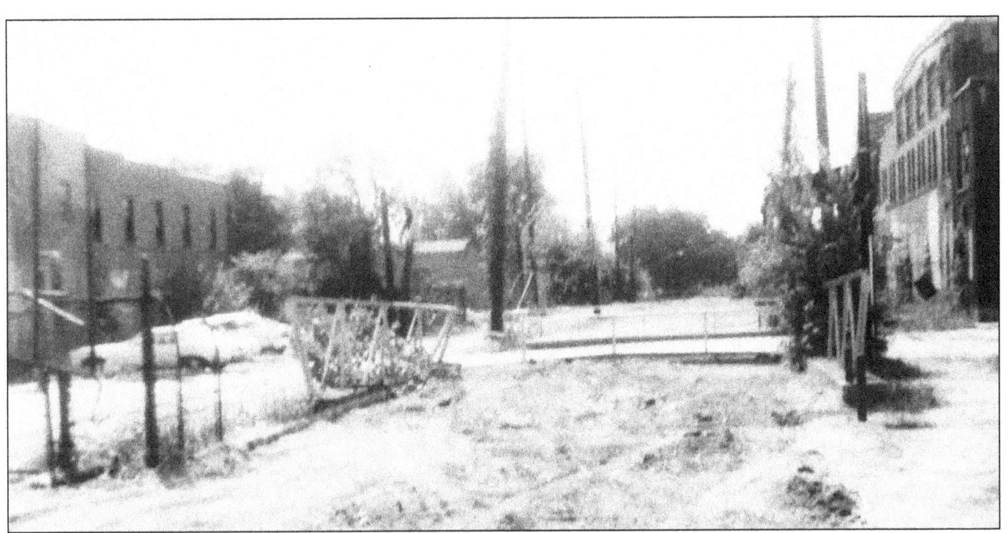

On September 12, 1983, that section of the old Hydraulic, south of Central Avenue, was finally filled in, largely with dirt excavated for the YMCA addition.

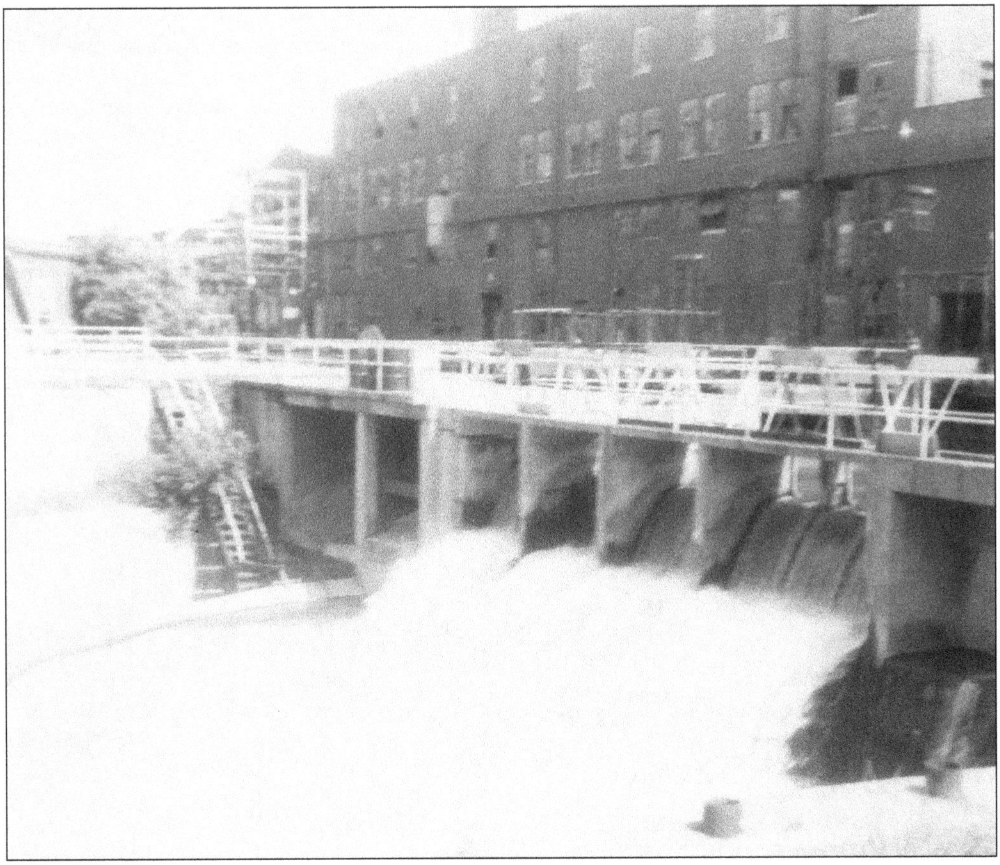

The water then left by way of a raceway (shown here) behind the Sorg Paper Mill on to the river. But on May 13, 1993, the State Dam which fed the Hydraulic collapsed, thus stopping the flow of water in the historic landmark.

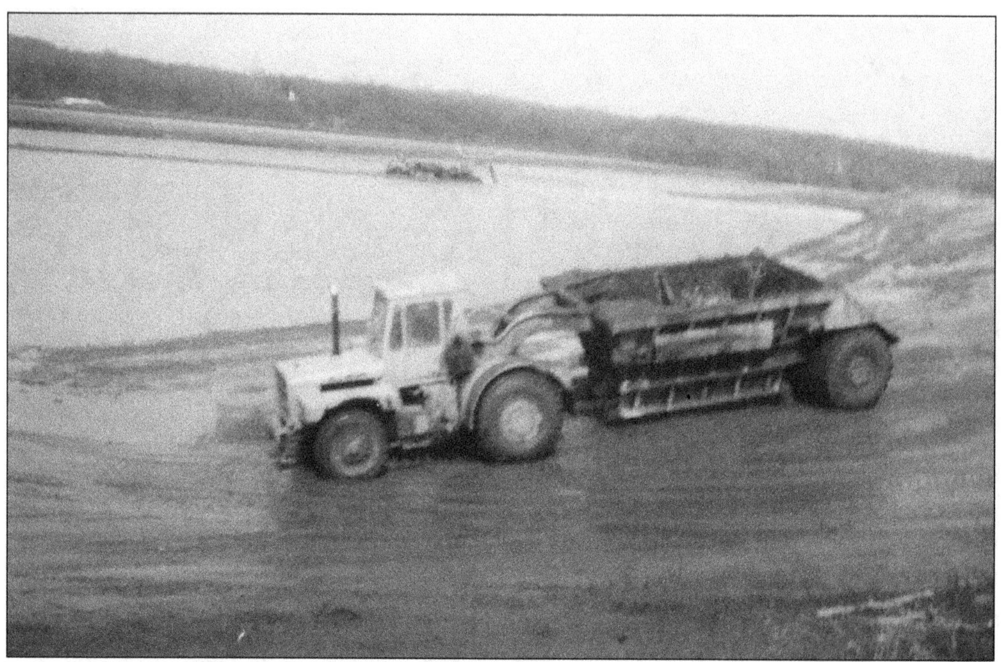
Natural occurrences often cause havoc. When the State Dam collapsed after almost two centuries, it later caused the silting up of Lake Middletown, a city Bicentennial project, which was completed in 1994. Shown here is the lake under construction, an idea first conceived in 1922.

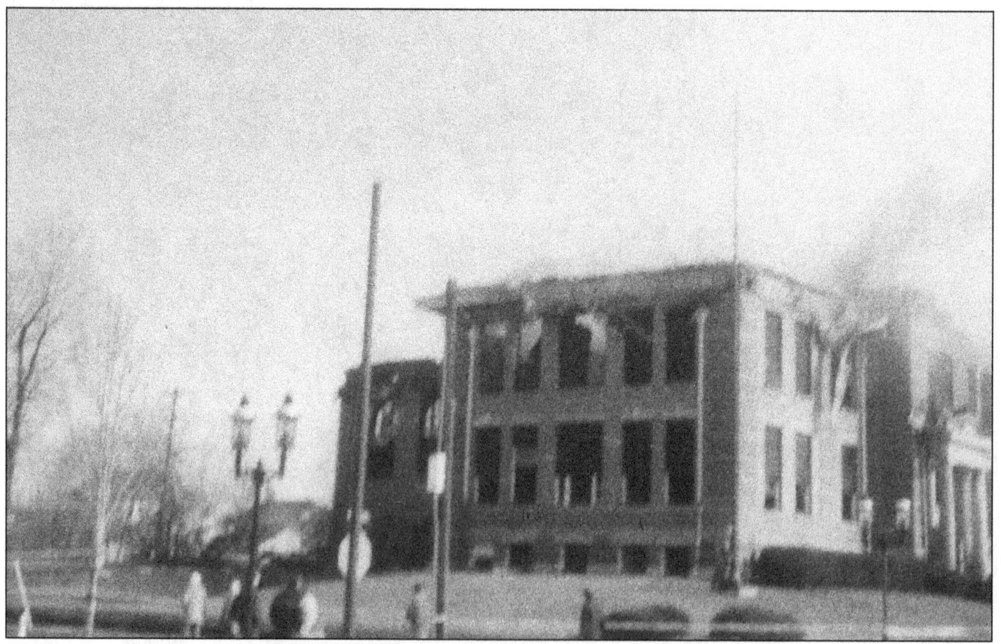
The old city building, which was originally the city's first high school building (1909-1930), burned on January 8, 1984, as shown in the photo. Another historic school building, South, was destroyed by fire on April 25, 1965. The massive Miami-Carey building burned March 11, 1972.

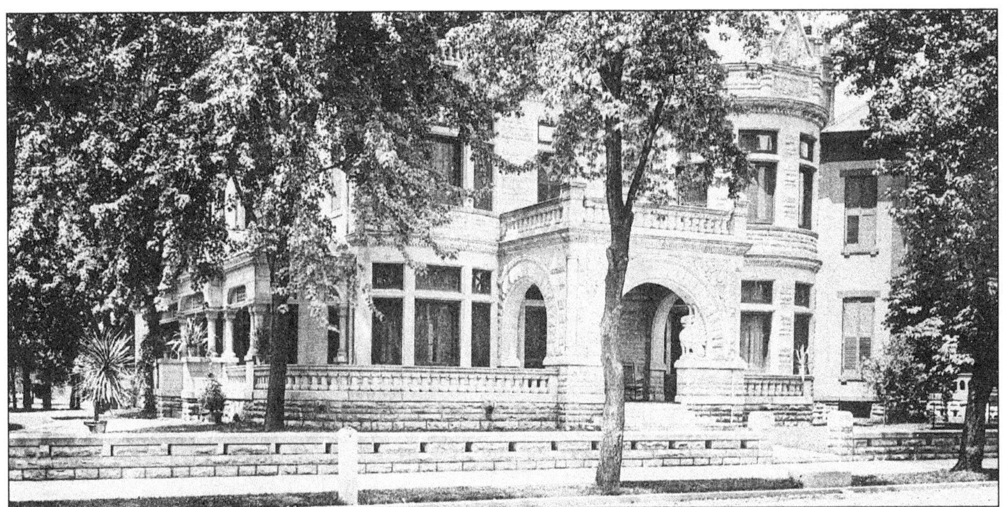

While fire wiped out many historic landmarks, so did the wrecking ball, as was the case of this old home, which once stood at 230 South Main Street in the midst of the historic district. It was purchased from the Charles F. Gunckel estate in 1902 by George M. Verity. After his death it was torn down for park space.

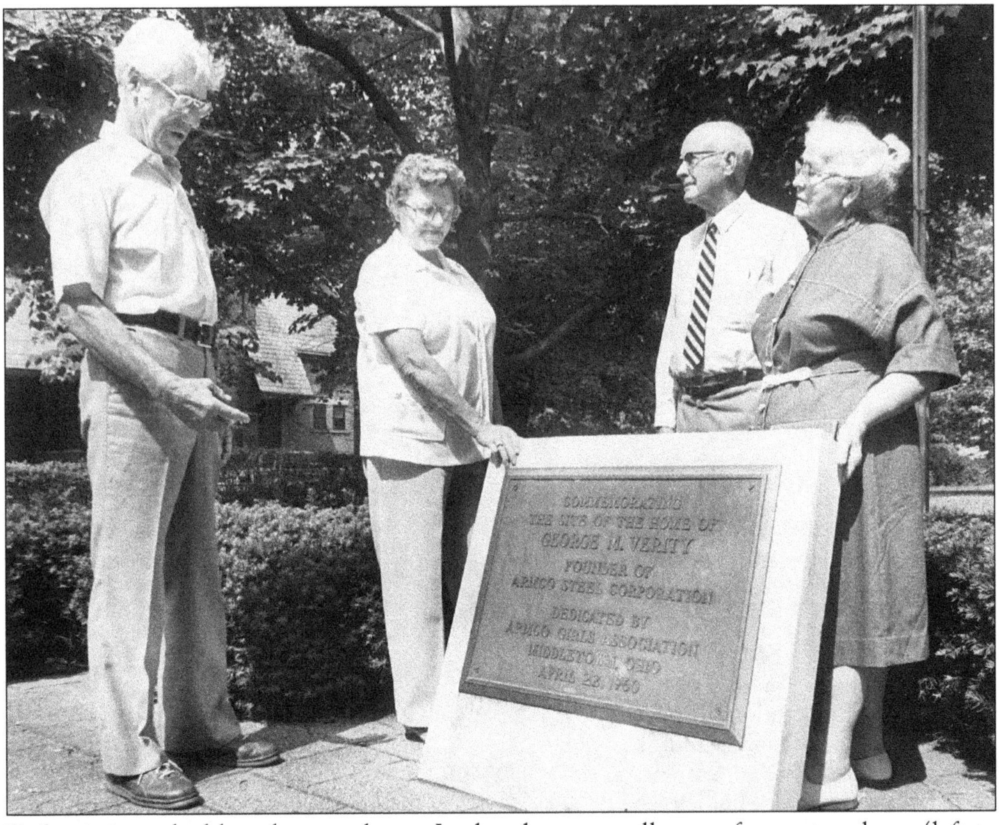

Today it is marked by a bronze plaque. In the photo a small group from a tour bus—(left to right) Ruth Oglesby, Harvey Apple, and Florence Black—examine it as Francis Burk explains its significance. Burk is a past president of the local historical society.

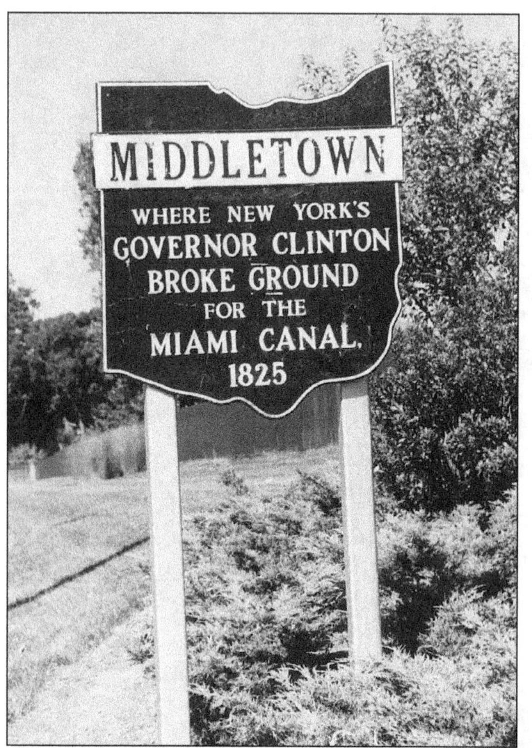

During Ohio's statehood sesquicentennial celebration in 1953, the general assembly encouraged the placement of historical markers at corporation limits. This is Middletown's official marker. Ohio is now planning its Bicentennial in the year 2003.

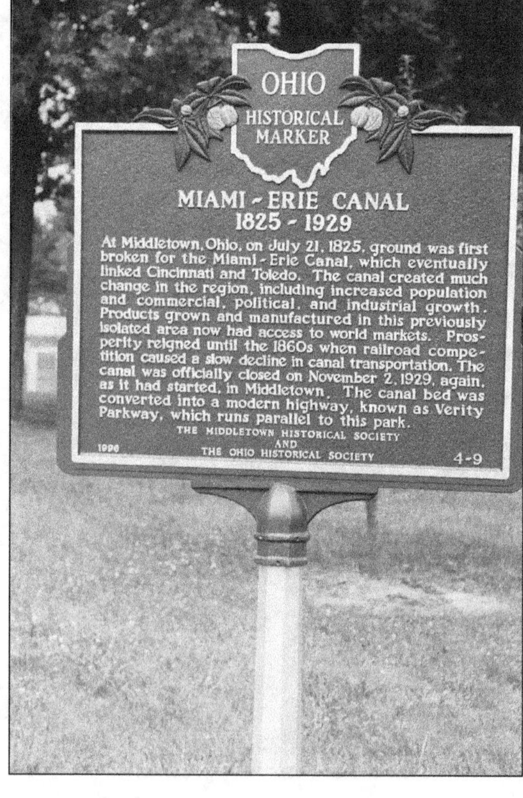

The Ohio Historical Society approved the bronze marker with more detailed information. It was erected in 1996, with funds from the Russell D. Stevens Jr. Foundation. Everett Sherron of the Middletown Historical Society has photographed all the city's markers in illustrating his brochure, "Middletown Markers."

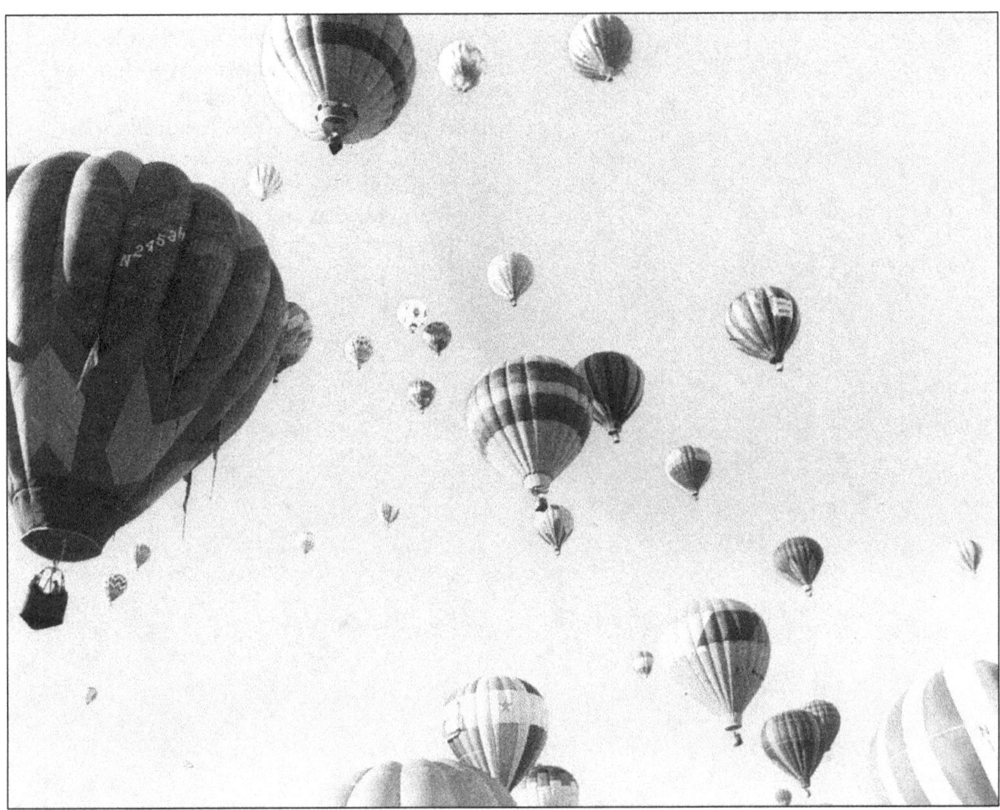

For three years, 1992–1994, during mid-summer, the Balloon Federation of America hosted the U.S. Hot Air Balloon Championships at Middletown. One hundred of the nation's best balloonists competed for the championship. It was based at the Hook Field/Smith Park complex. Another hundred fiesta flyers also took flight. The Friday evening kick-off program featured a balloon glow, during which the beautiful balloons, tethered to the ground, were inflated and lit up by their propane burners. The brilliant colors and designs of the balloons shone in the night, while the Middletown Symphony Orchestra, under Director Carmon DeLeone, provided the musical background. During their summer interlude, the colorful, soaring balloons lifted the spirits of all. Only wind currents would determine their path.

Somehow, it all seemed a preview for the Millennium, as we soon will soar off into the clear blue sky in a new adventure, not knowing what the future holds.

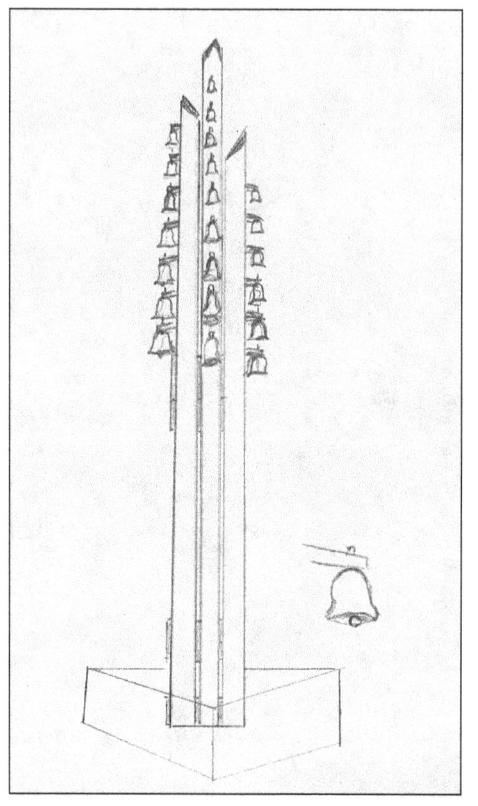

As the millennium approaches, the Casper family has provided Middletown with a new carillon as a memorial to Jack A. Casper. It will be located in the City Center Plaza in front of the Senior Citizens Center and the City Building. The drawing shows the carillon as some visualize it. Its construction should be complete at about the time this book appears.

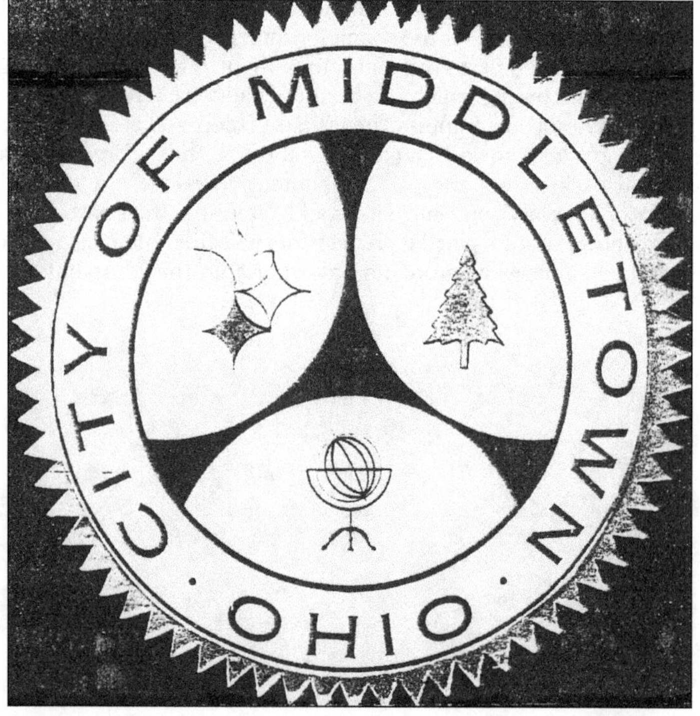

This is the official emblem of the city, adopted in 1964. It was designed by R. Paul Christiansen of the Department of Community Development to represent the major activities of Middletown. The Steelmark is symbolic of the steel industry, the tree of the paper industry, and the globe of the local Miami University Campus. The city flag also incorporates the seal, which is placed on a white background.

www.ingramcontent.com/pod-product-compliance
Lightning Source LLC
LaVergne TN
LVHW081548100826
845153LV00004B/339

* 9 7 8 1 5 3 1 6 6 5 6 6 1 *